LIBRARY CATALOGUING AND MULTIMEDIA LIBRARIES

LIBRARY CATALOGUING AND MULTIMEDIA LIBRARIES

By

Rakeshkumar Shantilal Prajapati

B.Lib., M.Lib.

Librarian

Swami Vivekanand Sarvoday Bank Education College

Mehsana (Gujarat)

(India)

DISCOVERY PUBLISHING HOUSE PVT. LTD.

NEW DELHI-110 002

Published by:
Tilak Wasan
DISCOVERY PUBLISHING HOUSE PVT. LTD.
4383/4B, Ansari Road, Darya Ganj
New Delhi-110 002 (India)
Phone : +91-11-23279245, 43596064-65
Fax : +91-11-23253475
E-mail : discoverypublishinghouse@gmail.com
sales@discoverypublishinggroup.com
parul.wasan@gmail.com
web : www.discoverypublishinggroup.com

Reprinted: 2019
First Edition: 2014

ISBN: 978-93-5056-427-1

Library Cataloguing and Multimedia Libraries

Printed at:
Dynamic Printers
Delhi

Preface

The primary functions of a library are to collect, organize, preserve and deliver information to the users. With the passage of time, several techniques and technologies have emerged for handling the information more speedily and effectively. Invention of printing in the second half of the 15th century started a revolution in spreading thought and scholarship. Later, still pictures, moving pictures, sound recordings discs, sound tapes, micro-computers and view data and optical storage systems were introduced in the commercial market which had an ever-lasting impact on publishing. Slowly all these recording media, used for storing information, were introduced in the libraries. All these forms were acquired and stored separately because the information retrieval methods used were different for each forms of the media. As a result combining information from different forms became difficult.

In 1940s, efforts were made by Dr Vannevar Bush to integrate all these forms and he designed a mechanical device, called 'Memex', for storing, organizing and retrieving information received in various forms. Those days librarians used to collect non-book material and call them as multimedia collection. However, there was no single platform on which all the forms of information could be stored and retrieved. During the late 1980s, computer specialists succeeded in integrating the text, graphics, animation, audio, and video information on a computer after converting them into digital media called 'multimedia for publicity purposes'. This is a major achievement in the field of publishing, which directly influenced both librarians and users.

This book covers a wide range of library cataloguing and multimedia libraries issues and attempt to introduce the subject in a comprehensive way. It avoids the narrow focus and considerable complexity of many other books in this area where in depth treatment is required. If the book opens the student's eyes to the problems, it would have surely served its purpose.

—*Author*

Contents

1

Multimedia Catalogue

INTRODUCTION

The RAI television and radio archives contain several hundred-thousand hours of programmes, stored on various media formats, most of which are obsolescent. The present yearly growth is estimated at about 60000 new supports for TV production, and about 40000 new supports for radio. A traditional method of organising this bulk of archive data does not allow for an efficient exploitation of programme content in the production environment, where the retrieval and delivery times play a crucial role. In particular, the manual handling of traditional storage media is incompatible with today's requirements and expectations.

In 1994, RAI started a project for the migration of endangered material from the old and obsolete supports to new ones, performing at the same time a new and complete re-classification of this material. Moreover, at the beginning of 1997, an interdepartmental project was launched whose goal was the digitisation and redocumentation of all the material owned and produced by RAI.

The project, managed by the Director of the *Audiovideoteche* department, has been subdivided into several sub-projects that relate respectively to the development of:

- A multimedia catalogue;
- A compressed TV library;
- An uncompressed TV library;

- Compressed and uncompressed radio libraries;
- A security system.

Access to the present archive requires many steps, several of which are manually managed. The overall procedure – from consultation of the programme catalogue, to delivery of a copy of the material – can sometimes take several days. The new system that RAI is developing will drastically reduce this time, through the development of a *Multimedia Catalogue* and the automation of the library management functions. Such a system will be available to internal users and, in general, to other people working in the production environment, as well as to external users such as researchers in social sciences.

The role of the new catalogue is that of a comprehensive search tool that will allow users to locate the required footage among the bulk of archived material. The catalogue will contain not only textual information, but also still pictures that relate to TV programmes, and the associated audio. From the catalogue, it will be possible to address not only programmes, but also segments and shots. The description given in this object will usually refer to documentation about TV material, as this represents the most general case, but it applies equally to radio and photo material with minor modifications.

GENERAL DESCRIPTION OF THE NEW ARCHIVE ARCHITECTURE

The archive can be subdivided logically into three main subsystems: the catalogue, the video libraries and the audio library, as indicated in fig. 1.1.

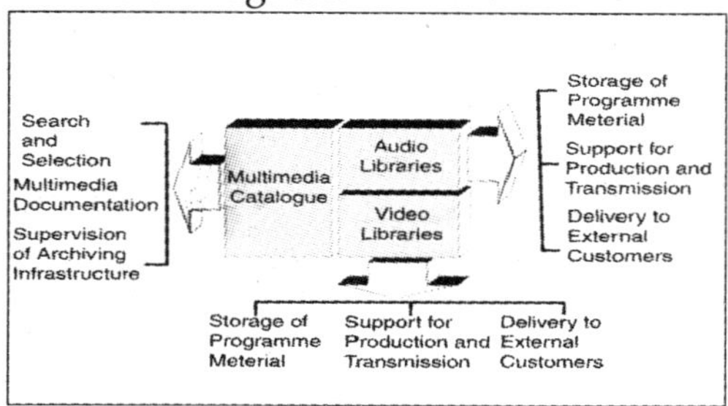

Fig.1.1. Functional Block Diagram of the RAI Archive.

The catalogue includes the documentation that relates to the Radio and TV materials, consisting of text and multimedia objects, audio and keyframes. The functions supported are: searching, navigation and previewing of the programme, and segment documentation – where a *segment* is a temporal part of the programme, having a close semantic meaning. The libraries store the physical copies of the content and their role is the preservation and handling of the media.

The catalogue and the libraries must be kept aligned so that the user, after querying the catalogue and locating the programme segments of interest, can send the relevant identification information to the appropriate library and receive a copy of the selected material without requiring any further viewing operations. The alignment between the catalogue and the libraries can easily be obtained when the catalogue is populated by means of documenting the materials previously stored in the libraries, because the correct material identification and temporal references can immediately be determined. In the case of a parallel feeding of the catalogue and libraries with pre-recorded material or from on-air feeds, the alignment between the catalogue and libraries is more delicate and must be considered attentively.However, this second case offers more freedom in the organisation of the archive workflow, as there is no need for tight coupling between the two subsystem input operations. The catalogue can be accessed on the RAI intranet by a vast number of concurrent users, via a web browser. Access to the libraries is restricted to a limited number of people in the production environment, both for copyright reasons and for keeping the network loading under control. The selected material can be delivered to the requester in several formats according to the connection available: as a file, as a TV video stream or as a tape.

ARCHIVE POPULATION STRATEGY

The strategy followed in order to populate the new system with TV material is twofold:

- Documentation and digitisation of all the programmes daily broadcast by the three RAI national channels;

- Digitisation and redocumentation of endangered legacy materials from the archive.

The first activity is done using a pipeline originated at play-out, where live programmes are recorded for archiving. At the same time, all the materials are digitised and compressed, and the multimedia information to be included in the catalogue is extracted. The advantages with this strategy are that no additional tapes are moved to and from the archive for documentation and digitisation purposes, and there is no need to generate and deliver copies of the programmes to the *documentalists*. The link between the various versions of a programme is then represented by the transmission time, which is the same at any acquisition station. The migration to digital formats and the redocumentation of the legacy materials is done selectively using an urgency policy, i.e. the most endangered materials are processed first.

THE VIDEO LIBRARIES

Information technology (IT) offers a versatile and future-proof way of storing and managing audio-visual materials as files, with features such as format independence which is hardly achievable with dedicated audio-video equipment. Unfortunately, storing the whole RAI TV archive at full CCIR 601 quality would require several tens of petabytes of mass storage – a real challenge even for the most advanced systems in use today.

Therefore, the adopted solution for the time being is that of maintaining a full-quality video library, named the *master library*, which is mirrored by a low-quality IT-based library, named the *fast library*. The latter contains MPEG-2 compressed video that can be used for viewing, disaster recovery, TV production not requiring very high quality, etc. The master library contains analogue and digital video, stored on conventional video supports. At present, the master library is not managed in a completely automatic way. The sup ports are stocked on pallet boards contained in a warehouse.

The locations of the supports and pallets are available on a computer system, and the movement of pallets is performed by robots. In the fast library, the material is organised in files and stored on two different memory levels. The first level consists of on-line hard disk memory, while the second level is constituted by robotised tape memory.

A caching process manages the transfer of materials between the first and second memory levels. The use of two memory levels enables an analyzis of costs and performance to be made. In fact, due to the large amount of video material we have at RAI, a memory system based only on disks would be extremely expensive.

On the other hand, the access time of material stored on tapes is not satisfactory, particularly if the number of concurrent accesses is high. A compromise is obtained using both tape and disk memories, where the latter acts as a cache for the former. The material is transferred from tapes to disks when required, and is transferred from disks to tapes when not in use and when disk capacity is required.

THE AUDIO LIBRARY

The application of computer technologies has enabled RAI to develop an Audio Master Library that holds – in digital form and in very high quality – the contents of all the radio programmes and the vinyl records and CDs This system is composed of three main parts, connected via flexible high-speed networks.

The "Trascrizioni" subsystem is responsible for the digitisation of the existing archived materials. The audio signal is converted to digital linear PCM in stereo, at 48 kHz sampling rate, with 24 bits per sample.

The system implements several features that allow for a drastic reduction in the digitisation costs:

- Automatic check of some significant features of the digitised sound. These parameters can reveal certain errors that can be proposed to the operators for acceptance.
- Automatic control of the media players;
- Systematic quality verification made by the operators on the most important parts of every document. This

will include the critical points revealed by the computer.

- Statistical checks on the complete documents.

The "Grande Archivio del Suono" (GAdS) subsystem is the master audio library that is responsible for the conservation and handling of the digitised material, based on a robotic archive with a capacity of 350 Tbyte in DLT tape format.

The audio files are formatted according to the AES/EBU BWF standard. The "Isole di Produzione" are clusters of interlinked workstations that are used with specific kinds of production.

These workstations are also linked to the *Grande Archivio del Suono*. From these workstations, it will be possible to control the process with high-quality standards, and without having to move around either the people or the media.

BASIC ARCHITECTURE OF MULTIMEDIA CATALOGUE

The multimedia catalogue must serve two roles. In its first role, the system should act as a repository for the multimedia objects and information that is gathered and generated during the various phases of the documentation process; in this role, the system interacts with the documentalists.

Its second role is the publication of the final product to the user; it should support searching, navigation and pre-viewing of the documentation, and managing the links with the content libraries. As a consequence of the different constraints relating to these two roles, an architecture based on two coupled subsystems has been selected.

The first subsystem, called the *Documentation Catalogue,* acquires the multimedia objects, and supports the documentation and validation phases.

The second subsystem, called the *Publication Catalogue,* receives the validated programmes, and supports the services aimed at the users, *i.e.* searching, navigation, previewing and links to the libraries in order to request the downloading of the content.

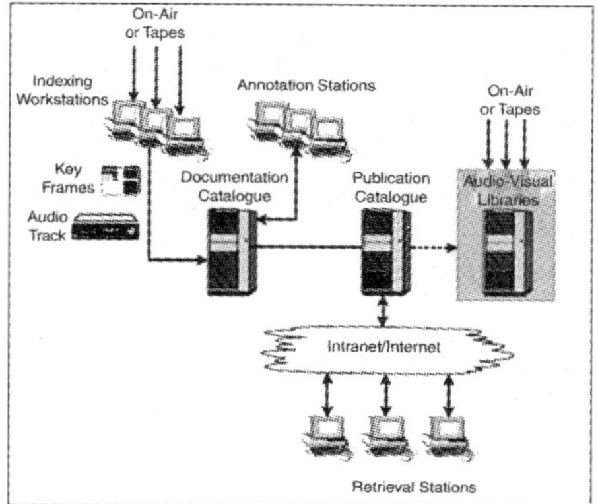

Fig.1.2. Basic Archiltecture of the Multimedia Catalogue.

Documentation Catalogue

The functions relating to the multimedia Documentation Catalogue are:

- Acquisition of multimedia objects;
- Merging of multimedia objects into programme items;
- Indexing and documentation of the programmes;
- Programme validation;
- Transferring of the validated programmes to the Searching Catalogue.

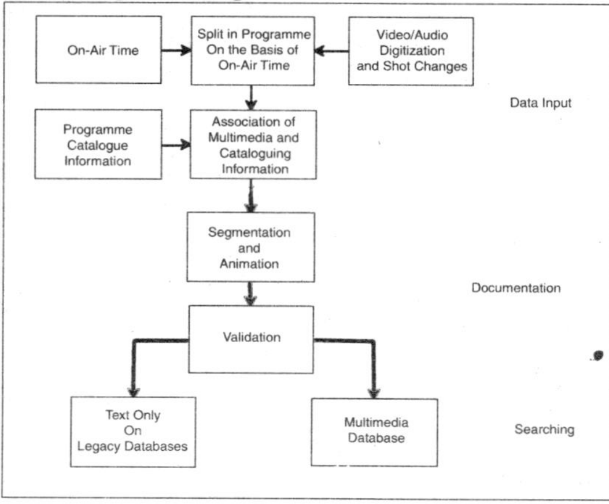

Fig. 1.3. Functional Block Dlagram of the Documentation Catalogue.

Multimedia Object Acquisition

The acquisition station is based on a custom bi-processor workstation which receives at its input a composite video signal and a temporal reference, and which performs in real-time the following activities:

- Digitisation and compression of the audio;
- Detection of shot changes;
- Extraction of a keyframe for each shot;
- Association of the starting time and duration of the shot with each keyframe.

When the acquisition station is fed with on-air signals from the broadcast channels, no programme information is available at this stage.

Thus, the keyframes and audio are labelled with their acquisition time, and further processing is required to subdivide this stream into programme items. The output stream is sent to the Documentation Catalogue server.

Subdivision of Multimedia Objects into Programme Items

In the Documentation Catalogue, the continuous flow of multimedia objects is processed in order to create programme items in the database. At present, this operation is performed manually, supported by information about the transmission start and end time of each programme, automatically loaded from an administrative database.

The available precision–sufficient for administrative operations–is not adequate for a completely automatic segmentation of programmes; therefore, an operator is required to refine the cut points.

This step is simplified in the digitisation chain for the legacy materials as there is very often a one-to-one correspondence between tapes and programmes. In this phase, a programme entity is created in the database, binding the multimedia information with some basic classification information, such as the name of the programme, the credits, identification codes of the programme, corresponding tape in the master library, etc.

Indexing, Documentation and Validation

The documentation of programmes is performed by outsourcing this work to a number of contracted companies. A general architecture has been individualised to include independent documentation islands that are connected to the Documentation Catalogue via a dedicated network.

In this way, the multimedia objects are transferred from the Documentation Catalogue to a server located in each documentation company, and then connected via a LAN to the individual documentation stations.The produced documentation is sent back to the Documentation Catalogue and added to the corresponding programme item in the database. The documentation must be validated subsequently by the archive department, before its publication.

Transferring of Programme Items to the Publication Catalogue

The validated, documented, programmes are transferred to the Publication Catalogue and then made available to the users by means of search, navigation and previewing functions.

Publication Catalogue

The Multimedia Catalogue must be able to manage the documentation relating to TV, radio, papers and photos stored in the various RAI libraries. Considering that RAI owns a huge amount of material that is increasing very rapidly, the Multimedia Catalogue would also have to be very large. A single database supporting the whole catalogue would consist of a very large number of records and would have a predictably poor performance.

Consequently, it has been decided to partition the database according to the type of material, while maintaining the capability of searching in parallel across all the partitions. The expected advantages are a large reduction in the size of each database, and a corresponding reduction in the number of concurrent users on each partition. This will lead to an increase in performance, a higher flexibility and a better scalability of the system. An additional cost to be sustained will arise from the need to maintain a distributed database which is, by its very nature, more complex than a centralised one. The user stations can be linked to the Catalogue by means of local or geographical networks, using web interfaces and standard browsers. The coding of the multimedia information has been carefully chosen in such a way that it uses minimal network resources while maintaining sufficient quality for the services provided.

Selected Technology

The documentation structure is modelled using an object-oriented approach. This structure has been mapped onto an *Object-Relational Database* (ORDB) that extends the entity-relation concepts with some features borrowed from the object-oriented technology. It is then possible to have tables of data addressed by means of the traditional SQL language, which allows for easy and efficient design and development of the searching functions, in combination with features such as user-defined data types and functions, and class inheritance.It is expected that this approach has the flexibility needed to support future releases of the system which include new requirements and new technologies. When compared with a traditional relational database, ORDB technology has proven to be very effective in the implementation of navigation functions in the media objects that make up the documentation of the programmes.

DATA MODEL

The material is logically structured according to a data model that considers a *programme* belonging to a *series* which, in turns, belongs to a *product*. The programme can be divided up into *segments* which are composed of *shots.*

These different levels are defined as follows:

- *Product*: A collection of collections, constituting a complete television programme or "title". It can also be defined as "all the programmes with the same title";
- *Series*: A set of programmes related to the same product;
- *Programme*: A media object with a unique timeline. It can be part of one or more collections, and can be sub-divided into one or more segments. A programme can also be defined as "an episode of a product";

- *Segment*: Part of a programme with a closed semantic meaning;
- *Shot*: A shot of video extracted from a programme, usually using automatic segmentation tools, according to some technical criteria, e.g. a scene change, a dissolve, a wipe.

Annotations are associated with the first four levels of data, i.e. the product, series, programme and segment levels. This structure is very general and can support recursive documentation that includes re-uses of the material. A typical case is shown in figure which depicts segments included within segments.

Each programme item comprises still pictures, compressed audio, formatted fields and free text. The still pictures consist of keyframes extracted from the TV programme, scaled to ¼ size and JPEG compressed.

The audio is derived from the programme soundtrack, compressed using MPEG layer-3 at 8 kbit/s. The formatted fields and free text include: the classification information, automatically downloaded from legacy databases; a minimal documenation generated in the production phase, and the annotation typed in by the documentalist during the documentation phase.

USER FUNCTIONALITIES

Search

To determine which tools the search interface for the Catalogue must offer to its users, an analyzis of user types must be performed.

At least two user classes must be considered:

- A generic user who accesses the Catalogue mainly for documentation purposes, without specialised information on its organisation;
- An expert user who is able to exploit every feature of the system, using complex queries.

Users belonging to the first class require a very friendly interface and the possibility of extending the search to many or all of the different types of material. On the other hand, users in the second class are, in the most part, professional researchers looking for specific materials to be included in new productions and therefore they need to locate the items in the shortest time, by means of comprehensive user interfaces. Furthermore, as different documentation fields are required for different kinds of materials, a query on the whole Catalogue must be based on the subset of documentation fields that is common to all the documentation typologies.

Based on the considerations, three searching levels have been considered:

- On the documentation of all the material, *i.e.* TV, radio, paper and photos;
- On the documentation of a single type of material, i.e. TV, radio, paper or photos;
- On the documentation of specific genres, *e.g.* TV fiction, dramas, magazine programmes, news, Radio news, etc.

The search at the third level is performed on all of the documentation fields, the formatted data and the free text. However, the search at the first two levels is performed only on free text and a limited subset of the formatted data. This subset contains the documentation fields available on all the material that is taken into account at that level. Clearly, this subset is more limited at level 1 than at level 2. The search can be composed using logical operators and by looking for either the exact word, a similar word or a synonym. The searching mode is set up by the user before starting the searching operation. The result of a search query consists of the number and list of the occurrences found. By clicking on such an occurrence, the navigation interface opens and the user is able to navigate within the selected programme.

Navigation

The results of a query can be any type of documented object, *i.e.* a product, series, programme, segment or shot.

These are all entry points to a graph of related objects, interconnected either:

- Through a structural link such as from a programme to its included segments;
- From one segment to the next one of the same programme, or;
- Through an association established by the documentalist, e.g. a set of news items on the same topic, or a programme and its script.

Therefore, after browsing the objects resulting from a query, the user can navigate across the graph of related objects. The user interface for navigation is illustrated in figure. On the left of the window is displayed a list of the segments included in the programme: it consists of the most representative keyframes, the title of the segment, and its duration.

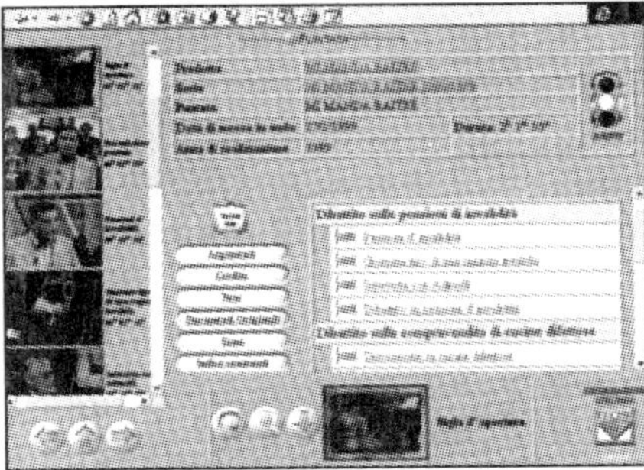

Fig.1.4. Navigation Interface at the Programme Level.

At the top of the window, the Product, Collection and Programme titles are shown. The duration of the episode, as well as the production and on-air dates, are also indicated.

By clicking on the buttons in the centre of the window, a documentation area is displayed. The picture at the bottom of the window shows the index of the programme segments, organised by content. The round buttons at the bottom of the window are used for navigation. Using this interface, it is possible to display information relating to a selected segment, as shown in figure.

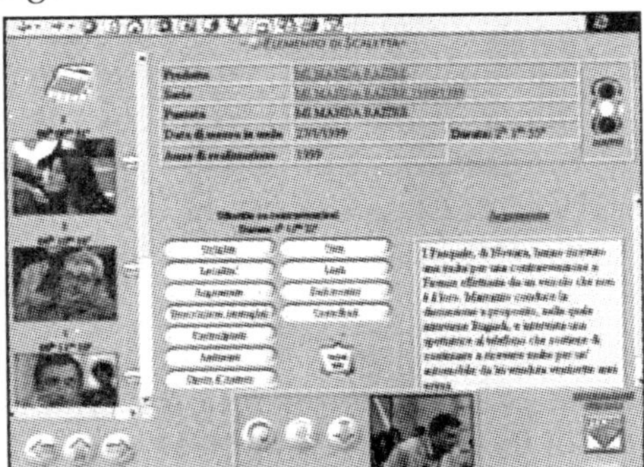

Fig.1.5. Navigation Interface at the Segment Level.

The page structure and the basic information relating to the Product, Collection and Programme at the navigation level are the same as for the Programme level. The keyframes in the left panel refer now to the most significant segment shots.

A selection of the most important shots is carried out by the documentalist in order to limit the number of displayed pictures and to reduce the downloading time. In any case, if required by the user, the complete list of shots can be displayed. The documentation areas associated with the segment object contain information that is specific to the segment, including segment description, video content description, participants list, location, environment, etc.

In the top right corner of the programme and segment interfaces, there is a traffic light icon. It indicates the presence or absence of legal constraints on the use of the material. Normally, the materials in the Catalogue are owned by RAI and are available for internal reuse but, occasionally, the allowed use may be constrained according to specific contracts. In the case of a yellow traffic light, the situation has to be cleared with the legal department. At the segment level, a previewing function is available. To limit the database size and keep the network occupancy as low as possible, the preview is obtained by displaying the keyframes for the duration of the relative shots, in synchronisation with the soundtrack.

"Palinsesto" Interface to Browse Undocumented Programmes

The complete documentation process, from the capturing of key frames to the uploading of the validated documentation to the Publication Catalogue, requires several days. For some genres such as news, the multimedia objects associated with the classification and broadcast date of the corresponding programme already constitute a valuable information source to some types of users.

Therefore, undocumented material is uploaded to the Multimedia Catalogue on the day following the transmission, without waiting for the completion of the documentation process. These materials can be accessed through knowing the relevant broadcast time or title. The enabled functions are: display of key frames; animation preview and display of the broadcast and classification date.

LINKS BETWEEN THE CATALOGUE AND THE LIBRARIES

The Multimedia Catalogue also contains an identifier of the files or supports which store the video and audio, as well as the initial timecode and the duration of every shot. Therefore, when accessing the catalogue it is possible to select a part of a programme on the basis of the documentation. The selected part is associated with the file or support identifier, and with the initial and final timecode. If the requested content is stored in a robotised library, the addressing parameters are transferred automatically to the library server which will:

- Locate the file,
- Extract the requested portion of the programme and
- Will make it available on the network.

It is possible to request each portion of a programme contained between two selected shots. If the requested content is stored in a traditional video library, a form will automatically be filled in with the parameters that refer to the material, and will then be transferred to the desk of the archivist responsible for the library, who will retrieve the requested content and send it on to the user.

2

Multimedia Systems in Libraries and their Applications

INTRODUCTION

The primary functions of a library are to collect, organise, preserve and deliver information to the users. With the passage of time, several techniques and technologies have emerged for handling the information more speedily and effectively. Invention of printing in the second half of the 15th century started a revolution in spreading thought and scholarship. Later, still pictures moving pictures' sound recordings discs; sound tapes, microcomputers and view data and optical storage systems were introduced in the commercial market which had an everlasting impact on publishing. Slowly all these recording media, used for storing information, were introduced in the libraries. All these forms were acquired and stored separately because the information retrieval methods used were different for each form of the media. As a result combining information from different forms became difficult. In 1940s, efforts were made by Dr Vannevar Bush to integrate all these forms and he designed a mechanical device, called-Memex', for storing, organisirig and retrieving information received in various forms. Those days librarians used to collect Non-book material and call them as multimedia collection. However, there was no single platform n which all the forms of information could be stored and retrieved. During the late 1980s, computer specialists succeeded in integrating the text, graphics, animation, audio, and video information on a computer after converting them into digital media called multimedia for publicity purposes. This is a major achievement in the field of publishing, which directly influenced both librarians and users.

MULTIMEDIA/HYPERMEDIA

Multimedia is a combination of some or all forms such as text, data, images, photographs, animation, audio and video, which are converted from different formats into a uniformat digital media and is delivered by computers. Unlike the analogue media the digital media which allows users to manipulate according to the needs, use at their pace, and interact at any point of the programme.

When a multimedia programme is developed in a hypertext environment, the resulting product is called 'hypermedia'. *So* multimedia would then be a part of the hypermedia. All hypermedia products are multimedia products but not vice versa. The basic difference between hypermedia and multimedia is in the organisation and linkages of the information fragments. The information chunks/fragments in multimedia are organised linearly whereas in hypermedia, these are organised Non-linearly with links to each other.

The main elements of the multimedia are:

- *Text*: Information about an object/event, etc; notes, captions, subtitles, contents, indexes, dictionaries, and help facilities.
- *Data*: Tables, charts, graphs, spreadsheets, statistics, and raw data.
- *Graphics*: Both traditional and computer, generated such as drawings, prints, maps, etc.
- *Photographic images*: Negatives, slides, prints.
- *Animation*: Including both computer generated, video, etc.
- *Audio*: Including speech and music digitised from cassettes, tapes, CDs, etc.

- *Video*: Either converted from analogue film or entirely created within a computer.

A multimedia system records, processes, stores and delivers all types of information in binary code the same way as a computer does. This is quite different from the traditional analogue technology of radio, TV, A-V tapes, gramophone records, or the combination of digital audio and analogue video in interactive video discs.

The main advantage of a digital format is the flexibility in combining, transmitting, manipulating and customising the elements of the multimedia according to the needs of the user. Basically, a multimedia system with have a powerful PC with high-end graphics processor, a sound card, CD drive, and multimedia extensions and drivers for playing digital audio and video.

Nowadays, major systems that are used for desktop multimedia design include IBM's PS/2, Apple's PowerMac, Commodore's Amiga, NeXT's Nextstation Colour, and Silicon Graphics IRIS Indigo. There are a wide variety of application software commercially available for all computer platforms. The most popular and inexpensive among all these are the Hypercard on Mac, and ToolBook on PC compatibles.

On the other hand, there are a number of authoring packages for high-end multimedia design. The popular ones include Macromedia's Director for both Mac and PC platforms and Icon Author for PC. Hypercard is a popular Hypermedia toolkit for Mac and is being used extensively in libraries for designing various applications during post 1980s and early 1990s.

APPLICATIONS OF MULTIMEDIA

Multimedia systems are being used for many purposes by different people in different organisations/offkes/environment. The main functions include media integration, storing, organisation and dissemination at different places in different ways. This chapter attempted in reviewing the use of multimedia for library and information services in various countries from the published literature.

Some of the general applications of multimedia are given below:

- Instruction/training and technical presentations
- Multimedia communications such as multimedia e-mail, personal conferencing, video phones, video conferencing, etc.
- Public information points/kiosks for libraries, museums, hospitals, tourists sites, monuments, etc.
- Medical information systems
- Multimedia databases, multimedia information banks
- Multimedia newsletters, multimedia books, other information resources
- Reference tools, e.g. Encyclopaedias, directories, etc.
- Archival systems
- Geographical information systems
- Electronic publishing and bookselling
- Point-of-sale displays,
- Product information catalogues
- Technical documentation, including engineering drawings, specifications, etc.
- Architectural information displays for example walk-through programmes for the new buildings or constructions/already constructed buildings/monuments,
- Entertainment, leisure, home
- Exhibitions such as conferences, trade shows, new product, facilities, museums, libraries, etc.
- Interactive displays in museums, hospitals, libraries, etc.

Tourism is one of the industries that has exploited the full strength of multimedia for developing tourist information systems for public and libraries.

Glasgow Online is one of the best tourist information systems designed by the University of Strathclyde during 1989 using Hypercard software. Afterwards several commercial multimedia information products were introduced in the market.

MULTIMEDIA APPLICATIONS IN LIBRARIES

Hypermedia, not only helps the users in providing information from different media on one platform but also saves on space, money, maintenance, operational inconveniences, etc.

The other advantages of multimedia in libraries are:

- It can help satisfying different information needs such as reference, enrichment, entertainment, leisure, etc.
- It can help meeting various types of information preferences of the users, such as scholarly, scientific, vocational, ' artistic, recreational, etc.
- Being in digital format, information can also be accessed by remote users on a network. It also helps in over coming the barriers of boundaries, proximity and physical rapacity of a library to accommodate users.
- It is interesting and easy to use over the existing form such as print, microforms, online, etc.
- Its control and interactivity helps the users and provides the benefits of books and human beings.

Electronic information, and multimedia in general, is about to become a vital part of our cultural heritage. Libraries have throughout the history ensured a democratic, independent and free access to the knowledge and intellectual value represented by conventional books. It is evident that this principle is also valid for electronic information and multimedia. The availability of multimedia information through,data networks may also open completely new ways for the libraries to obtain information for the common users.

AMERICAN AND EUROPEAN LIBRARIES

Many big libraries including the *Library of Congress* (LC), British Library, OCLC, etc. are building their collections in multimedia form. Apart from multimedia collection development in 1990, LC began the American Memory Project, aided by Annenberg Fund; the David and Lucile Packard Foundation; and others, for preparing multimedia CDs. This covered several kinds of information including country's historical books, pamphlets, photographs, folk songs, movies, genealogical works, etc. LC brought out the first part of this project America at the start of a New Century 1880-1920, as a CD. Similarly, Elmer E Rasmussen Library and 'University of Alaska started a Project Jukebox-a Hypercard-based Multimedia

Archival System. Project jukebox is used for archiving as well as providing access to recordings of oral history archives. For the past five years, many libraries in the developed countries started various projects such as archiving different forms of information, multimedia databases, multimedia catalogues, walk-through programmes, Instructional packages, electronic books, and digital libraries. There are a few surveys in the literature that are focused on the usage of multimedia technology in public libraries, academic libraries and special libraries. These studies primarily cover the use of multimedia CD-ROMs in libraries and also the use of world wide web and Internet.

INDIAN SCENARIO

Nowadays many librarians feels that the multimedia should be integrated into the regular services by the libraries. Even in advanced countries, libraries do not have a separate department or personnel responsible for multimedia products or services. For the past 2-3 years, use of electronic resources, particularly multimedia, in libraries has improved considerably. However, budget for multimedia products still seems to be less, but it is growing for bigger libraries situated in metropolitan cities.

Generally, for selecting multimedia products, libraries depend on retail stores displays, publisher's catalogues, reviews, advertisements, trade shows, demos, computer magazines and catalogues. The main type of multimedia products being sought in libraries are reference and educational. Other related categories include databases, electronic books, software and their training packages, entertainment, leisure, etc. Most of th'e libraries are using multimedia resources for reference service and instructional purpose. In this connection, a survey was undertaken by the author on the use of multimedia in Delhi libraries to have a clear picture of usage in Indian libraries particularly in Delhi. So far published results are not available in the literature. Overall, inspite of cost reduction in the multimedia hardware and software, use of the multimedia resources is limited to some of the national level institutions or organisations. However, the majority of the libraries are now setting up such facilities for their users. After the availability of internet in a very large scale in the offices, libraries, and houses, multimedia has become more popular, with the result most of the decision makers/financial authorities are realising the importance of multimedia in the daily life and particularly in libraries. American Centre Library, British Council Libraries and a few other libraries in Delhi are having good number of *multimedia PCs* (MPCs) for using Internet and multimedia resources to their users.

TYPES OF MULTIMEDIA SYSTEMS

MULTIMEDIA LIBRARY INFORMATION KIOSKS/ WALK-THROUGH PROGRAMMES

Improving accessibility to both collections and services has always been a concern of libraries. Several libraries made attempts to create plans and guides to help users. In this connection, multimedia is one of the best tools for creating electronic library guides or web library guides or electronic tours for their users. Many libraries in the US and Europe have started using hypermedia for designing library walk-through programmes for their users.

Reference service is one of the most visible services that can be provided by these systems. 1.1 one study, it was found that 44 per cent of reference questions were directional, 18 per cent were instructional, 32 per cent actual reference and 6 per cent were extended reference. In another study, it was found that 34 per cent of the queries are actual reference and 66 per cent are directional. So, Librarians designed Hypermedia Library information Kiosks for their users to provide quick reference and redeployed the reference staff in other library activities. Andruss Library Hypercard tour is one such hypermedia walk-through programme designed for library users to provide ready made reference. This programme does not tell the users where to find books on a specific topic, one has to still use the online or card catalogues which are briefly explained in this system, and also it is not an index to periodical or newspaper articles. However, these are described and their locations are given in this tour programme.

The Andruss Library has two catalogues for library material: a card catalogue for books, phone records, tapes, maps, and music scores; and a computerised catalogue called PALS. This tour programme helps the users by giving all the basic information that the library users require to use PALS. Sweet Briar College Library's Hvpermedra walk-through programme is another of this kind designed for the staff and students to provide information about the collection, catalogue, archives, services, and locations of various collections and responsible persons of various library services showing on the floor layout.

Some other important examples of multimedia library guide web library guides/electronic tours are:

- Electronic Library Guide in the University of Birmingham's main library, created 'using ToolBook
- Guide to South Bank University's Centenary Library, developed with HyperCard
- Guide to the Dickens House Museum Library, designed using Guide
- Multimedia Database of Tourist information developed using HyperCard by the Public Library of Gateshead Libraries and Arts Service
- Guide to the Edinburgh University Computer Services, designed using Guide
- Multimedia Library Tour of the Wayne State University Library, designed using HyperCard
- Multimedia Library Tour of the Sweet Briar College Library, designed using HyperCard
- Drexel Disk is a hypermedia walk-through programme to the Drexel University students, designed using Hypercard
- Multimedia Library Kiosk of the Defence Science Library, DESIDOC, designed using Hypercard.

INSTRUCTION/TRAINING

The role of multimedia in instruction has been well documented in several research experiments done in various discipline. So, librarians have started using multimedia as a tool to train their staff in the new library technologies/applications and also to the users to provide training about using library resources. The main advantage of using multimedia for training is its interactivity Hence,, it is being used by several schools, colleges, and universities for designing individualised library instructional packages for providing training to their users and also to provide in-depth subject training to their staff. The Paul Leonard Library at San Francisco State University desrgned a multimedia-based instructional programme on library skills to teach their users. This package is intended to serve as a prototype For subject tutorials using computing technology. This was integrated in the library skills modules being developed by the HyperCard Library Instructional Project. University of Tennessee, Knoxville libraries have made another hypermedia-based *computer-based training* (CBT) package for their new staff. To make this training more interesting, they have used pictures, animation, sound and graphics and iniplemented on Mac platform. The training programme covers library services, online catalogue, orientation to the libraries, circulation policy, access to journals literature, preservation of library materials, introduction to reference work, using e-mail, technical services, integrated online systems for libraries, and acquisition and processing library material's.

A few multimedia-based CAI packages designed using HyperCard used for library staff training/instruction are:

- *Illuminate* - a Multimedia-based CAI project about the University of Minnesota Library's OPACs.
- *Tour of the Internet* - a quick tour about the Internet
- *Information Access* - a library research skills tutorial for the university students
- *Hypercard-basedAACR2* - a self teaching CAI package for preparing catalogue cards
- *Hypercard-based University of Hawaii OPAC tutorial*
- *CatSkills* - an interactive Multimedia package to teach AACR2. It is a good professional training tool for students, beginners in cataloguing and working librarians. This multimedia CD is available in both Mac and Windows platforms. The Library Association, London is marketing this tool for $495

- *UGE 100 Library Skills* - designed by the Wayne State University Library
- *Teaching Mini Medline* - a training tool for Library users
- *STAR (Student Tutorial Access and Resources)* - CAI package designed for OSU Libraries
- *Hypermedia-based CBT package* for training the new staff of University of Tennessee, Knoxville libraries

SELF-LEARNING TOOLS

For people who need practical education in areas such as home ownership, vehicles repairing, etc, the multimedia CD-ROMs are a good medium for presenting the nuts-and-bolts tasks required to keep the house/machine functioning. For example, the House Repair Encyclopaedia provides a thorough compendium of well-illustrated repair guidelines, covering essential tasks such as stopping water leak, performing electrical wiring, pouring concrete, fixing a roof and patching the damaged walls and ceilings. Individual tasks are' depicted in animation, sound, video and providing far better information than the static pages of a book. The lnternet Resource Guide is an online book about lnternet that describes the various services available on it. Similarly many more commercial multimedia self learning tools are available in the market. Some of the important training applications available in libraries are National Geographic's Animal Samplings, ABC Golf, Music Data City, Cartoon Jukebox and Magic Flute, etc. These are self learning tools that any library can purchase and provide free education/ instruction to their library users. The linking capabilities of hypertext with multimedia provides an ideal learning environment for foreign languages. Addition of graphics, photographs, music, speech and video play a lot of impact on the learner's interest, speed of learning and retaining of information in their brain. Several popular multimedia packages were' designed for learning most of the European languages by foreigners, such as Think and Talk French/ Spanish/German and Introduction to Russian and Chinese, etc.

DIGITAF/ELECTRONIC LIBRARIES

Digital libraries are basically decentralised and easily extensible, able to support interoperability between different tools, applications and systems; support heterogeneity both in terms/forms of data and systems/tools supported; able to support a rich information seeking environment; and scaleable in terms of the size of the system. Digital information may include digital books, scanned images, graphics, data, digitised A-V clips, etc.

The first *Digital Libraries* (DL) project initiative was started, in 1995 in the following Universities in USA:

- University of Illinois Urbana-Champaign,
- Carnegie-Mellon University,
- Stanford University,
- University of California at Berkeley,
- University of California at Santa Barbara and
- University of Michigan.

Later on several organisations/universities/libraries in different countries started such projects. In the UK, an important DL projects were started by British Library is ELINOR-Electronic Library Project of De Montfort University, University of East Anglia, University of Bath, University College London, University of Wales, University of Ulster and University of Surrey. Some Digital Library related projects are listed below:

- IBM Digital Library provides a hardware/software solution for the libraries to develop their own multimedia digital libraries or multimedia archival systems. It is an integrated system for capturing, indexing, storage and retrieval of tabular, textual, audio, still images, and video data at compressed and full resolutions. A search engine that can combine parametric queries, free text searches, and Query by Image Content. Workflow processing to manage approvals and routing of data is also provided. !t has an integrated rights management including electronic watermarking, encryption, licensing, accounting, metering, and authentication. It is scaleable storage and network management system that allows libraries to grow without sacrificing the convenience of anytime, anywhere access. It also provides a hierarchical storage system to protect the assets from loss and ensure fast access to most frequently used media. A world-wide web client that facilitates the multi-search capability and delivers ranked results. This system has an integrated frame-accurate VTR control of continuous media. IBM Digital Library provides a way for libraries and users of content to store and retrieve multimedia information along with textual information that describes it. Regardless of who the end user is, IBM Digital Library allows the users to capture information and images quickly, find them when needed, and build them into new products quickly, whether it is today's broadcast, a new multimedia CD-ROM, magazine, or Internet product.

Some other important Digital Library:
Initiative projects and their site information.

- The Networked Computer Science Technical Reports Library - a collection of computer science technical reports from CS departments and industrial and government research laboratories.
- The Networked Digital Library of Theses and Dissertations - a project which aims to increase the availability of theses and dissertations by placing them online with the content in an accessible form. The works may be accessed through the Electronic Thesis and Dissertation Library.
- Library Without Walls - a broad based digital library project to make information available to researchers on their desktops on a network environment.
- Thesaurus Linguarum Hiberni - an interactive on-line searchable database archive of literary and historical materials in the various languages of early, mediaeval and modern Ireland.
- The Perseus Project - a collection on ancient Greek and Roman world. Perseus contains texts in Greek and its translation.
- The RYHINER - consists of more than 15,000 maps, charts, plans and views from the 16th to the 18th century, covering the whole globe.
- Project Bartleby - a public library on the Internet.

- Digital Libraries - a collection papers discussing digital libraries and their research efforts.
- The Visible Human Project - a complete, anatomically detailed, three dimensional representations of the male and female human body.
- National Digital Library the American 'Memory project, Special American Collections at the LC and Country Studies.
- Digital Library Programme at Tilburg University is to provide staff and students with excellent support facilities for teaching, learning and research.

MULTIMEDIA DATABASES

Now-a-days a large number of photographs, artifacts, audio recordings and textual $material in various collections are available in libraries. Multimedia is helping the librarians in integrating all the information from various forms/sources subject-wise and making meaningful multimedia databases both for day-to-day use and archiving. Mendocino County Library, Ukiah has developed a multimedia database of historical and cultural information that is relevant to the Californian Indians in that area. In addition to the historical photographs, this database is also having parts of oral histories from the state and local archives. Ultimately this library is trying to bring out a CD-ROM on 'Gathering together a Native American History'. Ancient Biblical Manuscript Centre in Claremont; California has ancient texts, photographs, negatives, related to the Bible. This centre has undertaken an ambitious programme 'Dead Sea Scroll Imaging Project', which involves digitising and reformatting photographic negatives for the past four years. The Centre has converted this collection into a comprehensive digital library and it has sophisticated search/ sort enquiries on Dead Sea Scrolls.

MULTIMEDIA INFORMATION RETRIEVAL SYSTEM

Hypermedia Information Retrieval System (HIRS) is a hypertext version of a large and comprehensive annotated bibliography of hypertext/hypermedia information. Compiled from a variety of sources including periodicals, academic journals and online informational databases, it is intended for educational and training purposes only and no warranty is made as to the suitability of anything included in this stack for any specific purpose. HIRS was created in association with Project Rivendell, at the University of Toledo. Rivendell focuses on the application of hypertext/hypermedia research to address training and educational needs. It is an interdisciplinary centre for applied hypermedia research serving as the focal point for the collection, synthesis, evaluation, and dissemination of the most current research available for using hypermedia to solve instructional problems in a variety of learning settings. HyperKRS is another commercial package being used for developing hypermedia-based information retrieval systems.

MULTIMEDIA CATALOGUES

Interactive multimedia Catalogues are electronic forms of catalogues distributed in the mail-order catalogue market. Printed catalogues are one of the important information sources particularly in technical libraries. These catalogues consume large percentage of postal carrier bags. Today, the interactive multimedia catalogues offer a high volume of information on a small disk. Several international publishing companies are also bringing out their catalogues in interactive multimedia CD-ROMs. For example, CD-ROM Catalogue Shopping, SW. Catalogues, Macromedia Showcase, Silverplatter Directory of Electronic Resources, etc. Under the *Colorado Alliance of Research Libraries* (CARL) System, Denver Public Library has designed a Kid's Catalogue is for children. The Kid's Catalogue designed to capture the imagination and the natural curiosity of children and connect them with intellectual and emotional delights of information. This catalogue was designed in *graphical user interface* (GUI) using Hypercard software. It was found that this catalogue made a considerable impact on the children's usage of the library collection. The Hans Helgesen Elementary School Library, British Columbia, Canada have also developed a Hypercard-based school card catalogue for the school children. Hypercataloguer is a Hypercard-based cataloguing tool. It can take text, graphics, animation, audio and video information for preparing multimedia-based digital catalogues. Several libraries are using multimedia Catalogues and OPACS' in their libraries for various purposes.

MULTIMEDIA INFORMATION RESOURCES

The kinds of multimedia systems/information resources available in libraries and information centers include:

- CD-ROMs.
- Video discs.
- Laser discs.
- Audio 8 video cassettes.
- Web.
- Databases on servers.
- Digital video.

Many big publishers have now converted their reference books including, Encyclopaedias, dictionaries, handbooks, etc. from the traditional print form to multimedia format. Thus libraries have a choice of selecting either print or multimedia publications.

Some of the multimedia publications are listed below:

- *Encyclopaedias*:Crompton's Interactive Encyclopaedia, 1998; Britannica CD 98 and Britannica Video CD; Encyclopaedia Americana 98; Grolier Multimedia Encyclopaedia, 1998; World Book Multimedia Encyclopaedia; Microsoft Encarta 98, etc.
- *Dictionaries and Directories*: Oxford English Dictionary; Webster English Dictionary; The Dictionary of Living World; National Geograpic's Mammals; British Birds; Microsoft Dinosatlrs, etc.
- *Reference Manuals*: MIT Movie Manual; interactive Graphics Documents; The Manual of Medical Therapeutics, etc.
- *Year Books*: The Guiness Disk of Records
- *Reference Books*: Earth Quest; World Climate Disc; interactive Periodic Table, etc.
- *Electronic Books*: Manual of Medical Therapeutics; The Electronic Whole Earth Catalogue; Microsoft Musical Instruments; Introduction to Classical Music; The Oxford Textbook of Medicine on CD-ROM, etc.

- *Electronic Newspapers/Journals*: The Times/Sunday Times/The Guardian; Times, Newsweek; Multimedia Tech for Electronic Newspapers; Integrated Multimedia Environment; Music and Multimedia Publishing; ST and Medical Publishing for Electronic Delivery, etc.
- *Multimedia Fiction*: Nowadays several Multimedia fiction books/packages are available for all levels of people. For example, The Manhole, a children fiction takes the kids to a fantasy world with talking animals and dragons where magic bean stalks grow into the sky.

GEOGRAPHICAL INFORMATION SYSTEMS (GIS)

Additional multimedia information, visuals, audio and video can be associated along with landmarks and other points of interest in a Geographical Information system?. For example, GIs multimedia application in The National Capital Planning Commission (NCPC), Washington, DC, uses online video clips and images of buildings along with their maps. In India, Bangalore Online, is a multimedia GIS applications designed with Maplnfo software. Similarly Escorts, India developed multimedia GIS for several cities in India. Number of commercial GIs reference tools are available in the market for libraries for their ready reference..

ELECTRONIC PUBLISHING

The emergence of CD-writers and recordable CDs has solved some of the problems at the libraries in storing/archiving their less used materials. Multimedia tools along with CD-writers made possible in publishing information from different sources in a most easy to use and acceptable form to the library users. Now several big libraries started publishing their special collections, image databases, OPACs, etc on multimedia CD-ROMs. It is one of the most viable alternatives to paper-based publishing.

MULTIMEDIA ARCHIVAL SYSTEM

Multimedia Archival System are mostly developed by the national museums, publishing houses, movie production companies, etc. The Design Museum located in Butler's Wharf in London has stored information regarding 250 artifacts, 40 designers, 25 manufactures and 11 monuments on Mac using Hypercard. The museum of London has over 3 million archaeological files on 7 gigabite storage space. Similarly ABC News has a very large size Mac-based video archival library for developing hypermedia applications. Project Jukebox is another Hypercard-based multimedia archival system for archiving multimedia information resources in the library.

MULTIMEDIA USE IN MUSEUM LIBRARIES

Multimedia systems allow images, sounds and text to be combined in imaginative new ways to be transmitted in digitised formats and to be stored and reproduced or networked for wide public access and use. To accelerate the multimedia digitalisation of collections, to ensure their accessibility to the public and to stress its value as a learning resource for schools and universities. Global co-operation will help museums and galleries to increase public interest in their collections and to exploit their resources for the benefit of further enrichment. The target users will be students, teachers, researchers, general public as well as curators and the end-users of the multimedia services provided by museums and galleries. Many American, European and Indian libraries are already using Multimedia in their libraries for providing information services to their users and interactive museums displays.

Examples of Indian multimedia museum guides are:

- An interactive Multimedia guide of the National Museum of Natural History designed using Director
- An interactive Multimedia guide of the National Rail Museum designed using ToolBook.

CALL NUMBER DIRECTORIES

A Call Number Directory programme was designed using Macintosh's Hypercard at the Science and Engineering Library. The Science and Engineering Library houses materials pertaining to the life and physical sciences, computing, mathematics, and nursing on seven floors. This programme helps the users in locating the information and also the physical locations of the books in different floors showing the pictures of those floors, stacks, etc.

LIMITATIONS OF MULTIMEDIA

Even though Multimedia systems have many advantages introducing such systems into offices, schools, colleges, universities, and homes is not easy task. The problems or limitations of multimedia technology are in two areas.

TECHNOLOGY

- The requisite hardware/software to setup a multimedia content creating facility is still very expensive and requires large investments.
- A wide range of multimedia software is not available to integrate, control, coordinate, manage and adapt different media for the latest human computer interfaces.
- There is a lack of support software facilitating the authoring, composition and production of multimedia content.
- Poor support technology in the area of, multimedia data and document storage and manipulation.
- Lack of proper search and pattern recognition capability for locating information from multimedia databases.
- Lack of software support technology for group decision making and cooperative work, especially in application of multimedia technology to cooperative decision making and work.
- Converting all the multimedia resources into digital multimedia and storing is difficult.
- Time being, there is no full-fledged established hardware/software multimedia technology solution for design and development of a large size realtime multimedia digital library.
- Existing distributed networks do not support real time multimedia services.

SKILLED MANPOWER

- Lack of trained manpower for the development and management of multimedia databases
- Vast amount of work required to create an hour interactive multimedia content
- Good multimedia content creation requires multi-disciplinary disciplinary knowledge, multi-technological skills and experience.

The main barrier to the widespread use of multimedia technology is the absence of standardisation among the various platforms and between hardware and software. For the time being there is no full-strength application of the multimedia information system, however, several universities are working in exploiting the full strengths of multimedia, such as natural language processing, realtime A-V content retrieval along with text and date, and implementing such a system in a network environment. The market is dominated by multimedia CD-ROMs, multimedia databases, reference tools, etc. The effectiveness of these systems will depend on various factors such as well developed software programmes, information content and development of new information handling skills. The requirements of the effective management are the support of the senior manager, the professional qualifications, knowledge about IT technology, interpersonal skills and learning models and frameworks and how to use these new resources and to be effective in the information needs of an organisation.

MULTIMEDIA TRENDS IN LIBRARY AND INFORMATION SERVICES

After the introduction of e-mail and internet in libraries, use of information in digital form has increased many folds. There is a considerable change in-libraries in their acquisition of library collection, organisation and providing services to users. The prospects for the development of a multimedia market have been transformed in the past two years by the explosive emergence of the internet and the digital revolution in the converging, IT, telecoms and entertainment sectors. There will be major changes in distribution networks and the implications of multimedia on the economy will be profound. The Internet has shown that there is a huge market for multimedia applications. The most exciting developments will come. from what is known as networked multimedia-the distribution of information using both telecommunication and broadcast technologies. It is currently multimedia packages/products such as CD-ROMs and hand-held videogames-which are the favoured methods of distributing multimedia, mainly because communications networks cannot deliver the same level of functionality. However networks are rapidly being upgraded to distribute graphics, sound and video and should soon take over from packaged multimedia. Products which can be transmitted digitally such as CDs and books are already facing major challenges. Paper publishing may never be completely replaced by electronic distribution but the cost savings for content producers may be too large to ignore. Value in the multimedia market will move away from infrastructure provision, where the network operators are strong, towards service provision and packaging which require innovation and new skills for libraries and information services. Consequently, new types of companies are poised to wrench control of the multimedia market from the network operators who will have to act quickly to gain the skills necessary to compete in the higher value areas of the market. Their alternative is to be left with high volume, but low profitability infrastructure provision.

CONCLUSION

Now many inexpensive hypermedia software are available in the market for Macs and PCs. The cost of both the hardware and software are also going down considerably. However, in India, introduction of computers and latest technologies such as multimedia, CD-ROMs, etc., is limited to the big and affluent libraries in the metropolitan cities only. It may be due to the unawareness of these technologies, insufficient funds, lack of skilled manpower, etc. Unless all the Indian Library Schools introduce the latest,technologies in their: syllabi and the teachers get trained, it will not be possible to change the present scenario of the libraries. Multimedia is a boon to the libraries, it is up to the Indian librarians how they use it in their libraries to improve the services. DESIDOC has designed a Multimedia Library information Kiosk for its user. Similarly others can also start designing for their libraries. Since, it is proven technology, it is up to Indian librarians/libraries to implement these technologies in their libraries and make optimum use to improve the user services as early as possible. In this information technology society, the future users require to access a variety of multimedia information sources in a manner that is simple, easy, and independent of time, place and subject discipline, for the purpose ranging from augmenting and refreshing memory, to learning, decision-making, and creating or uncovering new knowledge. The time is not too far in this cyber world and all these dreams will be realities in the coming 21st century.

3

Digital Libraries on the Internet

INTRODUCTION

The Internet and the Web have been growing in leaps and bounds over the past few years, accelerating the problem of information explosion, a well-known phenomena to all of us. According to Nature, the publicly indexable Web contains an estimated 800 million pages as of February 1999, encompassing about 15 terabytes of information or about 6 terabytes of text after removing HTML tags, comments, and extra white-space. Indeed, the growing amount of Search Engines (SEs) that have popped up everywhere, reaching more than 2400 different SEs, enable us to access the cyberspace, but they also flood us with vast amounts of irrelevant information. Search engine coverage, relative to the estimated size of the publicly indexable Web, has recently decreased substantially, with no engine indexing more than about 16 per cent of the estimated size of the publicly indexable Web. It is interesting to note that 83 per cent of the Web sites contain commercial content and only 6 per cent contain scientific or educational content.

The object is structured as follows. This part presents the resource repository hierarchy, defines the notion of the library and the development from paper to digital libraries. The next part classifies digital libraries, compares between the different types and introduces the logical harvesting model. The part following provides additional aspects regarding digital libraries. A concluding discussion ends the object.

RESOURCE REPOSITORIES HIERARCHY

Both Search Engines (SEs) and Digital Libraries (DLs) are Internet Resource Discovery (IRD) Tools. We introduce a resource repositories hierarchy with two major paradigms: search engines and digital libraries, where each branches to categories. SEs can be classified into three categories: Basic-SE, Directory, and Meta-SE.

All the categories support search user interfaces, but with significant differences in their construction method:

- Basic-SE/Index - a tool that uses an automatic robot/crawler to gather metadata on items.
- Directory/Catalog/Guide - a tool that uses human judgement to collect and catalog items.
- Meta-SE - a tool that holds no database of its own, but rather queries Basic-SEs upon a user request.

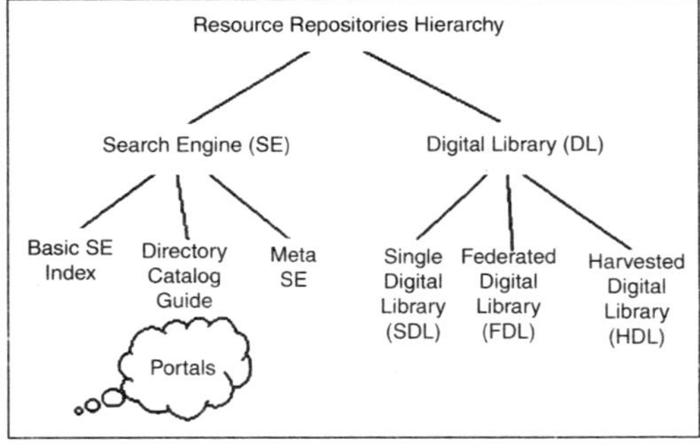

Fig.3.1 Resource Repositories Hierarchy.

LIBRARY

Before we delve into digital libraries, we define the notion of a library in general and of a digital library specifically.

Collection of Data Objects

A library holds a collection of data objects, also called holdings, items, resources, or just material.

The items can be:

- Books and journals.
- Documents (*e.g.*, HTML pages)
- Multimedia objects (such as pictures or images, tapes or video files, etc.).
- The library objects can be available locally in the library, or indirectly, by using a network to access them.

Collection of Metadata Structures

A library contains a collection of metadata structures, such as catalogs, guides, dictionaries, thesauri, indices, summaries, annotations, glossaries, etc.

Collection of Services

A library provides a collection of services, such as:

- Various access methods (search, browse, etc.) for different users.
- Management of the library (purchase, shelf arranging, computerisation, communication).
- Search (query formulation), browse, and consultation.
- Logging/statistics and Performance Measurement Evaluation (PME).
- Selective Dissemination of Information (SDI) or as it is called Push mode on the Internet.

Domain Focus

A library has a domain focus and its collection has a purpose. For example: art, science, or literature. Also, it is usually created to serve a community of users, and therefore is finely grained. For example: academic, public, special, school, national, or state library.

Quality Control

A library uses quality control in the sense that all its material is verified and consistent with the profile, or stereotype, of the library. The material is filtered before it is included in the library, and also its metadata is usually enriched (*e.g.*, annotated), etc.

Preservation

Libraries and archives have served as the central institutional focus for preservation, and both types of institutions include preservation as one of their core functions. The purpose of preservation is to ensure protection of information of enduring value for access by present and future generations. Preservation includes regular allocation of resources for persistence, preventive measures to arrest deterioration of materials, and remedial measures to restore the usability of selected materia ls.

FROM PAPER TO DIGITAL LIBRARIES

In any case, the Web and the SEs do not substitute the classical, loved libraries. Looking backwards, libraries can be classified into three types:

- *Paper/Analog Library (PL)* - the classical paper library with its card catalog;
- *Automated/Hybrid Library (AL)* - a paper library with a computerised catalog; and
- *Digital Library (DL)* - a computerised library in which most of the information is digital.

No one questions or disputes the long and lasting contribution of existing classical libraries. The concept of the paper library and the various services it provides are well established. The idea is that DLs should provide all these and more. We use the term 'integrated services' in DLs to allude to that. These integrated services will add services that are made possible by use of the digital medium such as: varied search techniques resulting in focused results, faster provision of relevant resources, and access also to multimedia resources. The problems of our regular libraries are well known and need not be detailed here. On the other hand, it is less clear to us what a digital library is and how it works-this is the subject of this paper.

CLASSIFYING THE DIGITAL LIBRARIES

We classify the digital libraries into three categories:

- Stand-alone Digital Library (SDL),
- Federated Digital Library (FDL), and
- Harvested Digital Library (HDL).

We now detail:

- *Stand-alone Digital Library (SDL)*: This is the regular classical library implemented in a fully computerised fashion. SDL is simply a library in which the holdings are digital. The SDL is selfcontained–the material is localised and centralised. In fact, it is a computerised instance of the classical library with the benefits of computerisation. Examples of SDLs are the Library of Congress (LC) and its National Digital Library (NDL), and the Israeli K12 Portal Snunit.
- *Federated Digital Library (FDL)*: This is a federation of several independent SDLs in the network, organised around a common theme, and coupled together on the network. A FDL composes several autonomous SDLs that form a networked library with a transparent user interface. The different SDLs are heterogeneous and are connected via communication networks. The major challenge in the construction and maintenance of a FDL is interoperability. Examples of FDLs are the Networked Computer Science Technical Reference Library (NCSTRL) and Networked Digital Library of Theses and Dissertations (NDLTD).
- *Harvested Digital Library (HDL)*: This is a virtual library providing summarised access to related material scattered over the network. A HDL holds only metadata with pointers to the holdings that are "one click away" in Cyberspace. The material held in the libraries is harvested (converted into summaries) according to the definition of an Information Specialist (IS). However, a HDL has regular DL characteristics, it is finely grained and subject focused. It has rich library services, and has high quality control preserved by the IS, who is also responsible for annotating the objects in the library. Examples of HDLs are the Internet Public Library (IPL) and the WWW Virtual Library.

COMPARISON

To emphasise the different aspects of this DL categorisation, let us get into the various DL types. In SDL and FDL, the items are electronically purchased or fully digitised/scanned. These items are stored in the local repository (in SDL), or in separate SDL repositories accessed using a network protocol (in FDL). Each SDL (and all together in a FDL) holds a huge repository containing both the items and some metadata structures to enable efficient retrieval. This material is updated every now and then, in a process similar to the one in classical library. It is important to note that composing a FDL out of SDLs requires interoperability capabilities, and the use of a common protocol. In contrast to the SDL and FDL, the HDL's items are gathered from the network. These items are scattered on many servers, and accessed via direct retrieval using standard protocols such as HTTP, FTP, etc. The HDL holds only metadata on the items, and therefore its repository is small and compact. Because the items that belong to the HDL can be updated any time by their authors, their summaries have to be dynamically refreshed in the HDL using computerised procedures that are triggered automatically or initiated explicitly by the IS. An interesting point is that the profile of a HDL can be changed by the IS to enhance the library contents.

HARVESTING MODEL FOR HDLs

As suggested, now describe our developed logical model for constructing HDLs. The model includes processes, data repositories (represented by rectangles) and auxiliary repositories (represented by parallelograms). The initiating IS invokes the Harvester with the DL harvesting request. The Harvester generates the initial DL profile and passes this as the harvesting query to the Locator component. The Locator uses various network search techniques to enrich the initial collection of URLs to be harvested. The next component to be invoked is the Gatherer. It uses each top-level URL, in a recursive manner, to gather all referenced resources from the network providers, and passes them to the Filtering component. The Filtering component is responsible for blocking the Non-relevant documents from reaching the focused DL. It uses various levels of filtering that all remaining documents have to pass to be considered relevant. A first level, for example, can use 'regular expressions' to match query keywords with the URL string tokens. A second level can use statistical techniques on the document itself, based on keyword counts and frequencies. A third level might use a Categoriser to classify the document and check if it belongs to the gathered DL categories. More levels or any geared combination of levels can ensure a cleaner DL devoid of 'noises'.

All relevant documents are passed now to the Summariser. It extracts a summary of the document, and passes a stream of summaries to the Broker. The Broker indexes the summaries and organises the DL. The IS builds for the DL a relevant topics-tree, possibly using advanced IR tools for categorisation and clustering. The Retriever provides the DL user with a user-friendly interface.

IMPLEMENTATION OF HARVEST/KATSIR SYSTEM

To demonstrate HDLs, we focus on the Katsir HDL based on the Harvest system, an initial/partial implementation of the harvesting model for HDL. Katsir is currently being developed in Bar-Ilan University (BIU) as cooperation between the Mathematics and Computer Science department and the Department of Information Studies. The Harvest system, developed mainly at University of Colorado, USA, is an integrated set of tools to gather, extract, organise, search, cache, and replicate relevant information across the Internet. With modest effort users can tailor Harvest to digest information in many different formats, and offer custom search services on the Internet. Moreover, Harvest makes very efficient use of network traffic, remote servers, and disk space. The Katsir system is based on the Harvest system. Katsir can be directed to build a focused DL, based on both local and networked harvested materials.

Katsir's enhancements over the original Harvest system are:

- *Hebrew support*: Full Hebrew support for both resources and interfaces was added to Harvest.
- *Improved user interface*: While Harvest's user interface supports keywords query, Katsir enable to user to retrieve information by keywords or conduct a guided tour by following a topics-tree that enables hypertext access to relevant materials.

- *Improved Graphical User Interface for the IS*: While the IS interface to Harvest is through Unix, using file editors to define harvesting options, Katsir implemented a GUI interface to define DL profile. The interface includes URLs for initialisation, harvesting options, ports selection, etc. It also employs the standard browsers Bookmarks/Favorites utilities to define the initial DL Harvesting URLs.

The initial Katsir system was developed and implemented in an educational environment as a response to the unique requirements of the Israeli educational system. This project was part of a drive to enhance and assimilate information and telecommunication technologies in Israel, based on the public Internet. Both researchers and students of the departments of Information Studies and of Mathematics and Computer Science at BIU were involved in the development of Katsir. Their cooperation in the framework of the demonstrative Gilo High-School project was complementary in knowledge and experience, and fruitful in its results. Moreover, the project itself was planned and executed with full cooperation of the Gilo user community. This begun in requirements analysis, in deciding the topics to be harves ted, in training the users in accessing the system, in conducting the control and evaluation process, and in reviewing and implementing the conclusions reached as part of the working methods of Katsir.

ADDITIONAL ASPECTS

PERSONAL DLs VS. PUBLIC DLs

All libraries can be personal or public, but this issue is mostly interesting in the implementation of HDL. HDL can support the harvesting of both personal and public DLs. A personal DL is one constructed for personal use by a seemingly only self-interested pers on. Here, the person is both the harvester and its user. The personal and library profiles could be related or even be the same here. A public DL is geared to a wider range of audience. The harvester here is the IS, but the users are many. The library profile supports the library (users) stereotype and is maintained by the library IS. A public DL supports a large audience and has to have a higher level of integrated services, including support for pull and push modes.

TEXTUAL DLs VS. MULTIMEDIA DLs

Most DLs nowadays are mainly textually oriented libraries. However, a major advantage of being digital is the option of supporting libraries that contain Multi-Media (MM) resources. One major problem with MM DLs is how to summarise MM resources. The methods for summarising MM resources are entirely different from textual ones; they include colour, texture, shape, objects, etc. for visual information; pitch, rhythm, etc. for vocal information. Also, the repository generated is different, requiring special tools, such as multimedia and object oriented databases. Another hard problem is intelligent search and retrieval of MM resources. Usual IR tools are textually oriented. Some techniques for MM contents search and retrieval have been developed for use in MM-SEs. These techniques includes query by example, and the tools are sketching or giving an image as example to the query for images and video or based on singing a melody or humming a few notes for audio.

There are several implementation of MM DL, few examples on the Web are:

- Webseek.
- Metaseek.
- Virage.
- Meldex.

However, most of these techniques are low-level using query by example or similarity measures, while DLs should also use higher-level methods based on object specification and recognition methods.

COMPOSING DLs

Another promising idea here is the composition of existing DLs to construct a coarser-grained DL. For example, we might have finely-grained DLs on the categories of Spaniels and Briards.

These two can be composed to a coarser-grained DL on dogs. If we had additional DLs on cats, we could then combine them to a mammal DL. And similarly, further compose a DL on the category of animals and so on. The DLs participating in a composed DL can be physically distributed of course. The DL composition process uses techniques of open networking, shared file systems, replication servers, and resource caching.

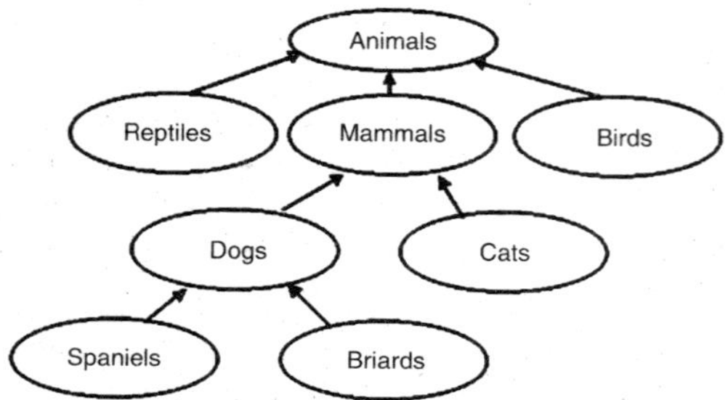

Fig.3.2 Composition of DLs.

Considering the vast amount of information, the Web is considered by many to be the world's ultimate virtual digital library-but is this solution the right one? We already confronted SEs with DLs to realise the differences between them. We can compare the different categories of SEs with the different categories of DLs. Basic -SE is similar to all DLs in the basic user interface, IR tools, and network access. Furthermore, Basic-SE is similar to HDL Since, they both hold metadata repositories rather than full items. A directory is even closer to a DL than a Basic-SE, Since, it is humanly compiled and therefore has quality control. But lets not forget it does not have domain focus and DL integrated services. Meta-SE is somewhat similar to FDL in the sense that both generate on-the-fly queries to other SEs/DLs to answer user queries.

SEARCH ENGINES VS. DIGITAL LIBRARIES

The Search Engine (SE) paradigm and the DL one are really located at the extremes of a spectrum of data repositories and types of search. There are two sides to each of these coins: the data repository construction side and the user information search side. As suggested, now discuss and contrast these aspects. As regards to the construction of SEs, this is a complex undertaking. It is clearly a long-term effort that is supported by commercial companies. The SE aims to build a quantitative global repository that represents as much information available on the Internet as possible or at least a large amount of it. The SE maintains various data structures, to represent its repository, like indices, directories, and catalogs. It also provides an elaborate user interface for search purposes. The SE continuously employs various types of robots to search out and index pages on the Internet and to dynamically update its provided repository. Let's look now at the user side of SEs. Assume that a user needs some information on a certain topic that currently interests him. So he summons on a whim of a second his favorite SE to search for any relevant information. The SE is invoked with an *ad-hoc* query composed of a supposedly appropriate combination of keywords. The SE will certainly return a lot of information, which is bound to overload the user.

He will then have to tediously sift through it all and manually filter the supplied references. The relevant information found will then be immediately used or temporarily kept in a cache for a short-term period of use.

Table.3.1 Search Engines vs. Digital Libraries - Server Side.

Measure	Search Engine	(Harvested) DL
Effort	Complex Undertaking	Medium
Emphasis	Quantitative	Qualitative
Content	Global/Shallow	Focused/Annotated
Repository	Huge	Small
Maintenance (Robots)	Continuously Updated Updated	Dynamically

Table.3.2 Search Engines vs. Digital Libraries - Client Side.

Measure	Search Engine	(Harvested) DL
Interest	Sudden	Lasting
Query	Ad-hoc	Sounder
Use	Short Term	Medium Term
Information Returned (coverage/recall)	A lot	Modest
Quality (precision)	Noisy	Clean
Sift/Filter	Manual	Not much needed
Distribution Mode	Pull Mode	Both Pull/Push

Consider now the process of harvesting (*i.e.*, constructing) a DL. A user, say an Information Specialist (IS), realises a well-thought out need to build a qualitative data repository on an important focused topic. He decides to invest by harvesting and maintaining a long-term DL, described by a set of specific categories.

So he interacts with an IS interface to carefully define his DL harvesting request. The DL is then harvested and made available to its users. It supports transparent user access methods using various data structures to enable efficient keywords search, touring a DL via a topics tree, and DB/SQL oriented views of the DL contents.

The contents of the DL are continuously kept current and the DL can be annotated and enhanced with additional relevant material. Let's check now on the use of DLs. A serious user will tend to often need information on a topic included in his areas of interest.

There is a good chance then that he already has access to a relevant DL, previously harvested. So he invokes the high-level DL interface and chooses an appropriate way to search this DL. The DL will return a reasonable amount of information (with high precision and recall) that the user can readily digest. The returned results will be made available at three levels of detail: first, a high-level summary (metadata); then, if requested, an additional abstract; and finally, if relevant, the referenced resource itself will be fetched and presented. Not much sifting will be necessary in any case. The relevant information can be further annotated by the user and later rediscovered whenever needed.

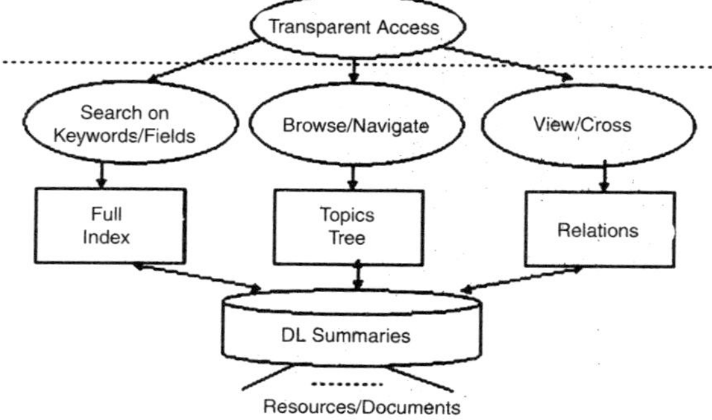

Fig. 3.3 User Access Methods and Data Structures in HDL.

So, to summarise, SEs necessitate a huge organisational effort, provide the user with too much noisy information, but are useful for a one-time shot for quickly needed information. DLs, on the other hand, require a modest support effort, provide the user with focused information, but have to be made available beforehand while excelling in quality and ease of use. It is important to note that these two paradigms are neither conflicting nor exclusive, but are complementary in nature.

CONCLUSION

Digital libraries and search engines on the Internet are similar in many ways yet differ in others. The direction they are all going seems somewhat alike, yet, more research should be carried out to determine the real trends. Further research can also probe into the versatile types of SEs and DLs and their generations. More exploration into additional aspects discussed here, like multimedia, composition of libraries, and DL profiles should take place to promote these issues for the benefit of the millions of users surfing the net.

4

Vital Technical Services in Academic Libraries

INTRODUCTION

Technical services departments in every type of library are affected by the state of modern librarianship. This is so most sharply for academic libraries. We have experienced a long journey of severe if unfair criticism, explicit or implicit threats of elimination, downsizing, and downgrading, and a deep experience of collective anxiety while our colleagues in public services and administration regarded us with suspicion and, simultaneously, we had to relearn our trade again and again. We seem to have come out of this prolonged trial period with our capabilities intact, our hearts filled with professional pride, and our expectations returned to normal within a revitalised profession. Researcher believes along with many others that our future is brilliant, that our work is as wonderful as it ever was, and that as suggested, have a better life during the coming decades. He want to discuss five urgent topics that have been suggested to me by colleagues and that are dear to me as a result of my own work in recent years. The five topics are: *access to information in print and Non-print media* with special emphasis on the question of remote storage; *leadership and management in library administration*; the *new standard for monographic and serial holdings of materials* in all formats; the *restructuring of MeSH by the National Library of Medicine*; and the *cataloging of computer files contained on discs.* Researcher has arranged them in the order stated so that he can move from the most general to the most particular. The first issue affects all media of publication on an international basis; the second is a vital problem for all employees at all libraries; the third issue implies an advance in bibliographic control at the national level, as the standard propounded is an American National Standards Institute (ANSI) standard which all American academic libraries should follow; the fourth issue is a technical question for American health sciences libraries; and the fifth issue is a problem for libraries that collect physical types of electronic materials. I will start with a philosophical discussion of resource management in libraries with space problems and the need to balance the acquisition of print and Non-print materials.

ACCESS TO PRINT AND NON-PRINT MEDIA

Nothing seems more urgent in the field of library administration than new ways of providing access to information. Administrators are eager to find these new ways because the advent of a torrent of information resources in electronic formats is something previously unknown in human history. We simultaneously marvel and despair at the newly available texts, graphics, audio, and video files in a variety of "machine readable" forms. This torrent of resources calls for an originality of mind and vision with which to achieve clarity and decisiveness. Library administrators need to make bold decisions about how to handle these new forms of information, how to select organisations which sell or distribute them, how to contract archiving agreements for whatever must be preserved, how to survive the competition of rivals, and how to operate within the law.

While we welcome the perceived need for new and penetrating ideas in library administration today, we question the novelty of what we are discussing. I ask if the issues are truly new in any sense of the term, or if we are repeating what we have more or less forgotten about the past, both remote and immediate. we do not propose to review the remote past, but we do intend to cover the relationship between the immediate past and the coming future. The past can not be changed, but thinking about it in the present is fair and even necessary in order to have a clearer picture of the future. In addition to discussing preservation of electronic resources, Researcher also wants to address the issue of the storage and preservation of *Non-electronic* resources that we want to preserve.

We hope this approach will put the problem of shrinking storage space in context, while relating it to discussions of electronic resources. In brief, there is "nothing new under the sun" and that a fruitful way to address the question of remote access to library materials acquired in the past and "deselected" for reasons of lack of use and space is to think of it in parallel to the question of remote access to electronic materials in the present. In explicating this work to librarians, researcher proposes an alternative to the "horizontal thinking" we all tend to follow in considering problems, and thus attempt to look at the question of access to library resources, old and new, print, electronic, and anything else, in terms of "vertical thinking."

It is better to think about time, not as something discrete, passing from left to right on a flat plane in equal units, but in the vertical style of agriculture, architecture, theology, and other disciplines, wherein we think of the past as the ground of the present, and of the future as the outcome of our lives and choices in the present. Instead of a flat, equal movement from day to day, acquisition to acquisition, set of books to set of books, shelf to shelf, building to building, try to conceive of materials, collections, budgets, and history as an organic process that moves from its ground in time and life towards its immediate future. Instead of the mere accumulation of thousands of books, microforms, films, diskettes, etc., which boggles the mind, gathers dust, and needs to be divided because of space limitations, think of a university's physical property as an organism that lives in the midst of the collective mental existence of the university's faculty and students.

In this way, you might be able to look at your large collections as a beautiful but overgrown tree that needs trimming in order to keep it alive, strong, and beautiful. Your physical environment and your intellectual environment suddenly begin to mesh, and it may be as sensible to have a break under a group of trees in a quiet area of the campus as to have a meeting in some special room of one of the buildings which house a part of the library's collection.

Instead of throwing away all the older materials that have not been used for a certain number of years, you will keep a good amount of them in a remote storage facility with the understanding that classics, unique holdings, local materials, specialty items, etc., are as valuable as any new acquisitions recommended by your tenured faculty members, or the best looking and most complete, free or purchased, resources found in the almost infinite niches of the Internet which your reference librarians pursue every day.

Those preserved older books which you acquired some time ago are continuing to live their proper lives as the published treasures which they were and still are in their right new place, thanks to the intelligent decisions of your staff. Each one of them will be granted an assisted life in the nursing home that you have remodeled for the senior members of the collections.

As those books are either circulated again to the occasionally interested scholar, or remain in storage to help preserve the memory of academia, they should be living a full and dignified life in their own right. There may be even time and funds to have some of them rebound, deacidified, microfilmed, or digitised. Concerning criteria for deselection from the main collection or the just mentioned upgrading of their physical condition, again, the truth may be that there is nothing new to add to the established truth of previous library practice.

Statistical information about external and internal use at the library in recent years, quantified extra life from interlibrary loan reports, numbers of citations reported in citation indexes, considerations about numbers of copies, original and present day price, availability in print or lack of same, and holdings in member libraries of consortia to which the library belongs, are sufficient for making decisions. If anything could be added to that, I would point to the welcome new emphasis on Non-quantifiable or Non-measurable criteria. At last, the professional literature is again referring to qualitative criteria for deselection, such as categories of use, the importance of a particular edition or printing of a text, personal recommendations of specialists with profound and extensive knowledge of a given scientific literature, and others.

A set of quantitative and qualitative criteria regularly updated by the collection management librarians should suffice for the library to have a satisfactory policy in place for the benefit of all. In addition, and at the risk of being charged with a personal bias, researcher would argue that the ultimate key to the successful separation of the collections into two or more categories resides with the cataloging department of the library. All materials removed to permanent storage need to be faithfully and fully represented in the library's catalog. Any given copy of anything might as well be thrown out if it is not represented by an adequate bibliographic record and an accurate holdings record in the local OPAC. The only other possible solution, and a much more costly one, is the already mentioned digitising of the entire document and the addition of a hot link to it on the library's web catalog.

Let me try at this point to draw again the vertical model I have presented earlier:

- (Written Policies) RESOURCE MANAGEMENT (Staff participation)
- (Searching) INTERNET (Web Page Construction)
- (Selection) LIBRARY (Cataloging)
- (Deselection) STORAGE (Preservation)

Researchers have now added some terms on the left and right sides of the vertical triad in order to recover the use of the horizontal dimension, and to amplify the meaning of the three single terms he used first. Vertical, or, if your prefer, organic thinking, does not intend to deny the reality and appropriateness of horizontal thinking, but only to make it more vital and true by means of a radical change of perspective. Traditional library functions and processes, such as searching, acquiring, cataloging, processing, weeding, preserving, etc., still have and will always have room in any legitimate professional practice. The traditions we come from are alive and important. On the other hand, the negative views of some contemporary proponents of an extreme electronic approach to information seeking are unbalanced and perhaps even dangerous. As Michael Gorman has repeatedly argued, there have not been yet any formats that cannot be successfully subjected to normal Anglo-American cataloging standards. In spite of the suspect intentions of some authors and vendors, all Internet documents are accessible, reproducible, and controllable by traditional library means.

And every new conceptual advance or technological development can be taught by professional instructors to all sorts of learners independent of age, background, field of specialty, and so on. I believe that the recent creation of "headers" for documents written in standard markup languages and "locators" (less or more permanent) for resources which can be embedded in bibliographic records will soon allow more exact control of materials than we ever had dared to imagine. We are fortunate that the profession as a whole has conveniently forgotten the very recent fad that was so-called "cataloging simplification." The refined model displays a greater number of terms, and any of us could have a good time adding more, in the approximate shape of a tree with roots, trunk, and branches.

The total life of the tree is made up of the composite life of all its parts. As in nature, multiple relations among the parts are responsible for the specific vitality of the one tree that will represent each library system. Thus, again, the right storage collection is a vital part of the total life of the library. With the storage and library collections as a foundation, librarians and patrons should then continue to aggressively explore the Internet in search of documents, files, archives, etc.

The result of this exploration will replicate, complement, revitalise, change, and improve the print, microform, and audiovisual collections of the past. The introduction of new viewpoints, modes of access, ways of working, and revolutionary changes in teaching and learning techniques, while not easy for many in certain ways, are a necessity and a gift for all. Vertical thinking and living require effort and direction from human beings, properly grounded in the past, who cannot resist the pleasure of letting their minds grow. I have included a fourth term at the top of the tree, Resource Management, again to follow tradition, but also to argue that intelligent management of our means is the most we can do, and that such management implies our professional efforts to teach the best to the new generations. In that sense, you can relate standard terms like "Bibliographic Instruction" or "Education" to the term Resource Management. I will argue that, as in the case of storage, librarians have the responsibility of selecting which electronic resources are to be made available and which should not be included in the offerings that workstations present to patrons.

There are all the constraints of limited funds, hardware, software, instructors, space, and time, but it is our duty and privilege to balance those concerns with our responsible choices from the universe of electronic publishing. That choice is the core of our instructional task. Let us select with care any and all of the resources that are available at either the storage facility, or in the stacks of the library, or at the computer workstations in the library and elsewhere. In doing so, as suggested, have discharged our duty. Compare with my idea what Carol A. Mandel and Robert Wolven wrote recently about the Web: "Information on the World Wide Web could be likened to a library in which authors shelve their own books, haphazardly, rewrite them overnight, and move them from place to place without warning."

LEADERSHIP AND MANAGEMENT IN LIBRARY ADMINISTRATION

Before waiting of the particular areas of technical services, researcher want to add to the philosophical discussion of administrative issues a specific discussion of personnel administration, simply because there cannot be libraries without librarians, and if the librarians are not infused with "the spirit of the times", libraries will not fulfil the needs of today's library patrons.

Researchers with good reason, is deeply alarmed by the mania for change that has invaded many companies, the mental laziness of the American population that wants everything to be easy and quick, the dependence of many organisations on various management ideologies, the sad phenomenon of extensive job dissatisfaction among workers, the obsession with numbers alone, and the lack of understanding of the very purpose of many organisations by their own leaders. Instead of such ideas and others commonly on the horizon of our management practice, Secor proposes a moderate view based on the revitalisation of certain traditional values and an eagerness to readapt and renew at every turn as the world keeps evolving. Researcher summarises his long essay in the very direction of my defence of "vertical thinking" when he says to his audience, "I've pointed you back to your roots." Before continuing to discuss Secor's ideas let me draw a new tree arrangement of the fundamental terms in personnel administration:

- Human Resources
- Workers
- Managers
- Leaders
- Company History

Starting with a strong defence of the need for a true self identity on the part of all members of a company's staff, researcher proposes a new idea of leadership which should make us rethink our notions of the relationship between leaders and followers. Armed with an awareness of the company's origin and nature, leaders are responsible for the introduction of change while watching out for the company's stability, and for the creation of a team in which everybody gets retrained as the changing content of each person's work demands and in which everybody contributes willingly to the total effort according to his or her own abilities.

Researcher writes, "If it's a team sport, then personal and interpersonal training is part of the conditioning." And, "Skills training and personal and interpersonal effectiveness training are critical building blocks for personal and organisational renewal." If one wants to disagree with the idea that a company's life is a "team sport" and prefers to believe it is an individual's privileged domain only, then there is no need to continue this discussion.

But if the fundamental notion of "team sport" is granted, then he point about the radical need to think and learn continuously and to renew oneself, whether we are talking of leaders, managers, or workers, should be at the center of a new theory of management for the contemporary company. Then, more specifically, He neatly distinguishes the concepts of "leader" and "manager" as pertaining to two quite distinct skill sets and personality types, and asserts that any healthy organisation needs to have some of both if it wishes to endure. The leaders are charged with the creation of a credible vision for the future and they must try to understand that human nature means the workers will feel uncomfortable with the tensions that accompany all change.

Capable managers will also be needed to bring about the change involved and help all workers adapt to it. And, of course, old and new workers will have to be employed to carry out the business of the company, following the lead of the leaders, and responding to the management of the competent managers, in a spirit of full participation and never of blind submission. Leaders, managers, and workers should join in the pursuit of the legitimate goal of the organisation and for the good of all, the company itself, and its customers. It seems to me that researcher must have been thinking about libraries when he wrote, "Most organisations do need to make fundamental changes in how they do business so that they can adapt faster and faster to their changing environments." Our library environments seem truly to change faster and faster, and thus far we librarians have failed to respond faster and faster to such changes.

The reasons for this are obvious. The responsibility for this failure rests with all of us - leaders, managers, and worker alike. First, our leaders often do not know how to lead, do not care for stability but only for abstract change and newness, do not communicate to library managers and workers clear visions that need to be shared by all, do not empower their managers with the proper responsibility, and do not respect the humanity of their workers. Second, many library managers do not care to manage but want to lead only, do not help their workers to adapt to the continuous changes, and do not attempt to understand the organisation's purpose and goal but care only to produce high figures and stay out of trouble.

And, third, too many workers do not want to work but only manage or lead in spite of their lack of qualifications for such tasks, do not join managers in any form to sustain a collective effort, and do not care about the organisation's past or future but are only interested in a self-serving, short-term benefit. To correct this situation, we need to go back to the drawing board, and for that we have the scheme presented by my new tree for the vertical organisation of a library's life.

Researcher would suppose that most persons trying to draw this tree of personnel would have placed the workers at the root level and the leaders at the branch level. We do not call certain powerful employees "top" executives for no reason. However, Since, the role of the leader is the decision-making that provides direction to the life of the organisation, we need to correct our customary incremental thinking and properly situate the "leaders" at the root level. Their work infuses the whole organisation with the vital substance which flows through all its parts. "Managers" do fit in the middle where we draw the tree's trunk. They must be the strongest members of the staff, involved as they always are of necessity in sustaining the company's life, whatever the circumstances.

And the "workers" should be placed at the level of the branches. They can change departments, they sometimes waver in their endeavors, they are visible to outsiders, they grow rather obviously when they educate themselves further, etc. When things are well in a company, we all know it has to do with having good leaders and managers first, but, also and decisively, with having good workers on the front line. Whether these workers are mechanics, programmers, or masons, the point is the same always. So, we do need "top" librarians in all good libraries - "top" reference specialists, "top" catalogers and indexers, "top" searchers, etc. Most companies today have a human resources department to watch over the workers and their human needs and to help with many delicate management issues and help "leaders" communicate with "managers" and "workers" In so doing, they are responding to the true reality of the organic life of a company in spite of our collective faults in thinking.

Without the fundamental direction of the "leaders," there will not be a tree or company at all but, instead, the company will wither away (as it is the case with many in the real world of economic and social competition, and whether or not they have tried "downsizing" or "reengineering.") Without "managers" who sustain the whole edifice of the organisation, wellrooted in the vision shared by the "leaders" from its roots, there will be chaos in the organisation. And without true "workers" there will not be the product that makes a company recognisable and appreciated. In the case of a library, the "leaders" can be the directors of national associations or consortia as well as the local heads of the largest libraries. The "managers" are, independent of their titles, the directors or head librarians of the smaller (school, public, special, corporate) libraries or the department heads of the sizable academic libraries. And the "workers" are the beginning professional librarians, the best of the paraprofessional staff, and even the expert veterans in all sorts of specialties whether degreed or not. The relationships among all of them, their understanding of the roles they play in library organisations, and their commitment to a vital vision of the place of libraries is what makes or breaks the real and effective existence of libraries in our society.

NEW STANDARD FOR MONOGRAPH AND SERIAL HOLDINGS

Having presented a model for vertical thinking about organisations, and having discussed the general issues of access to materials and personnel administration, I want to discuss next a more particular topic that is closely related to the issues of access and storage. That topic is the extremely important new ANSI standard Z39.71 for the display of holdings of both monographs and serials in all media, physical or electronic, and whether manual or automated means are used to keep records. This new standard was approved unanimously by National Information Standards Organisation (NISO) representatives after very careful consideration by many organisations and it has just been readied for publication. The importance of the standard lies in its direct and positive confrontation of some mistakes of our past and its responsible attitude towards new ways of delivering information.

It reverses the old separation of serial and Non-serial publications, and thus it justly proclaims to have made obsolete the two earlier standards for the display of holdings for those two sorts of publications. It also claims to apply to the display of holdings statements of bibliographic items in any format at either summary or detailed levels, or even a mix of the two for libraries that cannot create fully detailed holdings statements for their older publications.

It is independent of any particular cataloging system or code, and it leaves librarians free to choose among several alternatives to make practice possible under different local needs and possibilities. This is the same spirit of the latest revisions of AACR2 and new documents like the 1994 *ALA Guidelines for Bibliographic Description of Interactive Multimedia*. At last, the participation of all of us in the field, and in particular in technical services, is now continuously requested and appreciated. In this case, the standard was developed in full consultation with many specialists in American libraries. The main goal of standard Z39.71 is to make holdings statements consistent in all sources for such data and therefore make it possible to communicate the data across computer systems.

The standard, however, only addresses the display of holdings, not their communication. The latter is the job of the MARC holdings format, and the acceptance of Z39.71 will require some changes to that format. The recommendation is that catalogers and serials librarians must adopt the directions of Z39.71 as fully as local circumstances allow, and try to use its four levels of specificity intelligently. While single part titles can be satisfactorily recorded at the first level, multipart titles, titles with supplements, indexes, accompanying materials or any other sort of secondary bibliographic units, and serial titles—all still represented by a single bibliographic record—can only be satisfactorily treated at the second, third, or fourth levels of specificity. The second level provides only "general" information about holdings.

The third level provides a compressed summary statement of holdings. The fourth level provides detailed holdings information, either compressed or itemised, which, it seems to me, will deliver completely successful retrieval by computer in every conceivable case, no matter what complexity the record might include. For the purposes of my organisational model, the two older standards were another expression of horizontal thinking, while the new standard makes more sense from the point of view of vertical thinking..

RE-STRUCTURING OF MeSH

While the Z39.71 standard is an important new tool for descriptive cataloging, the restructuring of MeSH—*Medical Subject Headings*—the medical vocabulary of the National Library of Medicine (NLM) represents an important advance in subject analysis. The 1999 version of MeSH was prepared by the Cataloging Section of the NLM to exploit the capabilities of their new Voyager library automation system.

The new MeSH proposes to overcome the old difference between cataloging and indexing that has been an impediment for medical librarians and their patrons. NLM will now perform subject analysis in cataloging the same way as it does in indexing. This should result in a new equality in the treatment of all materials relevant in medical information seeking. No longer will there be two parallel systems: one for the analysis of journal articles by indexers and another for the analysis of books, audiovisuals, and computer software by catalogers.

Beginning in 1999, any document in any format will be analysed the same way, with subject headings distributed mostly in terms of descriptors subdivided topically, while earlier form, linguistic, and geographical subheadings will become genre, language, and geographic descriptors. Uptodate automated systems will be able to retrieve and combine such new headings with more powerful and accurate results. In keeping with the same spirit of liberty and participatory responsibility, NLM has opened a dialog with other medical libraries to present them with three choices for the use the new vocabulary structure depending upon local traditions, computer characteristics, and relationships among libraries.

Recognising that many medical libraries are associated with other types of libraries in many university systems, the first choice still allows for the stringing of headings and subheadings done in previous years, a technique which is much closer to the style of LC subject analysis that will continue to appear in most bibliographic records of those universities. The second choice is to comply with NLM's new practice. A third, intermediate choice is a hybrid of the other two that might take advantage of the strengths of both systems. I have taken the position that, if at all possible, medical libraries should follow NLM's lead and convert to its new practice as soon and as fully as possible, given staff retraining considerations, the economics of conversion, etc. The advantages of a unitary system of subject analysis that covers the article databases, the indexes, and the online catalog seem to me enormous.

In terms of my proposed vertical model, the new use of MeSH should represent the revitalisation of the branch of practical knowledge that is cataloging in its relation to the branch we call indexing and to the main trunk of all library work. The pruning of the previous MeSH will be a painful procedure, but it should result in a more rational and vital tool which will serve us well for years to come. An example of the greater intellectual correctness of the new vocabulary is that, at last, the topical subheadings epidemiology and ethnology will be exclusively related to geographic subject headings. On the other hand, in spite of the change a few years ago of the two topical subheadings legislation and statistics to legislation and jurisprudence and statistics and numerical data respectively, catalogers in many medical libraries have still been using them as equivalent to the form subheadings legislation and statistics and in practice applying only or mostly the form subheadings.

This change illustrates the need to reform the structure of the vocabulary. One cannot substitute a form subheading for a more precise topical heading and then expect success in the retrieval of pertinent literature. Discussions of laws are not enough like a collection of the texts of those laws, and the same applies to the second case about statistical data. The classical concatenated string of headings and multiple subheadings is an extreme example of horizontal thinking, with all its advantages and disadvantages. By contrast to LC vocabulary, MeSH has always had a built-in tree structure of concepts related vertically, and now it will be cleaned and polished as horizontal strings are replaced by vertical sets of subjects that apply to a given document. If only we could now go further and also clear up the horizontal relations among the various trees to make MeSH the perfect "forest."

POLICIES FOR CATALOGING COMPUTER FILES ON DISC

Another, and still more specific, example of the need for vertical thinking is in the development of policies for cataloging Non-audio compact discs, *i.e.*, CD-ROMs. We face an interesting situation with compact discs. On one hand, we do not look at them with the same awe of a few years ago, when their novelty and characteristics made them a hit among librarians as well as the public at large. On the other hand, they still are being published and distributed in large quantities and in many fields, from pornography to scholarship and anything in between. If anything, it appears that more and more of our traditional materials are either accompanied by a compact disc or are reissued in this contemporary technology.

The pressing issues for libraries seem to be their preservation and "fair use," which has led to discussions about the necessity or convenience of arranging a new collection of discs at the reserve desk. The bibliographic character of CD-ROMs is also an issue, including traditional questions such as monograph or serial, accompanying material or independent publication. By now, LC has prepared draft interim guidelines for cataloging electronic resources (excluding Internet documents). Their proposals seem quite reasonable and sufficient, and, if followed prudently, they provide the basic elements for a local policy on compact discs.

In practice, the most difficult aspect may be establishing whether the material is a reproduction (whether with the same title of the original or not) or a new publication. After that, it is a question of determining whether the disc stands alone or is part of a larger package. If the disc is truly a separate publication which stands on its own, a new bibliographic record must be prepared, with the MARC fields 007, 300, 516, and 538, which will fully describe its physical characteristics and the hardware required to use it. If the disc is accompanying material for another published item, then its physical description must be subsumed in subfield e of the 300 field for the primary bibliographic unit, and an 006 field should also be included to reflect that relation between the two. One should not conflate these approaches with the excuse that the primary bibliographic unit is not present or that it has not been possible to establish what is the case. It has been said that the difference between the two kinds of discs can be clearly shown by asking whether the publication "is" a disc or "has" a disc.

This also illuminates the added problem of discs that are only forms of advertisement (then the book "has" not a disc), or are part of a multimedia package (then the package "is" not just the disc). The ultimate goal has to be, as always, the full level cataloging of any disc worth adding to the collection, and of course the provision of means to insure proper preservation of the materials. A new factor in the situation with optical discs is that, instead of being used at readers placed around the library, many libraries are now mounting them on local networks to make them available to several patrons simultaneously. Some librarians even want to put them on the Web to make remote access possible, but this appears to be prohibitively expensive. If they are added to the Web, MARC fields like 538 - System Requirements and 856 - Electronic Location and Access would have to be adjusted in order to keep users informed of the physical or electronic availability of each product. LC's guidelines call these two uses of discs "directly accessed" and "remotely accessed" electronic resources and they cover both of them equally.In terms of my model of vertical thinking and management in libraries, it is horizontal thinking when discs are looked at as an intermediate technology between print (*e.g.*, books, indexes, etc.) and remotely accessed electronic resources. Every day we have more discs to catalog, separately or as accompanying material, because publishers avail themselves of this technique of reproduction for many purposes, without having it replace or be replaced by something else. As a successful technology, discs will continue to have their place in library collections, which helps keep healthy the live trunk of the green trees libraries are.

CONCLUSION

We have now completed an excursion through five issues that loom large in the immediate horizon of technical services operations in academic libraries. This excursion probably needs to be repeated with other issues of equal importance that I have not dealt with in this paper. As we moved from the general to the specific, we were moved more and more clearly from the historical roots of our field to the branches which it sustains in our time. Technical services has much to offer the profession and the academic world of research and learning generally. But we need to keep pruning our limbs during the proper season in order to keep up with the demands imposed on us, and the continuous development of technology.

There may be or not be anything "new under the sun" but, the proven prescription for a bride, with a slight alteration which still rhymes, is applicable to the state of affairs in our field. Cataloging, encoding, communication, retrieval, and use of bibliographic resources in all formats entail "something old, something new, something borrowed, something to do." And if we want to prove our critics wrong, as suggested, do it until it is "blue". In summary, cataloging titles in a new format, using a restructured vocabulary for analysis of medical materials, adhering to a new standard for the display of collection holdings, deselecting the titles least used and managing humanely involve "something borrowed," "something new," and "something old." What we have to do with all those elements is to practice our technical services specialties as the branches of knowledge they legitimately are while being conscious of the vitality of the profession as a whole. Without knowledge, libraries, continuous growth and development, and our dedication to our specialties there is no life of the mind, there is no humanity. But to remain truly human and alive first of all means, as Freud and many other sages have impressed upon us, that we stand erect on our feet and, thinking "vertically," looking beyond the horizon.

5

Cataloguing and Processing

LIBRARY ORGANISATION

STANDARDS

Most small, private, or classroom library collections do not need a formal system of library organisation as the individual books can be easily located. As the collection becomes larger, access becomes problematic unless some method of grouping is devised. Many different systems address this problem. For most school libraries, the international standard is the Dewey Decimal Classification (DDC) scheme and either Sears List of Subject Headings or the Library of Congress Subject Headings. Descriptive cataloguing is defined by rules outlined in the Anglo-American Cataloguing Rules (AACR2). Refer to the latest editions of these resources to obtain the most current practices in cataloguing. Every item in the collection must be described using a standard format.

The same basic components are contained in each description. Always cited in the same order, they must employ consistent punctuation. Such standardisation of procedures enhances the local, national, and international exchange of bibliographic data and is essential in computerised systems. To a computer, Hamlet and Shakespeare are just a string of characters. The machine will fail to recognise one as a title and the other as an author unless it is told where each is located in a descriptive record and how each will be introduced. If schools intend to exchange bibliographic data on a local or provincial basis, they should conform to the standards outlined in this document. The exchange of bibliographic data or information can occur in a number of ways, one of which is participation in a union catalogue. Historically, union catalogues have progressed from manual card and paper files to on-line shared databases to catalogue records electronically linked via Internet. Union catalogues form one of the main building blocks of resource sharing or shared services such as interlibrary loan, cooperative cataloguing, cooperative preservation, and cooperative collection development activities. Standards must be used by libraries and library systems to participate in union catalogues.

EDUCATIONAL RATIONALE

For students and staff to make the most effective use of the school's educational resources, the nature, extent, interrelationship, and location of these resources must be clearly identified. School libraries do not exist in an information vacuum but are part of a growing information network. Therefore, they should be provided with access to systems that are compatible with national and international standards. The process of standardised cataloguing and classification results in the creation of a library catalogue.

In a school library, the catalogue is a tool to:

- List, according to a consistent plan, the print and Non--print resources available in the school
- Describe print and Non-print resources
- Direct users to similar materials
- Record purchasing and publishing history
- Indicate the location of the resources
- Assist students in obtaining the skills of information retrieval

The catalogue enable users to:

- Retrieve information efficiently
- Increase understanding by students and staff of information retrieval systems
- Plan, order, and check resources efficiently
- Develop information retrieval skills that are transferable from one school library to other school, public, college, university, and special libraries.

NON-STANDARD SYSTEMS

In-house devised methods of library organisation are to be discouraged. These Non-standards-based solutions result in the following:

- Students and staff requiring training in the specific use of the collection, the knowledge of which is not transferable to other libraries
- Systems becoming inconsistent over time with changes in Personnel
- Cataloguing becoming useless when an attempt is made to convert it to a standard machine readable format

METHODS OF IMPLEMENTING STANDARDS

In applying these standards, school libraries and school divisions/districts which do not have centralised cataloguing have a number of options.

They may:

- Do their own original cataloguing
- Obtain derived cataloguing
- Purchase commercially produced cataloguing
- Use any combination of the above

Wherever possible, commercially produced cataloguing should be attained. No matter what options are used, consumers of cataloguing should be knowledgeable in terms of what to look and ask for about the standards. This recalls the importance of the training in cataloguing required to ensure consistency and accuracy. School libraries must be familiar with cataloguing standards and should establish local cataloguing policies.

Original Cataloguing

Original cataloguing refers to cataloguing an item by examining certain parts of it to obtain information needed to describe it. While original cataloguing allows for on-site, immediate, and locally applied cataloguing, there are some concerns.

These include:

- Original cataloguing is time-consuming for the cataloguer and the data processor/typist. The teacher-librarian's time can be much better spent working with teachers and students. In addition, library technician and library clerk time in school libraries is usually at a premium.
- Lack of library technician and library clerk time usually results in a backlog of materials which have not been catalogued or processed fully. These materials cannot be used by staff or students.
- Inexperienced cataloguers spend long hours misapplying rules. Thus, the advantages of using a standard system are often negated and re-cataloguing is often necessary at a future date.
- Cataloguing is an expensive process when done by unqualified personnel. If the hours spent by cataloguers and data processors/typists were costed out, it would become apparent that commercial cataloguing is more economical.

Derived Cataloguing

Derived or copy cataloguing refers to the process of cataloguing items by using existing bibliographic records obtained from various sources and altering those records to conform to local cataloguing standards.

Cataloguing information may be found in:

- Cataloguing-in-publication (CIP) data found within the item
- Book catalogues
- Non-book catalogues (*e.g.*, microfiche and CD-ROMs)
- Electronic catalogues (*e.g.*, the Internet). An on-line directory known as Hytelnet provides a well-organised means by which to browse through library catalogues or databases worldwide. Two telnet addresses worthy of mention are: 1) telnet locis.loc.gov (Library of Congress, mainly books) and 2) telnet dra.com (Library

of Congress—Data Research Associates, Inc., mainly films and videos). Two important Uniform Resource Locators (URLs) for web-based searching are: 1) http://lcweb2.loc.gov/ammem/booksquery.html (Library of Congress) and 2) http://library.usask.ca/hywebcat/.

While derived cataloguing does result in definite cataloguing savings, both in terms of cost and time, it should be noted that catalogue cards still must be typed manually or cataloguing records must be entered manually into an automated library system. Furthermore, cataloguing standards and formats may vary from catalogue to catalogue. This will also affect the amount of editing required to meet locally established practices.

Commercial Cataloguing

Commercial cataloguing refers to cataloguing services now being offered by a number of firms. It may take the form of simplified cataloguing records for only certain titles to customised cataloguing for specialised collections. Care should be taken in choosing commercial cataloguing that follows national and local cataloguing standards.

The advantages to purchasing commercial cataloguing include:

- Requiring less expertise on the part of the teacher-librarian (the main task for the school library staff may be in filing the cards in a manual environment or loading MARC records in an automated environment)
- Converting a card catalogue to an electronic format enables the school to have it done by a commercial vendor
- Improving consistency
- Centralising cataloguing reduces time spent duplicating the cataloguing for the same titles

Many jobbers or wholesalers routinely offer cataloguing for a nominal fee. Libraries considering automation in the future will want to consider ordering MARC catalogue records along with card sets. This investment in the future allows the school to stockpile MARC data for the automation project. It also greatly reduces the amount of time required to complete the recon, or retrospective conversion of the catalogue.

Combination

Most schools opt for a combination of commercial and original cataloguing, purchasing commercial cataloguing whenever possible, and doing original cataloguing for items in the collection for which commercial cataloguing is not available.

UNION CATALOGUES

Centralised cataloguing in a divisional or district processing centre can result in a union catalogue where the print and audiovisual materials of that network of libraries are known. Union catalogues achieve uniformity throughout the system, avoiding duplication of effort and promoting resource sharing.

RULES AND AUTHORITIES

The set of rules that currently outlines international cataloguing standards in most English-speaking countries are in the Anglo- American Cataloguing Rules(AACR2). Because AACR2 contains provision for a number of options, and because the rules are open to various interpretations, this document has been compiled to suggest the minimum level which should be followed by schools cataloguing materials for use in Manitoba.

ANGLO- AMERICAN CATALOGUING RULES REVISED (CONCISE AACR2)

Descriptive cataloguing is defined by rules described in the American Library Association's Concise AACR2—1988 Revision.

An outline of these rules follows:

- The Description of Library Materials
- General rule (0)*
- Title and statement of responsibility area (1)
- Edition area (2)
- Special area for serials, computer files, maps, and other cartographic materials and music (3)
- Publication distribution, etc., area (4)
- Physical description area (5)
- Series area (6)
- Note(s) area (7)

- Standard number (8)
- Headings, Uniform Titles, and References
- Choice of access points (21-29)
- Headings for persons (30-44)
- Geographic names (45-47)
- Headings for corporate bodies (48-56)
- Uniform titles (57-61)
- References (62-65)

CLASSIFICATION AUTHORITIES

All materials should be classified to the levels outlined in the most current edition of The Abridged Dewey Decimal Classification and Relative Index. This one volume edition contains the same basic numbers as the full edition but permits the possibility of expansion should there be a need.

SUBJECT HEADING AUTHORITIES

The individual library may choose between Sears List of Subject Headings and Library of Congress Subject Headin(gsese Bibliography). The Sears Listhas long been the standard for school and smaller libraries.

For most school libraries it will suffice. The Library of Congress subject headings should be considered only for larger libraries. All other situations cannot support the cost. Changes in technology may justify the use of Library of Congress subject headings in the future. Commercial vendors will provide the opportunity to select one or the other or both. When cataloguing is purchased, both Sears and Library of Congress subject headings should be requested. Then when the records are loaded, Sears would be used for the present time. The school library must update its edition of Sears regularly. Additional Canadian subject authorities may be derived from the National Library of Canada's Canadian Subject Headings and the Sears List of Subject Headings: Canadian Compani(osnee Bibliography).

The National Library of Canada's Canadian Subject Headings supplements the Library of Congress Subject Headin.g Ssears List of Subject Headings: Canadian Companiocnan be used in conjunction with the current edition of the Sears List of

Subject Headings. Assistance in the selection of French language subject headings may be found in Répertoire des vedettes-matièreavailable on microfiche, revised every six months, from Laval University Press.

Services documentaires multimedia (SDM) in Montreal publish the CD-ROM version known as RVM. SDM also publishes Vedettes-matière jeunesse which is an adaptation and simplification of Répertoire des vedettes-matière for materials aimed at young people aged 4 to 12. This product is available in paper, diskette, and on the Internet. The choice of subject authority is important in the construction of an automated catalogue. Sears, Library of Congres, sand National Library of Canada (NLC) subject headings are each flagged differently in an automated catalogue. MARC records often include both Sears and NLC headings. Any school library wishing to index its OPAC only with Sears headings would be required to set up the software to index only properly flagged fields.

DICTIONARIES

There is no single dictionary that has been designated as an authority for Canadian usage in cataloguing. This can create some difficulties in the creation of a MARC catalogue when the sources of MARC records may be using alternate spellings. A typical example is the American spelling of "labour" and the Canadian version "labour." The individual library must decide to accept American spelling or select any good Canadian dictionary and change. Consistency in spelling is a major factor in the production of a useful card catalogue or OPAC. The extra time and effort this requires may render the decision to convert American spellings to Canadian ones impractical.

ALA FILING RULES

ALA Filing Rules are the standard for manual card catalogues which should be followed. Automated catalogues result in filing and filing rules becoming redundant.

MARC CATALOGUING GUIDES

The National Library of Canada's Canadian MARC

Communications Format: Bibliographic Datnad the Library of Congress's USMARC Format for Bibliographic are useful tools for those working with MARC data. For the school library environment, it is recommended that a less technical guide such as Beaumont and Associates' Make Mine MARC (With Integrated Format) be used.

ORGANISING A SCHOOL LIBRARY

Organising a school library is challenging. The following steps are designed to simplify the project.

- Assemble all library resources from all areas of the school. Library personnel should avoid including
- Textbooks
- Sets of supplementary texts and readers
- Workbooks, lab manuals, or teacher's editions
- Multiple copies (six or more) of any book used as a class set
- Library personnel should weed resources that are
- Worn and damaged items
- Superseded editions
- Uncirculated for the past three to five years
- Unnecessary duplicates
- Non-fiction with old copyright dates and/or with inaccurate, Non-metric, condescending, stereotypical, or biased information
- Mend books in need of minor repair
- Sort four sections of resources (keeping duplicate copies of the same items together) into the following
- Easy books (picture books and easy fiction for Grades K-3)
- Fiction books (novels and short stories)
- Non-fiction books (books of fact, fairy tales, and folklore)
- Audiovisual
- Arrange easy books in alphabetical order by author on the shelves.
- Arrange fiction books in alphabetical order by author on the shelves

- Divide the Non-fiction books into broad groups using the 10 main Dewey classes as a guide. Remove any books that can be used as quick reference such as Encyclopaedias, dictionaries, almanacs, and atlases. Place them in a separate pile. These items will form the core of the library's reference collection.
- Easy books (arranged alphabetically by author)
- Fiction books (arranged alphabetically by author)
- Non-fiction books (roughly sorted into 10 broad Dewey subject groups with an eleventh group for reference)
- Audiovisual.

AUTOMATION

The first significant change in the way a library delivers basic service is automation. All school libraries are expected to be automated in the future. Data are the necessary ingredient for any computer to perform at its optimum. No other field in education has a better application for current computer technology than the library. The library has always been a database. In its new format the card catalogue becomes an OPAC (Online Public Access Catalogue). Searches which once were time-consuming can be done in seconds on a well-designed OPAC. In many ways, the traditional card catalogue has been as much a roadblock as an aid in education. The seldom understood innerworkings and cross- references of the card system are replaced by the far simpler keyword access of the modern OPAC. Students and staff, with some instruction, learn to manipulate large data files through the use of Boolean operators. By combining search terms such as author, title, subject, and abstract, the user is able to determine quickly where the appropriate information is to be found.

GETTING STARTED

Even if there is little or no funding in the budget for library automation, the school can begin to prepare itself for that eventuality. MARC records can be purchased for new acquisitions along with catalogue card sets. For these items there will be no need to worry about recon as the MARC data will be ready to load into the cataloguing module of your chosen automated library system.

Materials that are currently on the shelf present another challenge. Regardless of which library application software the library may eventually select, full MARC records are required. There are many sources of MARC records but not all records are of a good quality. MARC records derived from the Library of Congress or the National Library of Canada databases are uniformly good. Records from these sources require little or no editing because they are full records. Records derived from other sources, including some of the major jobbers, are not as consistent.

They often are not full MARC records and, invariably, they require some additional time and effort to raise them to the standard of the National Library of Canada or Library of Congress. Sometimes companies identify records as MARC when they are not (*e.g.*, Microlif records are not full MARC records). Libraries can prepare to automate by reading Selection of Automated Systems: Criteria for School Libraries in Manitaonbda Selection of Resources: Policies and Procedures for Manitoba Schools. These two documents are available from the Instructional Resources Unit, Manitoba Education and Training. French versions are available from the Direction des ressources éducatives françaises.

VISITATIONS

Many schools in the province have already converted their libraries to automated systems. Contact them and arrange a visit. The Instructional Resources Unit has a document available entitled Automated School Library Systems in Manitotbhat lists automated schools. Automated schools have learned a great deal and know how to avoid pitfalls.

Ask such questions as:

- Where to obtain MARC records?
- How much original cataloguing is necessary?
- How good is the data?
- How good is the application software?

- What were the difficulties encountered?
- Any vendor training? If so, is it useful?
- Is the vendor responsive to school needs?
- How much did the project cost?

WEEDING

A library benefits from judicious weeding. The most expensive part of any library automation project is the conversion of the old catalogue into a MARC format. Old textbooks, teacher editions, dated scientific materials, worn, torn, and yellowed items should be discarded before the conversion process begins; otherwise, much time, effort, and money can be wasted doing recon on these materials.

Note: The Instructional Resources Unit, Manitoba Education and Training, has a collection of old approved Manitoba textbooks. Before discarding such material from your school library, please contact this Unit to see if your material is wanted.

PREPARING THE SHELF LIST

The next phase is preparing the shelf list. If the shelf list has been catalogued up to the level described in this resource, recon is much easier. The more complete the shelf list, the simpler the task of matching against an existing database. If the shelf list is not up to standard, then the task becomes more difficult. It may become necessary to recatalogue many books entirely.

The shelf list may be:

- Sent to a commercial jobber who attempts to match the information on the card with an existing bibliographic record such as one from A-G Canada Ltd. (formerly ISM Library Information Services), or another local resource, TKM in Brandon
- Matched in-house using one of the compact disc MARC databases
- Matched online against the holdings of a bibliographic vendor (*e.g.*, A-G Canada Ltd., and TKM)
- Entered partially in-house on diskette and sent off to a bibliographic vendor who attempts to match the

"skeletal records" against their MARC database (TKM offers such a service)

If the shelf list does not include ISBN (International Standard Book Number) or Library of Congress numbers, arrange for volunteers to begin adding this data to the shelf list cards. The presence of this information greatly increases the chance of getting a "hit" and subsequently reduces the time and cost of deriving MARC records. Contact the Instructional Resources Unit, Manitoba Education and Training, for a copy of the publication Commercial Cataloguing and Processing Services for Books and Audio Visual Mater.

DESCRIPTIVE CATALOGUING

Cataloguing and classification are used to develop an index of the library collection to enable users to determine the availability of resources. Create a card or manual system with two different files (using 3 × 5 inch cards) that have

- A shelf list file for staff use
- A dictionary catalogue for use by staff and students

SHELF LIST

The shelf list is an inventory file and forms a complete record of the materials owned by the library. It should be housed separately from the regular catalogue. It is called a shelf list because its cards are arranged in the same order as the materials on the shelves.

DICTIONARY CATALOGUE

The dictionary catalogue, an index to the library collection, should be located in the main part of the library. The file is called a dictionary catalogue because its cards are arranged alphabetically. To create these files, information on each book or item in the collection has to be collected, assigned, and recorded. Four basic steps are involved that are similar either to creating a manual card catalogue or to gathering information for an automated system.

The steps are to:

- Record the bibliographic information for the item
- Assign classification numbers

- Assign subject headings
- Determine other indexing terms

PREPARATION FOR CATALOGUING

As this information is collected or assigned, record it on 3 x 5 inch pieces of paper. As the catalogue cards are typed from these slips, they are sometimes referred to as "Typing Slips" or "T-slips." A T-slip is required for each item. When completed, the cards are data processed/typed and filed. An alternative to this T-slip method is the use of one of the commercially-available systems that allows the user to generate complete card sets from the input of this initial shelf list information. The cataloguer may also choose to work directly from the item, by penciling in the Dewey number, underlining the main entry, and writing subject headings on the reverse of the title page. This avoids the use of T-slips.

DESCRIPTIVE CATALOGUING

Descriptive cataloguing consists of two elements: describing the physical item, and determining the main entry and added entries. The key elements determining main entry, correct formatting of the entry, and physical details of the entry are shown. The proper punctuation, layout, and style of cataloguing are shown rather than explained.

To help those who are automating their systems, the examples provide both the card and MARC formats. Describing a book is recording the bibliographic information for each book on a 3 × 5 inch T-slip. This information is recorded exactly from the title page of each book. Follow the punctuation style precisely as it is described and illustrated in this resource. Write or print information clearly to enable the data processor/typist to process it accurately.

Levels of Detail in the Description

The details in the level 2 AACR2 specifications include:

- Exact spacings and punctuation
- The elements of cataloguing and their spatial relationships.

1st Indention: 9 Spaces from left Margin
2nd Indention: 13 Spaces from left Margin

Added Entry.
(Do not Leave a Line Space)
Call Main Entry.
No. Title Proper [GMD]--Parallel Title: Other Title Information/ First Statement of Responsibility.--Edition Statement / Statement of Responsibility Relating to Edition--Place of Publication : Publisher, Data of Publication,
Extent of Item : Other Physical Details; Physical Dimensions + Accompanying Material.--(Series: Numbering).

Notes
ISBN

1. Subject Headings. 1. Added Entries. II. Title. III. Series.

Fig. 5.1 Complete Details.

In older records, you will often see the "1" and "0" follow the MARC 100 field tag. The "1" and "0" are indicators. The "1" indicates a single surname while the "0" indicates there is no relationship between the main entry and the subject of the item. This is the most common format encountered during a recon. Any book with an author follows this same format in a MARC record. In current practice, the record indicator is not used.

- $a = a tag delimiter

In most systems, the local call number will appear as 090 or 092. For standardisation in this document, 090 has been used in all examples.

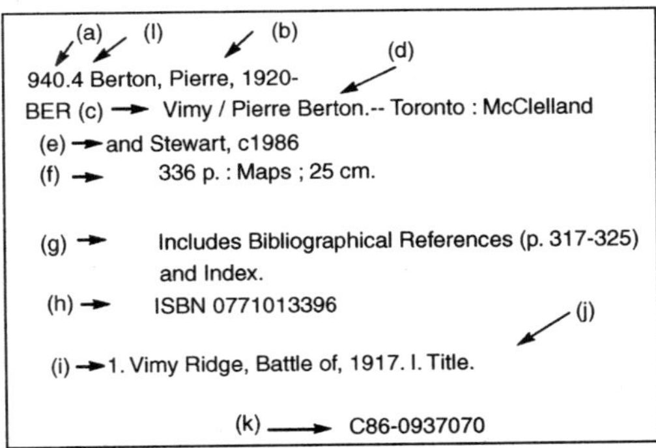

Fig. 5.2 Explanation of the Card Layout.

Notes:

(*a*) = Classification number (Dewey class)

(*b*) = Main entry (person's name)

(*c*) = Title

(*d*) = Statement of responsibility

(*e*) = Publishing details (imprint)

(*f*) = Physical description (statement includes the extent of the item, the physical details, and details of accompanying materials)

(*g*) = Notes

(*h*) = ISBN (International Standard Book Number)

(*i*) = Subject heading (topical)

(*j*) = Added entries

(*k*) = National Library of Canada Control Number or Library of Congress Card Number

(*l*) = Call number

MARC Example:

NLC Control #	016		$a860937070
ISBN 020			$a0771013396
Cat. Source 040			$aCaOTUbengcCaOTUdCaOONL
Dewey Class 082		04	$a940/.4
Local Call # 090			$a940.4 BER
ME: Pers. Name	100	1_	$aBerton, Pierre,$d1920-
Title	245	10	$a Vimy/$cPierre Berton
Imprint	260		$a Toronto: $bMc Clelland and Stewart, $cc 1986.
Phys. Descript.	300		$a336 P: $bmaps :$c 25 cm.
Note: Bibliog.	504		$aIncludes Bibliographical References (p. 317-325) and index.
Subj. Topical	650	_0	$a Vimy Ridge, Battle of, 1917.

Fig. 5.3 Mark Exaple.

Choice and Form of Main Entry

The first task facing the cataloguer is to determine the choice of main entry. The general principle of main entry is to enter a work under the person(s) or corporate body responsible for its intellectual content. In the case of books the chief source of information is usually the title page. Record the information exactly as it appears on the title page. Information appearing elsewhere in the item may be used in the catalogue entry.

Take care to ensure the consistent spelling of the author entry within the catalogue (in current practice, editors and compilers are never given a main entry although they were in the past). In current practice, authors are always entered under the commonly known name (*e.g.*, Mark Twain is under Twain, Mark rather than Clemens, Samuel Langhorne). The general rule for titles of nobility is to employ the most commonly used name. An aristocrat may be entered under his or her family name or title (*e.g.*, the Duke of Wellington is entered under his title rather than his family name).

Author Main Entry (Card Example)

The author's name appears on the top line of the card four lines from the top of the card and indented nine spaces from the left margin to allow for the entry of long Dewey numbers. The surname is given first, followed by a comma, and then the given names of the author in the usual order. Inclusion of birth and death dates is optional.

E Bourgeois, Paulette.
BOU Hurry up, Franklin/ Paulette Bourgeois: illustrated by Brenda Clark.--Toronto : Kids Can Press, c 1988
[30] p. : col. ill. : 22 cm
ISBN 1550740164 (pbk)
1. Turtles---Fiction. 1. Clark, Brenda. II. Title.

Fig. 5.4. Card Example.

Author Main Entry (MARC Example)

Personal name main entries are placed in the 100 field of the MARC record.

ISBN	020		$a 1550750385
Dewey Class	082	1_	$aE
Local Call #	090		$aE BOU
ME : Pers. Name	100	1_	$aBourgeois, Paulette
Title	245	10	$a Hurry up Franklin/$cPaulette Bouthroid ; illustrated by Brenda Clark.
Imprint	260		$a Toronto : $bKinds Can Press, $cc 1988
Phys. Descript.	300		$a [30] p. : $bcol. ill. :$c22 cm.
Subject	650	_0	$aTurtles$xFiction.
AE: Pers. Name	700	1_	$aClark, Brenda.

Fig. 5.5 Marc Example.

- The 100 is the field of interest in this example.
- The $a precedes a name subfield. All MARC fields have subfields.

Corporate Body Main Entry (Card Example)

On occasion, the school library may have materials that are the products of a corporate group such as associations, governments, business firms, and conferences. Rule 21.1B2 of AACR2 defines a corporate body as an organisation or a group that acts as an entity and is identified by a particular name.

When a corporate body is responsible for the intellectual content of a work, the main entry is listed under the corporate body. It is rare that a school library finds itself in possession of large numbers of government documents or works emanating from corporate groups. If there is doubt on the part of the cataloguer, main entry is by title. Always enter governments and government departments and committees under the name of the country, province, or local jurisdiction.

027 Manitoba. School Library Media Program Curriculum
MAN Committee.

Selection of Automation Systems : Criteria for School Libraries in Manitoba / Manitoba. School Library Media Program Curriculum Committee.---Winnipeg, MB : Manitoba Education and Training, c 1991.

47 p. : 28 cm.

ISBN 0771109865

1. School Libraries--Automation

Fig. 5.6. Corporate Body Entry (Card Example).

Corporate Body Main Entry (MARC Example)

Corporate main entries are placed in the 110 MARC field.

ISBN	020		$a0771109865
Dewey Class	082	0_	$a027/.8/02854
Local Call #	090		$a027 MAN
ME: Corp.	110	1_	$aManitoba. $b School Library Media Program Curriculum Commitee.
Title	245	10	$aSelection of Automation systems :$bcriteria for school Libraries in Manitoba/$cManitoba School Library Media Pogram Curriculum Committee.
Imprint	260		$aWinnipeg. MB :$b Manitoba Education and Training. $b Manitoba Education and Training. $cc 1991.
Phys. Descript.	300		$a47 p. :$c28 cm.
Subj. Topical	650	_0	$a School Libraries $xAutomation

Fig. 5.7. Corporate Body Entry (Marc Example).

- The 110 is the MARC field tag of interest in this example.
- The $a precedes a name subfield.
- The 245 title field provides a typical example of how subtitles are treated in MARC records. The $a introduces the title proper, Selection of automation systems. It is followed by a "space:$b." The $b introduces the subtitle criteria for school libraries in Manitoba. It is followed in turn by the statement of responsibility field. The punctuation is "space/$c" followed by the statement of responsibility—in this case the School Library Media Programme Curriculum Committee.
- *Note*: The classification number has been reduced to 027. Most school libraries have a limited number of works on library automation. Therefore, further subdivision of the classification number is redundant.

Personal Name Added Entry (Card Example)

If there is more than one author or an illustrator listed on the title page, record only the first author as the main entry. An added entry is made for the second author or illustrator. If three or more authors appear on the title page, main entry is by title.

```
E     Bourgeois, Paulette.
BOU     Hurry up Franklin / Paulette Bourgeois ; illustrated by
        Brenda Clark.--Toronto : Kids Can Press, c 1988
          [30] p. : col. ill. ; 22 cm.
      (Card not Shown in Full.)
```

```
        Clark, Brenda.
E       Bourgeois, Paulette.
BOU     Hurry up, Franklin / Paulette Bourgeois ; illustrated by
        Brenda Clark.---Toronto : Kids Can Press, c1988
          [30] p. : col. ill. ; 22 cm.
        (Card not Shown in Full.)
```

Fig. 5.8. Personal Name Added Entry (Marc Example).

Personal Name Added Entry (MARC Example)

The tracings for individuals such as editors, illustrators, and secondary authors are entered in the 700 field. The field may be repeated as often as necessary. If an individual or corporate body has been recorded in the statement of responsibility area, it is traced in the appropriate 700 or 7 field. Corporate added entries follow the same general format but are entered in the 710 field.

ISBN	020		$a1550740385
Dewey Class	082	1	$aE
Local Call #	090		$aE BOU
ME: Pers. Name	100	1_	$a Bourgeois, Paulette.
Title	245	10	$aHurry up Franklin / $ Paulette Bourgeois ; illustrated by Brenda Clark
Imprint	260		$a Toronto :$b Kids Can Press, $cc 1988.
Phys. Descript.	300		$a[30] p. :$bcol. ;$c22 cm.
Subject	650	_0	$a Turtles $xFiction
AE. Pers. Name	700	1_	$aClark, Brenda.

Fig. 5.9. Personal Name Added Entry (Marc Example).

Note the 700 MARC field tag in this example.
The "1" which follows the 700 field is an indicator. The "1" indicates a single surname.

Main Entry by Title (Card Example)

If no author is listed, or three or more persons or corporate bodies are listed, the main entry is by title. Make an added entry only for the first author named. The remaining authors or corporate bodies are not recorded by name in the statement of responsibility but grouped under the heading; neither are they traced. Works entered under title are typed in a form called a hanging indention. The main entry begins on the fourth line from the top of the card. The call number begins on the fourth line and is indented one space from the edge of the card. The title begins nine spaces from the left margin and is continued at the second indention.

031.02 The Canadian World Almanc and Book of Facts 1991.
CAN -------Toronto : Global Press, c1990.
725 p. ; ill. , Maps ; 21 cm
ISBN 0771539754 (pbk)
1. Almanacs, Canadian (English).

Fig. 5.10. Main Entry by Title (Marc Example).

Main Entry by Title (MARC Example)

Title main entries are placed in the 245 field.

ISBN	020		$a0771539754 (pbk)
Dewey #	082	0_	$a031/.02219
Local Call #	090		$a031.02 CAN
ME : Title	245	04	$aThe Canadian World Almanac and Book of Facts 1991.
Imprint	260		$a Toronto : $b Global Press, $cc 1990.
Phys. Descript.	300		$a725 p. ;$bill., Maps ; $c21 cm.
Subj. Topical	650	_0	$aAlmanacs, Canadian (English)

Fig. 5.11. Main Entry by Title (Marc Example).

Note the 245 MARC field tag in this example.

The "0" and "4" which follow are MARC field tag indicators. The "0" indicates that there is no author given and the main entry of the work is by title. The "4" indicates the number of Non--filing characters.

The $a is a subfield which precedes the short title/title proper.

In the 650 field, the indicator "5" denotes a National Library of Canada heading.

Books with Editors or Compilers (Card Example)

Books without a clearly identifiable author are treated as title main entries. In cases where an editor or compiler is named as responsible for the work, main entry is again by title. Note that the title of the item is recorded first in the statement of responsibility area and is followed by the editor. The editor is traced at the bottom of the card. The indention pattern is different when the T-slip begins with the title. The second and succeeding lines are indented two spaces under the first line.

```
971  The Junior Encyclopedia of Canada / James
003    H. Marsh, Editor-in-chief,--Edmonton : Hurtig, c 1990.
JUN    5 v. : col. ill., Maps, Ports. ; 29 cm.
       Includes Bibliographical Refences
       ISBN 0888303343 (Set)
     1. Canada--Distionaries and Encyclopedias. I. Marsh,
     James H.
```

Fig. 5.12. Books with Editors or Compilers (Marc Example).

Books with Editors or Compilers (MARC Example)

ISBN	020		$a0888303343 (set)
Dewey Class	082	0_	$a971/.003220
Local Call #	090		$a971.003 JUN
ME : Title	245	04	$aThe Junior Encyclopedia of Canada /$cJames H. Marsh, Editor-in-chief.
Imprint	260		$aEdmonton:$b Hurtig, $cc 1990.
Phys. Descript.	300		$a5 V. ;$bcol. ill., Maps, Ports.; $c29 cm.
Note; Biblio	504		$AIncludes Bibliographical References.
Subj. Geog	651	_0	$a Canada $xDictionaries and encyclopedias.
AE: Pers. Name	700	1_	$aMarsh, James H.

Fig. 5.13. Books with Editors or Compilers (Marc Example).

Again the 245 MARC field tag is the subject of attention.

The "0" and "4" which follow the field tag are indicators.

The "0" indicates there is no author and the main entry is by title.

The "4" indicates the number of Non--filing characters, in this case four.

The $a precedes the title proper and is followed by a "space/$c" and the name of the editor of the work. As the editor is traced here in the statement of responsibility area, he must be recorded in the 700 field as an added entry.

Books with Retellers or Adaptors (Card Example)

In cases where there is an adaptor, this individual is given the main entry and an added entry is given to the original author (if there is one). This situation is commonly encountered with the works of the Brothers Grimm and Hans Christian Andersen.

Smith, Bob.
The Little Mermaid / Hans Christian Andersen; Retold by Bob Smith.--New York : Alfred A. Knopf, c1988
[24] p. : col. ill. ; 24 cm.
(Card not Shown in Full.)

Fig.

Andersen, Hans Christian
Smith, Bob.
The Little Mermaid / Hans Christian Andersen ; Retold by Bob Smith.--New York : Alfred A. Knopf, C 1988.
[24] p. : col. ill ; 24 cm.
(Card not Shown in Full.)

Fig. 5.14 Added Entry.

Books with Retellers or Adaptors (MARC Example)

Local Call #	090		$a398.2 SMI
ME : Pers. Name	100	1_	$aSmith, Bob
Title	245	14	$aThe Little Mermaid / $c Hans Christian Andersen ; Retold by Bob Smith.
Imprint	260		$a New York : $bAlfred A. Knopf $cc 1986.
Phys. Descript.	300		$a[24] p. : $b col. ill. ; $c24 cm.
AE: Pers. Name	700	1_	$aAndersen, Hans Christian.

Fig. 5.15. Books with Retellers or Adaptors (Marc Example).

Note: The 245 MARC field tag is the key in this example.

The "1" and "4" after the 245 field tag are indicators.

The "1" indicates there is an author. The "4" indicates the number of Non- filing characters.

The $a is the subfield which is followed by the title proper. It is followed by a space/$c and the statement of responsibility area. Even though Hans Christian Andersen originally wrote the work it is retold here by Bob Smith. For this reason Smith is placed in the 100 main entry field. Andersen is traced as an added entry in the 700 field.

The indicator in the 700 field is a "1"which denotes the presence of a single surname.

Cataloguing Format

Once the form of the main entry has been determined add the title information to the T-slip.

Title

- The title is recorded on the next line and is indented two spaces under the author.
- The first letter of all proper names is capitalised, otherwise lower case letters are used except for the first letter of a title.

- Subtitles follow the main title and are preceded by a space-colon-space (:).
- The full title is the beginning of the "title paragraph."

Statement of Responsibility

- A statement of responsibility is required for persons or bodies with major responsibility for the item (*e.g.*, an author, corporate body, illustrator, editor, translator). If the person or body named in this first statement of responsibility is recognizably the same as that chosen for the main entry heading and the rest of the statement consists only of the word "by," omit the statement.
- A first statement of responsibility follows the title and is preceded by a space-slash-space (/). Each additional statement of responsibility is preceded by a space-semi colon-space (;). A statement of responsibility is required when there is an author(s), an illustrator, or an editor being traced.
- Any author, editor, illustrator, and corporate author, who may be recorded in this area, should be traced at the bottom of the card, although this is at the discretion of the library. Added entry cards are produced for inclusion in the catalogue.

Edition

- The edition statement, if necessary, is next.
- It is preceded by a period-space-dash-dash-space (. .).
- The edition statement is included to indicate a revised edition or a numbered edition. Use abbreviations: Rev. ed., 3rd ed.

Place of Publication, Distribution Area

- In this area, information regarding the place of publication, the name of publisher and date of publication is recorded. Collectively this is known as the imprint. This information will generally be found on the title page. The area is preceded by a period space-dash-dash-space. (- -).

- The city of publication is noted first. Transcribe the first named place as the source of the publication. The rule holds even if two or more places are named. *e.g.*, Toronto
- If the city of publication is uncertain, supply the probable place in the language of the chief source of information, followed by a question mark. The city is to be enclosed in square brackets when the cataloguer is uncertain.

Name of Publisher, Distributor

- Record the name of the publisher or distributor next. It is preceded by a space, colon, space (:). Give the name of the publisher in the shortest form in which it may be understood. e.g. Toronto: University of Toronto Press
- The publisher's name may be shortened to eliminate terms such as Ltd., Co., and Inc.

Date of Publication

- The date follows the publisher and is preceded by a comma-space (,).
- If there is no date on the title page, select the most recent copyright date. These dates are most commonly found on the back (verso) of the title page. Do not use the printing date, unless there is absolutely nothing else.
- If no publication date is available, provide an approximate date of publication. These approximate dates are to be surrounded by square brackets. *e.g.*, probable date or decade uncertain
- The date completes the title paragraph.

Physical Description

- Begin a new paragraph for the physical description and indent it two spaces. The information for this area may be taken from any source.
- Record the last numbered page, leave a space and then record the abbreviation.

- The last numbered page of a preface paginated with Roman numerals should be recorded, followed by a comma, then followed by the last numbered page with Arabic numerals.
- Record the number of physical units, the components, and the total playing time as appropriate. *e.g.,* 1 jigsaw puzzle (30 pieces), 4 filmstrips
- In the case of multi-volume works, record the number of volumes *e.g.,* 5 v.

Illustrative Matter

- Record the abbreviation "ill." after the number of pages when the book is illustrated with pictures, diagrams, drawings, tables, or maps.

Dimensions

- Measure and record the physical sise of the text in centimetres.
- Record items where the width is greater than the height.

Series Area

- The series, if any, is recorded next. It should be preceded by a period-space-dash-dash-space. (.—).
- Each series is enclosed in round brackets.
- An item which is a numbered part of a series should be recorded after the series title. Punctuation is space-semi-colon-space (;).

Note Area

- Leave two lines after the physical description before beginning note entries.
- Record here bibliographies or indexes, if present. Contents notes, summaries, multivolume works, in another language, audience level, and local note are also entered in this area. *i.e.,* Includes bibliographical references and index. MARC examples:
  - 500 $a Includes index.
  - 504 $a Includes bibliographical references and index.

Standard Book Numbers and Library of Congress Card Numbers

The last items to be entered as part of the physical description of the book are the ISBN, LC card numbers, and Canadian National Book Numbers (CNBN). While these particular numbers are of no use to the clientele, their presence saves the librarian countless hours during a retrospective conversion if they are included on the shelf list card.

These numbers are essential when searching for MARC records.

- ISBN begins on the line immediately following the last note.
- *i.e.,* 087287221 (pbk)
- MARC example: 020 $a0872872211 (pbk).

The Canadian National Book Number or Library of Congress card number is to be entered after the tracings in the bottom right hand corner of the shelf list card.

Multiple Copies of the Same Book (Card Example)

If the library possesses two or more copies of an identical item, note it on the T-slip. Record "c.1" (for copy 1), "c.2", etc. (for as many copies as the library has) in the near left-hand edge of the card near the middle of the card:

```
E     Hasler, Eveline
HAS     Winter Magic / Eveline Hasler ; illustrated by Michele
        Lemieux.---Toronto ; Kids Can Press Ltd., c1989.
         [30] p. : col. ill. ; 26 cm.

c.1
c.2
        (Card not Shown in Full)
```

Fig. 5.16. Multiple Copies of the work (Card Example).

Multiple Copies of the Same Work (MARC Example):

NLC Control #	016		$a890943109
ISBN	020		$a0921103719 (pbk)
Dewey Class	082	0_	$a833 /.914219
Local Call #	090		$aE HAS$cc.1
Local Call #	090		$aE HAS$cc.2
ME; Pers. Name	100	1_	$aHasler, Eveline
Title	245	10	$aWinter Magic / $c Eveline Hasler ; illustrated by Michele Lemieux.
Imprint	260		$a Toronto : $bKids Can Press, $cc 1989.
Phys. Descript.	300		$a[32] p. : $b col. ill. ; $c26 cm
AE; Pers. Name	700	1_	$aLemieux, Michele.

Fig. 5.17.Multiple Copies of the work (Marc Example).

SUBJECT HEADINGS

Subject headings consist of words, groups of words, or acronyms that are used to describe the subject of a work. As access points in the catalogue, these headings are extremely important in communicating the holdings of a library. Add subject headings to the T-slips to provide access to the intellectual content of the material. In selecting subject headings, the cataloguer decides what index terms appear in the dictionary catalogue for the book.

The chosen headings are numbered with arabic numerals and are recorded. It is important to use consistently the same terminology to designate a particular subject. For this reason, libraries have developed standard lists of subject headings.

The most commonly used lists in Canadian school libraries are the Sears List of Subject Headings and the Canadian Companion to the Searslist. A supplemental choice would be the most recent edition of the Library of Congress Subject Headings and the National Library of Canada's Canadian Subject Headings.

The latter two titles supply an expanded number of subject possibilities. Note that subject headings are never assigned from the Dewey Decimal Classification. Before assigning subject headings, the main subject or subjects of the book must be determined. This is done by examining the title, table of contents, description on the dust jacket, preface, text, and illustrations. The next step is to write down the subject and check to see if that choice is permitted in the standardised list. If the subject selected is not in the list, the related subjects must be consulted. It is possible, although not advisable, to add a local subject heading.

This should be done only when all other avenues have been exhausted.The standard subject lists represent a controlled vocabulary that has been carefully constructed over a number of years. Local subject creativity—if taken to excess—results in a garbled catalogue.

If local headings are added to the catalogue, write them in your copy of Sears or LCSH for future reference. Typically, two subject headings per item is sufficient for most school libraries, although there are occasions when three or more may be required to cover the scope of the item.

Select as specific a heading as possible. A book about bears should be given the subject heading BEARS rather than the general heading ANIMALS.

For a book about several different animals, the more inclusive heading ANIMALS should be used rather than separate headings for each animal mentioned in the text. Determining whether to use a specific or a general subject entry can pose difficulties.The introduction to Sears describes how to designate them correctly.The subject heading is listed at the bottom of the T-slip preceded by an Arabic numeral. Such a notation is called a tracing and tells the cataloguer what other cards exist. School libraries often find it valuable to include subject headings for Fiction and Easy materials. This makes it easier to identify storybooks about a particular subject or theme. In general, add the word FICTION as a subdivision of other subjects to indicate that the item is a work of fiction.

FICTION SUBJECT HEADINGS (CARD EXAMPLES)

	New Foundland--Fiction
F	Major, Kevin
MAJ	Blood Red Ochre/ Kevin Major.--Taronto : Dell, c1989. 147 p. ; 18 cm
	1. Newfoundland--Fiction. 2. Beothuck Indians--Fiction 1. Title.
	(Card not Shown in Full.)

Fig. 5.18. Fiction Subject Headings (Card Example).

	Turtles--Fiction
E	Bourgeois, Paulete.
BOU	Hurry up, Franklin / Paulette Bourgeois : illustrated by Brenda Clark.--Toronto : Kids Can Press, C1988. [30] p, : col, ill. ; 22 cm.
	1. Turtles--Fiction. 1. Clark, Brenda. II. Title.
	(Card not Shown in Full.)

Fig. 5.19. Fiction Subject Headings (Card Example).

Vimy Ridge, Battle of, 1917
940.4 Berton, Pierre, 1920-
BER Vimy / Pierre Berton.--Toronto : Mc Clelland and Stewart, c 1986.
336 p. : Maps ; 25 cm

Includes Bibliographical References (p. 317-355) and Index.
ISBN 0771013396

1. Vimy Ridge, Battle of, 1917. 1 Title

C86-0937070

Fig. 5.20. Non-Fiction Subject Headings (Card Examples).

CLASSIFICATION

A classification number now should be added to the T-slip. It appears in the upper left-hand corner opposite the author. In classifying library collections, numbers or letters are assigned to the books to represent the subject of the book. These notations, which are called "call numbers," are also used to arrange the books on the shelves. Generally library collections are separated into four major categories: Easy, Fiction, Non-Fiction, and Reference.

EASY (CARD EXAMPLES)

Easy books are normally found in every elementary school and include picture books and easy-to-read fiction suitable for children in the Early Years.

All Easy books take the notation "E." Easy books are usually arranged in alphabetical order by the first three letters of the author's last name. Where there is no author, the first three letters of the title are substituted. Please note that "a," "an," and "the" are to be omitted when filing by title (*e.g.*, for A Promise is a Promise, the book would be filed under the word "Promise").

E Andrews, Jan, 1942-
And Pumpkin Time / Jan Andrews.--Toronto : Groundwood, 1990.
[32] p. : col. ill. ; 25 cm.

(Card not Shown in Full.)

Fig.. (A)

E The Bye-bye Book.-- New York : Nelson,1994.
BYE 68 p. ; 19 cm.

(Card not Shown in Full.)

Fig.5.21. (B) Easy (Card Examples).

FICTION (CARD EXAMPLE)

Fiction materials are usually designated by F, FIC, or Fic and are also arranged alphabetically by the author's surname. Again, the first three letters of the author's surname are used. If no author is identified the first three letters of the title are employed.

F Major, Kevin.
MAJ Blood Red Ochre / Kevin Major.--Toronto : Dell, c 1989.
147 p. ; 18 cm.

1. Newfoundland--Fiction. 2. Beothuck Indians--Fiction

(Card not Shown in Full.)

Fig.5.22. (A)

FIC Korman, Gordon.
KOR The Zucchini Warriors / Gordon Korman. --- Toronto : Scholastic, C1988
198 p. ; 22 cm.

ISBN 059041335X

1. Football--Fiction. 2. Schools--Fiction. 3. Humorous Stories.
1. Title. 88-6720

Fig. 5.23. (B)

FIC The Laugh-a-day Gang.--Toronto : Kids Can Pess, 1995.
LAU 177 p. ; 20 cm.

(Card not Shown in Full)

(C)

Fig. 5.24. Fiction (Card Examples).

NON-FICTION

School libraries primarily use the Abridged Dewey Decimal Classification scheme to organise their Non-fiction materials. It is a hierarchical classification scheme which uses the decimal principal for subdivision. There are ten main classes into which all areas of knowledge are subdivided. Each main class is broken down into 10 subdivisions and each subsequent division is further broken down into 10 more subdivisions.

Examples follow:

- 900—History
- 970—North American History
- 971—Canadian History
- 971.2—Canadian Prairie History
- 971.27—Manitoba History

The Abridged Dewey Decimal Classification is frequently misused and some formal instruction in classification should be undertaken before attempting its use. Contact Red River Community College or the University of Manitoba, Faculty of Education, regarding courses and programmes.

Number Building in Dewey

As a general rule, the Dewey classification number should be kept as brief as possible. Assignment of class numbers begins with determining the general subject of the book and the treatment it requires. Clues may be gathered from the title, the table of contents, the description on the dust jacket, the preface and the text.

Titles can be misleading and classification by title alone is not recommended. If a book has two or more subjects try to determine which subject best describes the contents of the item. Then select the classification number accordingly.

The Dewey Decimal Classification scheme classifies materials primarily by a disciplinary approach to the subject. The subject "corn" as a farm product goes under the number for farming. "Corn" as a grain may go in a number in the Pure Sciences, the 500s.

"Corn" as a basis for designing decorative displays for fall goes in the 700s. Once the subject area of the book has been determined, a class number is assigned in the following manner.

Use the current unabridged or abridged edition of Dewey to:

- Turn to the outline of the ten main classes provided at the beginning of the classification scheme and determine in which main class the item belongs

- Turn to the outline of the 100 divisions of the 10 main classes, (also provided at the start of the classification scheme) and determine in which division of the main class the item belongs
- Turn to the schedules (*i.e.,* the detailed outline of the classification numbers) and select the most specific number for the item. For all but the very largest school collections, a maximum of three places beyond the decimal point, or the first logical break, should be sufficient

Non-Fiction (Card Example)

As with fiction materials, the classification number is completed with the first three letters of the author's last name. If there is no author, the first three letters of the title are used omitting "a," "an," and "the."

971 Marcotte, Nancy Sellars.
MAR Ordinary People in Canada's Past / Nancy Sellars Marcotte, -- Edmonton : Arnold Pub., c1989.
236 P.:ill. (Some Col.). Maps : 28cm.

(Card not Shown in Full.)

Fig. 5.25.(A)

551.4 Peters, Lisa Westberg.
PET Pet The Sun, the Wind and the Rain / Lisa Westberg Peters; Illustrated by Ted Rand, -- New York : Hold, c1988.
[32] p. : Col. Ill. ; 24 cm.

(Card not Shown in Full.)

Fig. 5.26. (B)

822.008 The Five Dances : Plays for Stage, Radio and Television/
FIV Edited With an Introduction by Arlene Sykes. --St. Lucia. Qld. : University of Queensland Press, c1977.
279 P.: ill.: 19 cm.

(Card not Shown in Full.)

(C)

Fig. 5.27 Examples of the Non-fication Classiffication.

Biography

A subject heading should always include the name of a person in a biographical work. These headings should include the full name of the individual and the person's birth and death dates, if applicable.

It is often necessary to consult reference sources such as a biographical dictionary or Encyclopaedia to determine the exact spelling of the person's name and the appropriate dates. Individual biographies about men are to be classified as 920.71. Individual biographies about women are to be classified as 920.72. The first three letters of the name of the person in the story are to follow the class number in the case of individual biography.

General collections of biography not limited by place, period or specific subject are to be classed as 920.02. Such collections are entered by title. In such cases the first three letters of the title will follow the 920.02 class number.(The Dewey classification optionally makes provision to class individual biography in 92 or B. Collective biography may be classed in 92 or 920 undivided.) Optionally, biographies may be classed in the specific subject area with which the person is associated.

920 White, Marjorie E.
.71 Robert Bateman / Marjorie E. White. -- Markham. Ont. :
BAT Fitzhenary and Whiteside, c1988.

48 P.: Ill (Some Col.); 23 cm, -- (Canadian Lives)

ISBN 0889028524 (Pbk)

1. Bateman, Robert, 1930- 2. Painters--Canada--Biography.
3. Naturalists--Canada--Biography. I. Title.II. Series.

Fig. 5.28. Biography Subject Heading (Card Example).

NLC Control#	016		$a890906556
ISBN	020		$a0889028524 (pbk)
Cat. Source	040		$aCaOTUbengcCaOTUdCaOONL
Dewey Class	082	0	$a759/.1/1219
Local Call#	090		$a920.71 BAT
ME:Pers.Name	100	1	$aWhite,Marjorie E.
Title	245	10	$aRobert Bateman /ScMarjorie E. White.
Imprint	260		$aMarkham. Ont. :$bFitzhenryand Whiteside, $cc1990.
Phys. Descript.	300		$248 p.:$bill.(Some Col.): $c23 cm.
Series	440	0	$aCanadian Lives
Subj.Pers	600	10	$aBateman.Robert,$d1930-
Subj.Topical	650	0	$aPainters$zCanada$xBiography.
Subj. Topical	650	0	$aNaturalists$zCanada$x Biography.

Fig. 5.29. Biography Subject Heading (MARC Example).

- The 600 personal subject field is used for biographies.
- The "1" and the "0" are indicators. The "1" indicates a single surname which is the most common format. The "0" indicates the subject is derived from a Library of Congress authority file.
- The $a is a subfield introducing the name subfield area.
- The 650 subject field is worthy of comment as well.
- The "0" is an indicator which notes this is a Library of Congress subject heading.
- The $a introduces the subject Painters.
- The $z is a subfield which denotes a geographic location, in this case Canada.
- The $x is a subfield which introduces a general subdivision in the Library of Congress Subject Headings, in this case Biography.

Reference

Most libraries will have a reference section for materials such as Encyclopaedias, dictionaries, atlases, and almanacs. These items are housed in a separate section for materials which normally do not circulate. To indicate an item as a reference book include the notation "REF" with the call number.

REF
971 Thef Junior Encyclopedia of Canada / James
.003 H. Marsh, Editor-in-Chief,--Edmonton : Hurtig, c1990.
JUN 5 v. : Col. Ill.. Maps, Ports. : 29 cm.

Includes Bibliographical References.
ISBN 0888303343 (Set)

1. Canada--Dictionaries and Encyclopedia.
I. Marsh, James H.

Fig. 5.30. Reference (Card Example).

ISBN	020		$a0888303343 (Set)
Dewey Class	082	0	$a971/.003
Local Call#	090		$a971.003 JUN;$bREF
ME:Title	245	04	$aThe Junior Encyclopedia of Canada /$cJames H. Marsh, Editor-in-Chief.
Imprint	260		$aEdmonton :$b Hurting, $cc1990.
Phys. Descript.	300		$a5 V. :$bcol. Ill., Maps, Ports,; $c29 Cm.
Note:Biblio	504		$aIncludes Bibliographical References.
Subj. Geog.	651	0	$aCanada$sDictionaries and Encyclopedias.
AE:Pers. Name	700	1	$amarsh, James H.

Fig. 5.31. Reference (MARC Example).

Oversised Materials

In many cases, libraries possess big books and oversised documents which do not fit comfortably on shelves. Frequently, these items are laid on their sides and gravity eventually pulls the text out of its binding.

A common solution is to create an oversised section in the library to house such items. To alert users to where these items are located, add the prefix OS above the call number. The result is greater longevity for the books and a neater overall appearance. An oversised item may be any monograph over 30 cm high.

OS
911 Times Atias of World History / Edited by Geoffrey Barraclough.
Tim --Maplewood, N.J, : Hammond, 1985.
360 P. : Col. ill. ; 36 Cm.

Bibliography: P. 113
Includes Index and Glossary.

1. Geography, Historical - Maps.I. Barraclough, Geoffrey, 1908-

(Card not Shown in Full.)

Fig. 5.32. Oversised Materials (MARC Example).

ISBN	020		$a0779135246
Dewey Class	082	0	$a911/.32
Local Call #	090		$a911 TIM ;$bOS
Me: Title	245	00	$aTimes Atlas of World History / $cedited By Geoffrey Barraclough.
Imprint	260		$aMaplewood, N.J, : $bHammond, $c1985.
Phys. Descript.	300		$a360 p. :$bcol. ill.;$c36 cm.
Note:Bibliog	504		$aIncludes Bibliographical References, Index and Glossary.
Subj. Topical	650	0	$aGeography, Historical$xMaps
AE:Pers.Name	700	1	$aBarraclough, Geoffrey, 1908-

Fig. 5.33. Oversised Materials (Marc Example).

AUDIOVISUAL MATERIALS

The cataloguing of audiovisual materials such as videorecordings, kits, computer software, and sound recordings follows the same general patterns as those for books. As with books, the cataloguer must still identify the title, the publisher, and date of production but many audiovisual items will not have identifiable authors. In cataloguing audiovisual materials the number of frames, the components of the kit, or the duration of the recording are identified rather than the number of pages. Guidelines for the cataloguing of online information resources are being formulated. This includes numeric databases, computer forums, discussion groups, mailing list servers, online public access catalogues, and full-text databases.

GENERAL MATERIAL DESIGNATION [GMD]

The General Material Designation [GMD] is included to alert the user that the item in question is not a book. It is appended in square brackets [ ] after the title and indicates the precise format of the item. As with the subject headings, only certain terms are to be used as GMDs.

The most common ones which are likely to be used in a school library are:

- Activity card — Kit (2 more media)
- Computer file (replacing — Map
- Machine Readable model — Model
- Data File, a~ the GMD for — Picture

- Computer software) Realia
- Chart Sound recording
- Filmstrip Transparency
- Game Videorecording

The Specific Material Designation [SMD] is a term indicating a special format of material (usually the format of the physical object[s]) to which items belong (*e.g.*, videodiscs and videocassettes). These SMDs are used in the 300 field. The procedures outlined in the chapters on classification and subject indexing are equally applicable to audiovisual materials.

The following examples illustrate some of the most common types of audiovisual materials likely to be encountered in school libraries and may be used as guides in cataloguing.

VIDEORCORDINGS

- Sources of Information
- Usually the main entry is by title.
- Physical Description Area List
- The number of videorecordings.
- Running time as stated on the item.
- Other details such as sound and colour.

Note Area:

- The presentation format such as VHS or Beta should be indicated in this area.

```
VR
971   The Newcomers: 1911[Videorecording].--
New      [S.1.] :Nielson-Ferms,Inc.for Imperial Oil Ltd.
         1 Videocassette (60 Min.) : Sd., Col,-- (Newcomers:
         Inhabiting a New Land)

         Format VHS.
         Summary:Looks at a Danish Couple in New
         Brunswick Who Cannot Decide Whether to Remain in
         Canada or Return to Denmark.

      1. Danes in New Brunswick -- Drama.  2. Canada--
      Emigration and Immigration -- Drama. I.Series.
```

Fig. 5.34. Videorecording (Card Example).

Note the use of the prefix "VR" above the call number to indicate a videorecording.

Dewey Class	082	0_	$a971
Local Call#	090		$a 971 New $bVR
ME:Title	245	04	$athe Newcomers: 1911$h [Videorecording].
Imprint	260		$a[s.1.]:$bNielson-Ferms, Inc. for Imperial Oil Ltd.
Phys. Descript.	300		$a1 Videocassette (60 Min.) : $b sd., Col.
Series	440	_0	$aNewcomers :$binhabiting a New Land
Note:General	500		$aFormat VHS.
Summary	520		$aLooks at a Danish Couple in New Brunswick Who Cannot Decide Whether to Remain in Canada or Return to Denmark.
Subj. Topical	650	_0	$aDanes in New Brunswick$xDrama.
Subj. Topical	651	_5	$aCanada$xEmigration and Immigration$xDrma.

Fig. 5.35. Videorecording (MARC Example).

The GMD is always placed in the 245 field of a MARC record directly after the title proper and before any subtitles. It is always preceded by an $h.

In the 245 field, the "0" and "4" are indicators with the "0" denoting a main entry by title and the "4" being the number of Non-filing characters. In the 245 field, $a is a subfield introducing the title proper.

The $h is a subfield introducing the GMD, in this case a videorecording. The 651 field is an example of a geographical subject heading rather than the more frequently encountered 650 topical heading.

Videodisc

While videodiscs represent a relatively new form of technology, they are to be treated like any other form of media.

- Sources of Information
- The main entry will usually be by title.
- Physical Description Area List:
- The running time as stated on the item.
- The number of frames.

- Other physical details such as the sise of the disc, sound, colour, and teacher guides.
- Note Area:
- As with computer programmes, a system requirements note is mandatory.

VD	Sea Creatures [Videorecording].
574	2nd. ed, -- New York : Phoenix Films, Inc., c1992
.92	1 Videodisc (24220 fr.) : sd., Col., 12 in. + 1 Teacher;s Guide.
Sea	
	System Requirements: 12 in. Videodisc Player Capable of Playing CAV Discs With Barcode Scanner.
	Summary: Interactive Videodisc Program Designed to Introduce Viewers to a Variety of sea Creatures.
	1. Marine Biology.

Fig. .5.36. Videodisc (Card Example).

Dewey Class	082	0	$a574/.9/2
Local Call#	090		$a574.92 Sea $bVD
ME: Title	245	00	$aSea Creatures $h [Videorecording].
Imprint	260		$aNew York :$bPhoenix Films, Inc., $1992.
Phys. Descript.	300		$a1 Videodisc (24220fr.) :$bsd., Col.:$c12in. +$e1 Teacher's Guide.
Note:System Details	538		$aSystem Requirements: 12 in. Videodisc Player Capable of Playing CAV Disks With Barcode Scanner.
Summary	520		$alanteractive Videodisc Program Designed to Introduce Viewers to a Variety of Sea Creatures.
Subj. Topical	650	0	$aMarine Biology.

Fig. 5.37. Videodisc (MARC Example).

COMPUTER SOFTWARE

The GMD "computer file" is used to describe a file containing data, programmes, or both, encoded for manipulation by a computer. Computer software is another area of specialised cataloguing. At best only a cursory introduction can be provided in a document of this type.

Information for the record is to be taken from the following sources in exactly this order —

- Title screen(s)
- Menus or other internal information
- Labels attached to the disk (verified)
- Documentation or manuals provided with the disk
- The container (verified)
- Other published descriptions of the file
- Other sources

Physical Description Area List:

- The extent of the item (*e.g.*, 1 computer disk or cassette).
- Sound and colour if applicable.
- The physical dimensions of the disk.
- 1 computer disk: sd., col.; 3½ in

Note Area:

- A system requirements note is mandatory. Include the make and model of the computer, amount of memory, name of the operating system, and any peripherals which may be required such as a mouse. The statement "System requirements:" must precede this information.

CF	
010	The Bibliography Writer [Computer file]--Version 4.0--
BIB	Chicago, Ill,: Follett, c1995.
	1 Computer Disk + 1 Guide.
	System Requirements: IBM or Capable, 386 or Higher; 4 MB of RAM.
	Title form Title Screen.
	1. Bibliography -- Design and Construction.

Fig. 5.38. Computer Software (Card Example).

Dewey Class	082	0_	$a010
Local Call#	090		$a 010BIB$bCF
Me:Title	245	04	$aThe Bibliography Writer$h [Computer File].
Edition	250		$aVersion 4.0.
Imprint	260		$aChicago,Ill.:$bFollett, $cc1995.
Phys. Descript.	300		$a1 Computer Disk + $e1 Guide.
Note: General	538		$a:System Requirements: IBM or Comparable, 386 or Higher; 4mb RAM.
Note: General	500		$aTitle form Title Screen.
Subj. Topical	650	_0	$aBibliography$xDesign and Construction.

Fig. 5.39. Computer Software (MARC Example).

Note the suffix "CF" in the 090 field designating the item as a computer file.

CR
567.91 Microsoft Dinosaurs [Computer File],--
Mic [United States] : Microsoft Corportation, c 1993.
1 Computer Laser Optical Disk : sd., Col. + 1User's Guide.
--(Microsoft Home) (Exploration Series)

System Requirements: IBM PC or Compatible
(386Sx or Higher Microprocessor) :4 MB of RAM,
2.5 MB of Hard-Disk Space: MS-Dos Operating System,
Version 3.1 or Later, Microsoft Windows Operating System.
Version 3.1 or Later; CD-ROM Drive; Audio Board, VGA
Displays (for 16-Colour Support) or VGA + Displays,
(for Full 256-Colour), Microsoft Mouse or Compatible Pointing
Device, Headphones or Speakers.

Title from Title Screen.

Summary: Presents Over 1000 Colour Illustrations and
Photographs of Dinosaur Images. Includes Spoken
Pronunciations, 200 Illustrated Articles With More Than
800 Pop-up Windows. Also Includes Animated Video Clips.

1. Dinosaurs.

Fig. 5.40. Computer Software (CD-ROM) (Card Example).

Dewey Class	082	0	$a567/91
Local Call#	090		$a 567.91 Mic$bcr
ME: Title	245	00	$aMicrosoft Dinosaurs$h [Computer File].
Imprint	260		$a[United States]:$b Microsoft: Corporation, Scc 1993.
Phys.Descript.	300		$a1 Computer Laser Optical Disk: $bsd., Col,:$c12 cm. +$el User's Guide.
Series	440	0	$aMicrosoft Home
Series	440	0	$aExploration Series
Note: System Details	538		$aSystem Requirements: IBM PC or Compatible (386Sx or Higher Microprocessor);4 MB of RAM, 2.5 MB of Hard-Disk Space; MS-DOS Operating System, or Later, Microsoft Windows Operating System, Version 3.1 or Later; CD-ROM Drive; Audio Board, VGA Display (for 16-Colour Support) or VGA+Display (for Full 256-Colour), Microsoft Mouse or Compatible Pointing Device, Headphones or Speakers.
Note: General	500		$a Title from Title Screen.
Summary	520		$a Presents Over 1000 Colour Illustrations and Photographs of Dinosaur Images Includes Spoken Pronunciations, Ambient Sounds and Growls and Nearly 200 Illustrated Articles With More than 800 Pop-up Windows. Also Includes animated Video Clips.
Subj.Topical	650	0	Sadinosaurs.

Fig. 5.41.Computer Software (CD-ROM) (MARC Example).

SOUND RECORDING

The GMD sound recording is used to designate any disc, roll, audio compact disc (CD), tape (reel-to-reel or cassette) on which sound has been recorded for reproduction.

Sources of Information:

- The item itself (*e.g.,* labels on records or cassettes)
- Accompanying material
- Container
- Other sources

Main Entry:

- Selection of main entry for sound recordings can be very complex. Consult Nonbook Materials by Jean Weihs for specific details and the Concise AACR2—1988 Revision.

Physical Description Area:

- Note—The number of cassettes, records, or reels.
- Playing speed.
- The recording mode (analog, digital)
- The dimension of the item should be listed, e.g. 12 in. for a typical 331/3 rpm disc.

Audio compact discs are usually 4¾ in. (or 12 cm) and are treated exactly the same as any regular recording.

CD
784.5 Turner, Tina.
TUR Private Dancer [Sound Recording]. -- Hollywood, Calif. : Capital, cp1984.
1 Sound Disc(39 min., 31 Sec.) : Digital, 4¾ in.

1. Popular Music -- United States. 2 Rock Music -- United States, 1. Title.

Fig. 5.42. Sound Recordings (Card Example).

Dewey Class	082	0	$a784/5
Local Call#	090		$a784.5 TUR$bCD
ME:Pers, Name	100	1	$a Turner, Tina
Title	245	10	$aPrivate Dancer$h[Sound Recording].
Imprint	260		$aHollywood,Calif.:SbCapitol, $cp1984.
Phys. Descript	300		$a1 Sound Disc (39 min., 31 Sec.) :$Digital;$c4¾ in.
Subj. Topical	650	0	$aPopular Music$zUnited States.
Subj.Topical	650	0	$aRock Music$zUnited States.

Fig. 5.43.Sound Recording (MARC Example).

A general note might be added to the 500 field to indicate that this is a compact disc.

KITS

A kit is an item containing two or more categories of material, none of which is identifiable as the predominant constituent of the item. The GMD "kit" is applied only to those media which are to be catalogued as a unit.

Sources of Information:

- As the chief source of information, use the part which gives the most information (*i.e.,* use the video, not the manual; the filmstrip, not the guide; the book, not the cassette).
- Secondly, use the part that is the unifying element (*e.g.,* the container or the manual).
- Thirdly, use other sources.

Main Entry:

- It is often difficult to determine authorship for kits. Main entry will be by author only if an author can be established as the creator of the kit as a whole. Usually the main entry will be under title if only partial authorship or no authorship can be discerned.

Physical Description Area:

- List the number and name of each part of the kit in their order of importance to the kit as a whole. List the contents in alphabetical order if importance cannot be determined.

```
KIT
549    Rocks and Minerals [Kit]. -- Ottawa :
ROC       National Film Board, 1988.
          1 Chart, 3 Filmstrips, 1 Manual , 13 Rocks and Minerals;
          in Container, 30×5 cm.

       1. Rocks.
```

Fig. 5.44. Kit (Card Example).

Dewey Class	082	0_	$a549
Local Call #	090		$a 549 ROC $bkit
ME:Title	245	00	$aRocks and Minerals$h[kit]
Imprint	260		$aOttawa :$bNational Film Board, $c 1988.
Phys.Descript.	300		$a1 Chart, 3 Filmstrips, 1 Manual, 13 Rocks and Minerals;$cin Container, 30×26×5cm.
Subj. Topical	650	_0	$aRocks.

Fig. 5.45. Kit (MARC Example).

Sources of Information:

- Information for the catalogue record should be taken from the following sources in this order:
- The item itself. Preference should be given to the title frame(s) rather than the leader frame(s).
- Container.
- Accompanying materials.
- Other sources

Physical Description Area:

- Frames in an unnumbered filmstrip are to be counted and placed in square [ ] brackets.
- Other physical details such as sound (sd), colour (col), or black and white (b & w) should be noted.
- The dimensions should be noted. Usually it is 35 mm.
- Additional materials such as guides should be listed.

```
FS
917.1 The Canadian Shield [Filmstrip]. --Ottawa:
Can        National Film Board, 1988.
           1 Filmstrip (40fr.):Col,; 35mm. + 1 Teacher's Guide.

       1. Canada -- Geography
```

Fig. 5.46. Single Filmstrip with Numbered Frames and a Guide (Card Example).

Dewey Class	082	0_	$a917/.1
Local Call #	090		$a917.1 Can $bfs
ME:Title	245	04	$aThe Canadian Shield$h [Filmstrip].
Imprint	260		$aOttawa :$bNational Film Board, $c1988.
Phys.Descript.	300		$a1 Filmstrip (40 fr,):$Bcol. $c35 mm. + 1 Teacher's Guide.
Subj. Geog.	651	_5	$aCanada$xGeography.

Fig. 5.47. Single Filmstrip (MARC Example).

```
FS
638.1 Honeybees [Filmstrip]: -- Toronto : Educational
HON      AV, 1988.
         4 Filmstrips (60 fr. Each):Col.; 35 mm + 4 sd.
         Cassettes (30 min.Each).
         Contents: The Queen bee -- The Hive -- The Setting --
         Problems in Production.
      1. Bee Culture. 2. Bees.
```

Fig. 5.48. Multipart Filmstrips (Card Example).

- For the example on the previous page the MARC record would appear as follows

Dewey Class	082	0_	$a638/.1
Local Call#	090		$a 638.1 Hon $ BFS
Title	245	00	$aHoneybees$h[Filmstrip].
Imprint	260		$a Toronto :$bEducational AV, $cc 1988.
Phys.Descript.	300		$a4 Filmstrips (60 fr.each) :$bcol. ;$c35mm. + $e 4 sd. Cassettes (30 min. Each).
Contents Note	505	0	$athe Queen Bee -- The Hive -- The Setting -- Problems in Production.
Subj. Topical	650	_0	$aBee Culture.
Subj. Topical	650	_0	$aBees.

Fig. 5.49. Multipart Filmstrips (MARC Example).

TYPING CATALOGUE CARDS

Automatic card generating systems are available as an alternative to typing the cards. If you must type catalogue cards, they are to be typed on 3 × 5 inch card stock which is readily available from any library supply firm. Each card should follow a standard format.

The catalogue cards are to be single spaced throughout, with the following exceptions:

- Double-spacing before the beginning of the first note
- Beginning the tracings at the bottom of the card but above the hole

The typist should set up the typewriter in the following way

- Margin 2 spaces from the left edge of the card
- 1st tab 9 spaces from left of card (1st indention), 11 spaces from left of card.
- 2nd tab 13 spaces from the left margin (2nd indention)

AUTHOR MAIN ENTRY

F Korman, Gordon.

Kor The Zucchini Warriors / Gordon Korman. -- Toronto: Scholastic, c1988.

198 P.;22 cm.

ISBN 059041335X

1. Football--Fiction. 2. Schools--Fiction. 3. Humorous Stories. I. Title.

88-6720

Fig. 5.50. Author Main Entry—Showing Indentions (Card Example).

Arabic numbers (1, 2, 3 and so on) are used in the bottom tracings to indicate subject headings. Roman numerals (I, II, III and so on) are used to indicate added entries which are entries beyond the main entry. Examples are added entries for an author, illustrator, translator, title, variant title, series, and so on.

- *Call Number* - Should begin on the fourth line from the top of the card at the left margin in block style.
- *Author* - Should be typed on the fourth line beginning at the first indention.
- *Title Paragraph* - (*i.e.,* title, statement of responsibility, edition, publisher, and date). Should be typed on the fifth line starting at the second indention. The second and succeeding lines of the title paragraph should commence at the first indentation.
- *Physical* - Begins at the second indention on the line Description following the title paragraph. Any extension of the physical description should start at the first indention of the next line.
- *Subject Headings* - Begin at the first indention as close to the and Tracings bottom of the card as possible. (Avoid typing through the hole at the bottom of the card.) Begin the second line of this paragraph at the first indention as well.

COMPLETE CARD SET

A complete card set for any item in the library consists of the following

- A shelf list card
- Main entry card
- A dictionary catalogue card (which goes into the card catalogue)
- One card for each of the subject headings and other index items listed as tracings at the bottom of the shelf list card (they go into the card catalogue)

Shelf List Card

The shelf list card is an inventory card and is kept in a separate card file in the library office or other safe place. It will indicate how many copies of the title the library has as well as what cards are in the dictionary catalogue for the book. This latter information can be determined from the tracings at the bottom of the shelf list card. Other information may be recorded, such as the accession number(s), price, and status of each copy (*e.g.*, lost, damaged).

E Bourgeois, Paulette.
Bou Franklin Fibs/Paulette Bourgeois; Illustrated by Brenda Clark, -- Toronto: Kids Can Press, 1991.

[32] P. : Col. ill.;23cm.

ISBN 155074385

1. Turtles--Fiction. 1.Clark,Brenda. II. Title.

C90-94941

Fig. 5.51. Card 1 - Main Entry, Shown in Full (Card Example).

Dictionary catalogue cards do not need to repeat the tracings listed at the bottom of the shelf list card. The first card typed for the dictionary catalogue, which in the case above is an author card, will be identical to the shelf list card up to the end of the physical description area.

This is the basic card. To create subject, title, and illustrator cards for the dictionary catalogue, make additional copies of the basic card, one for each subject heading and additional tracing. Type the subject heading, title, or the name of the illustrator at the top of one of these basic cards starting at the second indentation on the third line from the top of the card.

Subject headings are to be typed in CAPITAL LETTERS; while titles and illustrators are in upper and lower cases as required. Together, Figures below illustrate a complete typed card set of five cards. This particular book requires five cards to complete the set.

E Bourgeois, Paulette.
BOU Franklin Fibs / Paulette Bourgeois; Illustrated by Brenda Clark. -- Toronto : Kids Can Press, 1991. [32] P.: Col. ill.; 23 cm.

ISBN 155074385

1. Turtles--Fiction. I. Clark, Brenda.II. Title.

C90-94941

Fig. 5.52. Card 2—Main Entry (Card Example).

E Bourgeois, Paulette.
BOU Franklin Fibs / Paulette Bourgeois; Illustrated by]
Brenda Clark.-- Toronto: Kids Can Press, 1991.
[32] P.:Col. ill.; 23 cm.

ISBN 155074385

1. Turtles--Fiction. 1.Clark,Brenda. II Title.

C90-94941

Fig. 5.53. Shelf List (Card Example).

Clark, Brenda.
E Bourgeois, Paulette.
BOU Franklin Fibs/ Paulette Bourgeois; Illustrated by
Brenda Clark.---Toronto : Kids Can Press, 1991.
[32] p. : col. ill. : 23 cm.

ISBN 155074385

1. Turtles---Fiction. 1. Clark, Brenda. II. Title.

C90-949411

Fig. 5.54. Card 3—Name Added Entry (Card Example).

Turtles--Fiction
E Bourgeois, Paulette.
BOU Franklin Fibs / Paulette Bourgeois; Illustrated by]
Brenda Clark.-- Toronto: Kids Can Press, 1991.
[32] P.:Col. ill.; 23 cm.

ISBN 155074385

1. Turtles--Fiction. 1.Clark,Brenda. II Title.

C90-94941

Fig. 5.55. Card 4—Fiction Subject Added Entry (Card Example).

Franklin Fibs
E Bourgeois, Paulette.
BOU Franklin Fibs / Paulette Bourgeois ;Illustrated by
Brenda Clark. -- Toronto : Kids Can Press, 1991.

[32] p. : Col. ill.; 23 cm.

ISBN 155074385

1. Turties--Fiction. I. Clark, Brenda. II Title.

C90-94941

Fig. 5.56. Title Added Entry (Card Example):

TITLE MAIN ENTRY CARDS

When the main entry for an item begins with a title (and not an author), the format is slightly different. The title in this case begins at the fourth line at the first indentation; the extension is carried over to the next line at the second indention. Entries made in this fashion are referred to as hanging indentations.

```
CF
006  The Print Shop [Computer File].--San Fafael, Calif.:
.68     Broderbund Software, c1995.
PRI     1 Computer Laser Optical Disk ; 12cm. + 1 Guide
       System Requirements: 1BM PC or Compatible ; 2 MB of
       RAM, 2.5 MB Hard-Disk Space.
     1. Computer Graphics.
```

Fig. 5.57. Title Main Entry (Card Example).

FILING CARDS

ALA (AMERICAN LIBRARY ASSOCIATION FILING RULES)

For manual card catalogues, the ALA Filing Rules are the standard which are to be followed.

SHELF LIST

The shelf list file contains one card for each distinct item in the library and is arranged in the same order as the items on the shelves. Different shelf lists are created for materials in various locations such as Reference, AV and VTR. To file shelf list cards for the main collection, group them first into main categories: one for Easy, one for Fiction, one for Non-Fiction, and one for Reference cards.

- *Easy*: Arrange the cards in alphabetical order by author (or by title in cases where there is no author). Sub-arrange the books by the same author alphabetically by title.
- *Fiction*: Arrange the fiction cards in alphabetical order by author (or by title in cases where there is no author.) Sub-arrange the books by the same author alphabetically by title.
- *Non-Fiction*: Arrange the Non--fiction cards in numerical order by Dewey number, remembering that Dewey numbers are decimal numbers. The following is an example of a correct sequence

  971 971.004 971.2 971.24

- In cases where the library may have several different books by the same author, file first by Dewey number and then sub-arrange by main entry.

DICTIONARY CATALOGUE

- Interfile all author, subject and title cards in one alphabetical sequence.
- Alphabetise by the TOP line of the card. When the top lines are identical, sub-arrange by the next line on the card.
- Ignore the articles "a", "an" and "the" when they occur at the beginning of a title. These articles need only be considered in alphabetising when they occur in the middle of the heading. In French, ignore the articles "le", "la", "les" and "l' " only. "Du", "de", "d' " and "un(e)" will be filed under those articles.
- Alphabetise character space by character space. Blank character spaces come before character spaces with letters. Thus, shorter words come before longer words beginning with the same letters.

  e.g., The new mathematics New World Atlas Newman, Joan.
- Acronyms are field as single words. UNESCO The Union of Canada. Numbers expressed as numerals (arabic or roman) are filed according to their numerical value; this file is before the first alphabetical file (*e.g.*, before "A").

  e.g., 200 275 6000 Numbers that are spelled out as words are: Six thousand.
- Numbers that are spelled out as words are filed as spelled.
- Abbreviations are filed exactly as written, not as if spelled out.
- Apostrophes are disregarded and the word containing the apostrophe is filed as one word.
- Proper names with prefixes are treated as a separate words unless joined to the rest of the name directly or by an apostrophe without a space.
- Subject cards with dates as subdivisions are subarranged chronologically with the earliest date first.

PROCESSING

Once the cards have been prepared and filed, prepare the items for circulation. Use the following as a guide.

BOOKS

- Stamp the book with the school stamp
  - The fly leaf
  - The lower part of the title page
  - On the outside edges of the pages, with the book firmly closed
- Type a book pocket and card for each item according to the example given on the next page. Note that the author's surname and the first name are both typed. The same tabs that are used for typing the catalogue cards may be used to type the book card and pocket.
- Type the call number for each book on a label and attach it to the book. Cover the label with a mylar label cover. Both spine labels and mylar label covers are available from any library supply company. Be consistent in the placement of the labels.
- Most libraries prefer to paste the pocket in the back of the book so as not to cover title information found in the front. It is important to be consistent in the location of the pocket. If a library does put the pockets in the front, a blank page can be introduced to put the card on. Again be consistent about the use of the front or back. If date due slips are being used, attach one to the pocket below the typed title.
- Books with paper dust jackets should be covered with a plastic dust jacket for protection.
- If the item is to be circulated in an automated system the barcode should be affixed to the item and covered with mylar barcode tape. It is a good practice to write the barcode number on the inside cover in case the label becomes separated from the book. Systems typically employ portable barcode readers. Placement of the automated label on the cover, as opposed to

the inside of the cover, offers the practical advantage of not requiring that every book be removed and opened during inventory.

Pocket and Card for a Book

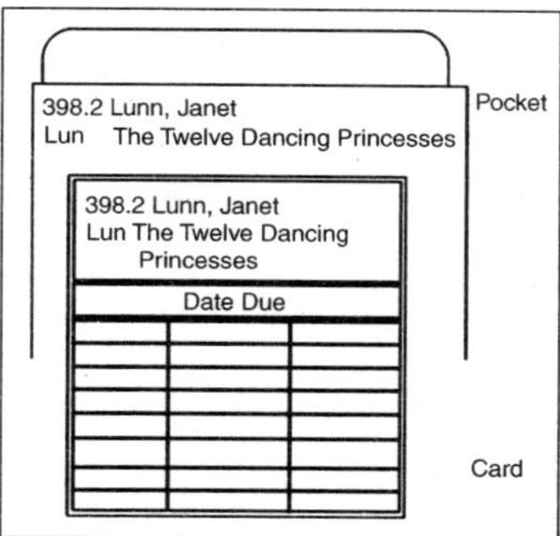

Fig. 5.58. Pocket Card.

AUDIOVISUAL MATERIALS

Audiovisual materials come packaged in so many diverse ways that it is difficult to detail the various means of processing.

In general, follow these steps:

- Stamp the item with the school stamp.
- Prepare a book card and pocket as if for a book and attach it to the box or container. It is a good idea to label the component parts of the box so when the item is returned it is easy to verify nothing has been lost or misplaced.
- Prepare the call number label and attach it to the box. Cover the label with mylar tape.
- If the item is to be circulated in an automated system, affix the barcode label and cover it with mylar tape. Write the barcode number inside the box in case the label is removed from the box.
- For compact sound discs and CD-ROMs, book cards, pockets, and barcodes should be attached to the containers. Any library-specific identifying marks (*i.e.,* call number and institution name) may be written on

the transparent centre of the disc as close to the hub and as clearly as possible. A fine point, permanent, silver metallic ink marker works well.

Pocket and Card for an Audiovisual Item

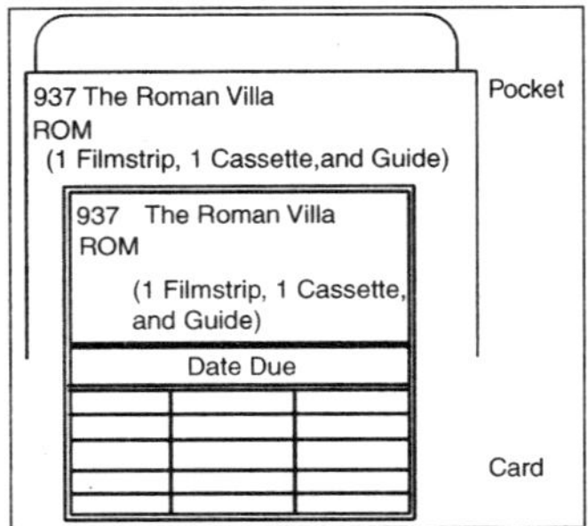

Fig. 5.59. Pocket and Card for an Audiovisual Item.

MARC CATALOGUING FOR MANITOBA SCHOOL LIBRARIES

MARC tapes, MARC format, MARC records and MARC compatible are terms which now dominate the lexicon of library literature. All school libraries and teacher-librarians who plan to automate will have to come to terms with MARC records. The purpose of this section of the guide is to explain what a MARC record is and to provide some guidelines for MARC cataloguing in the school libraries of Manitoba.

The importance of following this standard cannot be overstated. If school libraries are to share their cataloguing, and take advantage of the MARC databases available to assist in the recon task, it is essential to adhere to the following standards. The creation of MARC records would allow for the electronic access to bibliographic records, thus facilitating resource-sharing among school libraries.

WHAT DOES MARC MEAN?

A MARC record is a Machine Readable Cataloguing record. By "machine readable" is meant a record that a computer can read and interpret. The following pages will explain why MARC is important and how it is made possible. A cataloguing record is a bibliographic record, containing the information shown on the catalogue cards described earlier in this guide. Typically a record includes

- Describing the item
- Adding entries
- Arranging subject headings
- Labelling call numbers and shelf list information as well as additional information

WHY IS MARC NECESSARY?

Because computers cannot think or reason they must be provided with guides that enable them to interpret the data which has been inputted into them. The MARC record contains directories or guideposts before each piece of bibliographic information to tell the cataloguer and the computer what type of data is to be found in a specific field.

Author, title, and subject are examples of the various field types. Because the lengths of names and titles are usually different, the best library software allows for unlimited field lengths and an unlimited number of fields. Guidance on selection of automated library systems is found in a companion volume to this work. It is available from the Instructional Resources Unit, Manitoba Education and Training, and is entitled Selection of Automation Systems: Criteria for School Libraries in Manitoba

MARC TERMS AND DEFINITIONS

To understand what is being talked about when MARC records are being discussed one needs to be acquainted with the following terms: delimiters, fields, tags, indicators, subfields, and subfield codes.

Delimiters

With different kinds of keyboards, different keys are used to represent the delimiters. In some cases a $ is used, or (-) for Microlif records. For the sake of convenience, a $ will represent the delimiter in this document.

Fields

Bibliographical data is divided into a number of fields to facilitate retrieval: fields for authors, fields for titles, and so on. The fields are further subdivided into one or more subfields. For example, the place of publication, the publisher's name and the date of the publication are all included as part of the MARC field tagged "260."

Tags

A tag is a three-digit number which precedes each field in a MARC record. The tag identifies the field and the kind of data that follows to the computer.

The most frequently encountered tags for monograph and audiovisual resources are:

- Tag Field
- 010 LCCN
- 016 National Library of Canada control number
- 020 ISBN
- 040 Cataloguing Source
- 082 Dewey Decimal Classification number as assigned by Library of Congress (LC) or National Library of Canada (NLC)
- 090 Local Call Number
- 100 Author main entry field
- 110 Corporate main entry
- 111 Conference main entry
- 130 Uniform title main entry
- 245 Title field
- 246 Varying forms of the title
- 250 Edition field
- 260 Publication information
- 300 Physical description
- 440 Series statement—Title (traced)
- 500 General note area
- 504 Bibliographic note
- 505 Contents note
- 520 Summary or annotation
- 521 Audience level note

- 600 Personal name subject heading
- 610 Corporate subject heading
- 611 Conference subject heading
- 650 Topical subject heading
- 651 Geographical subject heading
- 690 Local subject heading
- 700 Personal name added entry
- 710 Corporate name added entry
- 740 Variant title
- 856 Uniform resource location (URL)
- 901 Local barcode number
- 903 Local price

A typical MARC field for the ISBN number would appear as:
020 $a0880223707

There are 999 fields which may be used in a MARC record, but only a fraction of the possible fields will ever be found in any single record. About 10 per cent of the tags are used over and over again and the MARC cataloguer will quickly become familiar with them.

Indicators

Two spaces follow each tag. One or both of these spaces may be used for indicators. In some fields, only the second space is used. Sometimes only the first is used and sometimes both are assigned. Consult the Canadian MARC Communication Format for details. Each indicator will be a number from 1 to 9. Each individual digit has a meaning. In the following example the first three digits are the tag (245 being the title field tag), and the next 2 digits "1" and "4" are indicators. The "1" is the first indicator and the "4" is the second.

245 14: $aThe trials of life $ba natural history of animal behaviour/$cDavid Attenborough.

The first indicator of "1" in the title field indicates that there should be a separate title entry in the catalogue. In the card catalogue environment, this means a title card should be printed for this item. A "0" as a first indicator means that this is a main entry by title and the cards should be printed with the traditional hanging indention. The second indicator displays the number of Nonfiling characters at the beginning of the field. For the example, The trials of life, the second indicator is set at "4" so that the first 4 characters (the "T," the "h," the "e," and the space) will be skipped and the title will be filed under "trials." Indicators act as signals to the application software. They define how the software should treat the information within a specific field. Should the library ever consider having authority control work (*e.g.*, correct/consistent spelling) done on their database by a large commercial vendor, correct use of indicators is critical.

Subfields are Marked by Subfield Codes

Most fields will contain several related pieces of data. Each type of data within a field is called a subfield, and each subfield is preceded by a subfield code. For example, the physical description field defined by the 300 tag typically contains a subfield for the number of pages, one for physical details such as illustration, and a further subfield for dimensions in centimetres.

300 $a234 p.:$bill.;$c24 cm.

Subfield Codes

Subfield codes are one lower-case letter preceded by a delimiter. Each subfield indicates what type of data follows it. In the example, the subfield codes are $a for extent, $b for other physical details and $c for dimensions.

USING THIS PUBLICATION

The following summary details the MARC tags most likely to be encountered by teacher-librarians during recon or original data entry. The list may appear intimidating at first but most MARC cataloguers will quickly become familiar with the meanings of the various tags. Not all fields will be found in every entry. Notes have been included indicating fields which are repeatable (R) or not repeatable (NR).

Examples are:

- ***Tags***—Will be followed by the names of the fields they represent. Repeatable fields (those which can appear more than once in any given record) will be followed by an "R," Non- repeatable fields (those which can appear no more than once in any given record) by an "NR."

- ***Indicators***—The use of the indicator is explained in the fields where they are used. Indicators are one digit numbers. Starting with the 010 field, two spaces are left for the indicators if required. Indicators are not required in all fields.
- ***Subfield Codes***—All the data in each field is divided into subfields, each of which is preceded by a subfield code. In almost all cases the subfield will be followed by a delimiter followed by a letter or a number. The name of the subfield will follow the code.
- ***Examples***—Examples will follow each field. In the examples a "0" = a blank space. For the sake of clarity one space will be left between the tag and the first indicator, one will be placed between the second indicator and the first subfield code, and one space between the subfield code and the subfield data.

MARC Leader

The MARC leader is the first block of data which appears at the top of a MARC record. The leader consists of a number of fixed fields and its primary importance is to provide information to the application software (*i.e.,* the OPAC) about how to process the record.

It consists of 24 fields and by-and-large the cataloguer will not be concerned with this area at all. The application software will normally record a control number and the date of entry automatically. This, of course, will depend upon the type of application software involved. Individual users should consult their software guides as to how to deal with this particular area. For the purposes of clarity the MARC Leader will not be included in any of the examples in this document.

MARC Fields

010 LCCN Library of Congress Card Number (NR):

- *Indicators*: Undefined
  Subfield most commonly used: $a
  Example: 010 __ $a910988

016 National Library of Canada's Control Number (NR):

- *Indicators*: Undefined
  Subfield most commonly used: $a
  Example: 016 __ $a860937070

020 ISBN International Standard Book Number (R):

This ten digit number is becoming the unique number by which books and their corresponding MARC records are identified. If the library should own both the hardback and the paperback edition of a book, the ISBN numbers may be repeated for this field. Typically a paperback edition will be indicated as (pbk) and noted after the ISBN.

Indicators: Undefined
Subfield most commonly used: $a ISBN
Examples:
020 __ $a0771034356
020 __ $a0771013396 (pbk)

040 Cataloguing Source (NR):

- *Indicators*: Undefined
  Subfield most commonly used: $a Cataloguing source
  Example: 040 __ $aDLC

082 Dewey Decimal Classification Number (R):

- *Indicator 1*:
  Type of edition (*e.g.*, 12th)
  blank—no edition information recorded
  0—Full edition of Dewey
  1—Abridged edition
  Indicator 2:
  Source of DDC number
  blank—no information provided
  0—assigned by LC
  4—assigned by agency other than LC

Non-Fiction Number Building in Dewey

Note: In many cases the call number selected by the Library of Congress or other cataloguing agency will be far longer than the school library requires. Rarely will a school library find it necessary to build Dewey Numbers three or more places beyond the decimal point. In cases where extremely long Dewey numbers are encountered the cataloguer in a school situation should feel free to truncate at three places beyond the decimal point or at the first logical break. The cataloguer may opt to truncate the call number at the slash or apostrophe as desired.

Subfield most commonly used: $a
Example:
082 04 $a960.4/31
082 04 $a960.4'31

Fiction

All fiction works in a school situation should be classed as F or FIC but not both. In many cases an 800 classification number will be encountered when deriving records from a MARC database. These items should be classed as F when encountered in a school library situation.

090 Local Call Number

The 090 field is used to indicate the local call number and if an item has a special location in the library. It is also used to alert users to copies of books which are located at other sites within the school division/district.

Local Call Number (R):
Indicators: Undefined
Subfields most commonly used:
$a Local call number
$b Special location within library
$c Number of copies held
$d Location within school division/district
Examples:
090 $a971 BER $bREF
090 $a328 VIC $bOS
090 $a659.4 DAY $c 2 copies $d
Crescentview School

100 Level Fields

Be aware that many indicators have been eliminated as of

January, 1995. These indicators are marked by an asterisk. The 100 level fields are reserved for author and uniform main entry by title. As there can only be one main entry, unlike many other MARC fields this one is not repeatable.

100 Personal Name Main Entry (NR)

(NR, as there can be only one main entry)

Indicator 1: Type of personal name
0—Forename only
1—Single surname (most common)
2—Multiple surname
3—Name of family
Indicator 2: Blank
Subfields most commonly used:
$a Name (surname and forenames)
$c Titles and other words associated with name
$d Date of birth and death
$q Expansion of initials in parenthesis (*i.e.*, a qualification of the name in a fuller form)
Examples:
100 1_ $aBerton, Pierre,$d1920-
100 1_ $aGiroux, Lionel,$d1878- 1967.

110 Corporate Main Entry (NR)

During a recon the cataloguer will encounter many examples of corporate main entries. A corporate body is an organisation or group of persons that is identified by a particular name (*e.g.*, an association, government, government agency, religious body, local church, conference).

Indicator 1: Type of Corporate name
1—Place or place and name
2—Name direct order
Indicator 2: Blank
Subfield most commonly used: $a Name
Example: 110 2_ $aManitoba Library Association

200 Level Fields

240 Uniform titles (NR):

In the absence of adequate authority tools to verify

alternatives properly, it is recommended that the 240 field not be used.

245 Title Statement (NR):

This is a mandatory field in all MARC records:

Indicator 1: Should the title be indexed as a title main entry?

0—No added entry; No author is given

1—Title added entry (most common; used when an author is present)

Indicator 2: Number of filing characters

0-9 The number of filing characters, including spaces (usually set at zero except when the title begins with an article)

E.g., for a title The Spanish Inquisition, the second indicator would be 4. The letters t, h, e, and the space following them are then ignored in alphabetising titles. The book would be alphabetised with the "S's."

Subfields most commonly used:

$a Short title/title proper

$b Remainder of title (subtitles)

$c Remainder of title page transcription

$h GMD (General Material Designation) used most often for media

246 (R) Varying Forms of Title

Indicator 1: 0 —No title added entry

1 —Title added entry

Indicator 2: Blank—no information provided

0 —Access for portions of title

1 —Parallel title

2 —Distinctive title

3 —Other title

4 —Cover title

5 —Added title page title

6 —Caption title

7 —Running title

8 —Title from spine

Subfield Codes: $a Short title/title proper

$n Number or designation (R)
$p Part or section (R)
$h General Material Designation
$b Other titles and other title information
$c Remainder of title page transcription
$f Designation of volume and issue and/or dates associated with the title
$g Miscellaneous information

Following are the types of titles which are included in this field—parallel, distinctive, cover, added title page, caption, running, spine, other.

Examples: Parallel Title; Title Statement —

245 00 $a Guide du camping au Québec = $bQuébec camping guide/$c Association des terrains de camping et caravaning du Québec.
246 11 $aQuébec camping guide

250 Edition statement (NR)

Indicators: Undefined
Subfields most commonly used $a Edition statement
Examples: 250 $a6th ed.

260 Publication, imprint/release (NR)

Indicators: Undefined
Subfields most commonly used
$a Place
$b Publisher
$c Date of publication
Example: 260 $aNew York:$bRandom House, $cc1991.

Note: For school libraries doing original cataloguing, it should be sufficient to record the first city listed on the title page and ignore subsequent cities listed.The same rule can be used in the case of multiple publishers. A "c" should precede the date in the entry if the date of publication is derived from the copyright date. The distributor should be added for all audiovisual materials as the source is often different from the producer. Describe the item in hand.

300 Level Fields

300 Level Physical Description or Collation (R):

The physical format of the item being described is recorded in this area. The physical description includes: the pagination or extent of the item, its physical details and details of accompanying materials.

Indicators: Undefined

Subfields most commonly used

$a Extent of item (number of pages)

$b Other physical details (*e.g.*, illustrations, maps, ports, etc.)

$c Dimensions (e.g. 24 cm.)

$e Accompanying material

Examples:

300 __ $axii, 300 p.:$bcol. ill.;$c24 cm.

300 __ $a2 computer disks;$c3 1/2 in.

300 __ $a4 filmstrips (60 fr. each): $bcol. and b & w;$c35 mm.

400 Level Fields

Series Statement/Added Entry—Title (R): This field is used for series that are traced in the catalogue. The name of the series will be found on the title page or elsewhere in the book.

Indicator 1: Undefined

Indicator 2: Non-filing characters

0-9 Number of Non--filing characters (for initial articles, including spaces).

Subfields most commonly used

$a Series title

$v Volume or number in the series

Examples:

440 _4 $aThe history of modern Europe

440 _4 $aThe ship;$v29

500 Level Fields

500 *General Notes (R)*: If a book has an index or the library desires to add some additional information it is recorded here.

Indicators: Undefined

Subfield most commonly used

$a General note (used when no specialised note field has been defined for the information)

Example: 500 __ $aIncludes index.

504 *Bibliography Note (R)*: If a work has a bibliography, discography or filmography it should be recorded in this field.

Indicators: Undefined

Subfield most commonly used

$a Bibliography/discography note

Example: 504 __ $aIncludes bibliographical references and index.

505 Contents Notes (NR): This field is typically used to trace the contents of multi-volume works. It should be preceded by the label Contents.

Indicator 1:

0—Contents (complete)

1—Contents (incomplete)

2—Partial contents (if items missing)

Indicator 2: Blank

Examples:

505 0_ $a1. The stars (24 min.). —2. The universe (25 min.)

505 1_ $av. 1. Report—v.3. DNA update.

505 2_ $av. 1. Claudius the god.

520 Summary Note, Abstract, or Annotation (R): This field is commonly found in MARC records derived from a source such as the Library of Congress. Summary notes are recommended in automated systems. A keyword search of a note field will greatly enhance the recovery of materials to meet the thematic approach often used by teachers. Summary notes should be kept concise.

Indicator 1: Usually blank

Indicator 2: Undefined

Subfield most commonly used $a Summary, abstract or annotation.

Example: 520 __ $aExplains the concepts of continental drift, vulcanism, and plate tectonics.

521 *Audience Note (R)*: Reading levels or intended audience levels are placed in this field if the levels are specifically stated in the item itself. All other methods are marginally reliable and useful at best.

Indicators: Undefined

Subfields most commonly used: $a Audience level

Examples:

521 __ $aGrades 3, 4, 5.

521 __ $aEarly years.

600 Level Fields

600 Subject Added Entry—Personal Name (R): This field is used for any subject heading which is a personal name. The form to be followed will be the same as if entering a personal name in the 100 field. This field is commonly used for the subjects of biographies and literary criticism.

Indicator 1:

Type of personal name

0—Forename

1—Single surname (most common)

2—Multiple surname

Indicator 2: Source of the subject heading

0—Library of Congress Subject Heading

5—National Library of Canada (NLC) English Subject Heading

6—National Library of Canada (NLC) French Subject Heading

7—Source of Subject Heading or Term Specified in Subfield $2

Note Regarding Sears Subject Headings: The National Library of Canada does not provide an assigned indicator for Sears headings. For libraries which change or edit records or do original cataloguing, an

indicator of 7 is used. Subfield most commonly used
$a: Name (surname and forename)
$q: Expansion of initials in parenthesis
$b: Numeration (Roman numeral and name used with the entry element of a forename heading)
$c: Titles and other words associated with the name (R)
$d: Birth and death dates
$t: Title
$x: General subdivision (R)
$y: Chronological subdivision (R)
$z: Geographical subdivision (R)
$2: Source of subject heading or term
Examples:
600 10 $aShakespeare, William,$d1564-1616$xComedies
600 10 $aNicholas$bII,$cEmperor of Russia,$d1868-1918.
600 10 $aDavidson, Donald,$d1917- $xCriticism and interpretation.
610 Subject Heading—Corporate Name (R): Corporate bodies, government agencies, or other organisations are placed in this field. The coding is similar to the 110 field used for Corporate Main entry.
Indicator 1: Type of Corporate name
0—Surname (inverted)
1—Place or place and name
2—Name (direct order) most common
Indicator 2: Source of subject heading
0—Library of Congress Subject Heading
5—National Library of Canada (NLC) English Subject Heading
6—National Library of Canada (NLC) French Subject Heading
7—Source of Subject Heading or Term Specified in Subfield $2
Subfields most commonly used:
$a: Name
$b: Subheading (R)

$d: Date of conference meeting, etc. (R)
$c: Place of meeting, conference, etc.
$t: Title
$x: General subdivision (R)
$y: Chronological subdivision (R)
$z: Geographical subdivision (R)
$2: Source of subject heading or term
Examples:
610 10 $aUnited States.$bArmy $xHistory$yCivil War, 1861- 1865.
610 20 $aCanadian Open Golf Championship Tournament$d(1968:$cToronto, Ont.).
611 Subject Heading—Conference or Meeting (R): If the conference itself is the subject of the book, then the established name of the conference should be placed in the 611 field.
Indicator 1: Type of conference or name of meeting
1—Place or place and name
2—Name (direct order)
Indicator 2: Source of subject heading
0—LC Subject Heading
5—NLC-English Subject Heading
6—NLC-French Subject Heading
7—Sears Subject Heading
Subfields most commonly used
$a: Name
$c: Place of meeting
$d: Date
$n: Number of the conference
Example: 611 20 $aConference on Library Technology$d
630 Subject Heading—Uniform Title Heading (R): The 630 field is not recommended for use by school library personnel unless they have had specialised training in it.
650 Subject Added Entry—Topical Heading (R): The bulk of all subject headings will be listed in this field. Topical headings include general subject terms, including the names of events or objects.

Indicator 1: Normally blank
Indicator 2: Source of subject heading or authority
0—Library of Congress Subject Heading
5—NLC—English Subject Heading
6—NLC—French Subject Heading
7—Subject Heading From Source Specified in Subfield $2
Subfields most commonly used:
$a: Topical subject heading
$x: General subdivision (R)
$y: Chronological subdivision (R)
$z: Geographical subdivision (R)
$2: Source of subject heading or term
Examples:
650 _7 $aMagic$2Sears
650 _0 $aAnimals.
650 _0 $aTaxation$zCanada.
650 _0 $aChurch and state in Germany$y20th century.
650 _5 $aInuit$zCanada.
650 _6 $aTimbres-poste$zCanada.
651 Subject Added Entry—Geographic Name (R): Places, natural regions, sites, parks, and political jurisdictions are placed in this field.
Indicator 1: Undefined
Indicator 2: Denotes the subject heading authority from which the heading was derived
0 —LC Subject Heading
5 —NLC-English Subject Heading
6 —NLC-French Subject Heading
7 —Subject Heading From Source Specified in Subfield $2
Subfields most commonly used:
$a: Geographic name (R)
$x: General subdivision (R)
$y: Chronological subdivision (R)
$z: Geographical subdivision (R)
$2: Source of subject heading or term
Examples:
651 _0 $aCanada$xBoundaries$z United States.
651 _0 $aUnited States$xHistory $xChronology.

651 _0 $aGermany$xPolitics and government$y1918-1933.

690 Local Subject Headings (R): It is not recommended that schools indulge in creating their own subject headings. As strange as many subject headings derived from Sears or the Library of Congress may seem they are the international standard. Cataloguers are strongly encouraged to use approved headings only. The 690 field is reserved for those rare situations where no suitable heading can be located in the standard list of subject terms. The indicators and subfields in the 690 area are identical to the other 600 fields.

700 Level Fields

700 Added Entry—Personal Name (R): Typically, tracings such as editors, illustrators, and joint authors are entered in this field.

Indicator 1: Type of personal name:

0—Forename only

1—Single surname (most common)

2—Multiple surname

3—Family name

Indicator 2: Type of added entry

Blank—No information provided 2—Analytical entry (used for someone involved with only a portion of the work)

Subfields most commonly used:

$a: Name

$c: Titles and other words associated with the name

$d: Date

$q: Qualification of the name (fuller form)

$t: Title of the work

Examples:

700 1_ $aGal, Laszlo.

700 1_ $aBerton, Pierre,$d1920-

700 1_ $aMillar, Ken,$d1915 —$tMoving target.

710 Added Entry—Corporate Name (R): Most school libraries can skip this field. It is used to add any additional corporate name which may be associated with the work. Coding for the field is the same as for the 110 main entry for corporate names.

Indicator 1: Type of Corporate name

1—Place or place and name

2—Name direct order (most common)

Indicator 2: Type of entry:

Blank—No information provided

2 —Analytical entry

Subfields most commonly used:

$a: Name

$b: Subheading (R)

$c: Place

$d: Date (R)

$t: Title of work

Examples:

710 1_ $aUnited States.$bArmy Map Service.

710 2_ $a Law Society of Upper Canada.

710 2_ $aFoundation for Inner Peace.$tA course in miracles.

800 Level Fields

856 Uniform Resource Location: This field is used for electronic location and access and contains information needed to locate an electronic resource, such as electronic journals and books. Indicators and subfields are being developed.

900 Level Fields

The local holdings fields are added to assist patrons in finding the material they require. The fields vary depending on the application software. For example, MicroCAT uses 090 for the call number and 595 for the local notes. BiblioFile and ISM use the 090 to 099 fields.

6

Use and Users of Electronic Library Resources

OVERVIEW

Libraries of all sizes and types are embracing digital collections, although most libraries will continue to offer both print and digital collections for many years to come. New purchases and purchases of journals, magazines, and abstracting and indexing services are heavily weighted towards digital, while digital books (e-books) are only beginning to become a presence in library collections. Libraries prefer digital collections for many reasons, including, but not limited to, the following: digital journals can be linked from and to indexing and abstracting databases; access can be from the user's home, office, or dormitory whether or not the physical library is open; the library can get usage statistics that are not available for print collections; and digital collections save space and are relatively easy to maintain. When total processing and space costs are taken into account, electronic collections may also result in some overall reductions in library costs. Such a dramatic switch from print collections to digital collec-tions has an impact on library users and users' perceptions of the library. Many researchers have attempted to predict or measure that impact through surveys, transaction log analysis, and other research techniques.

Librarians would like to be able to use the information and conclusions generated by the many research studies, especially because it is time consuming to conduct good research on their own and because the best measures of impact come after decisions are al-ready made and collections are converted. Unfortunately, the conclu-sions of various studies sometimes seem contradictory, and it may be difficult to judge which research studies offer valid and reliable find-ings. The opinion literature outnumbers the research literature, and it may be a challenge to distinguish fact from opinion.

The purpose of this report for the Council on Library and Infor-mation Resources is to help librarians identify reliable research stud-ies, to provide a synopsis of the good studies, and to present an anal-ysis of conclusions. A subtitle of the report might well be the same as the CLIR symposium held March 28, 2003, "What Are Users Telling Us?" Or, "What do user studies tell us about how and why library constituents of all types use digital library resources and are likely to use them in the future?" The goal of this report is to provide in-formation that librarians can use to make important decisions about collections, services, and product design. Also relevant to this topic is CLIR's January 2002 report "Usage and Usability Assessment: Library Practices and Concerns" by Denise Troll Covey. Although this introduction refers to the resources as digital re-sources or digital libraries, the less precise, but more commonly used terms electronic resources or electronic libraries will be used throughout as synonyms.

REPORT OUTLINE

Hundreds of recent publications focus on how users interact with or how they feel about electronic library resources. It is important, therefore, to state clear parameters of what is included in this report.

Only publications or reports of studies that meet the following parameters are included and analysed:

- Studies must focus on the use of both electronic resources and li-braries (electronic resources through the library, in addition to the library, or in comparison with the library). Studies that are mostly about the Internet, but include a substantive section on libraries (the Pew studies, for example) or those that are mostly about libraries in general, but include a substantive section on digital libraries (the LibQUAL+™ studies, for example) are also included. Internet use studies that do not focus on libraries are excluded.

- Studies or surveys that focus solely on librarians, library staff, library Websites, or publishers are excluded; only those that study library patrons are included.
- Studies that are limited to the behaviour of authors rather than readers are excluded.
- Only research studies are included. Opinion pieces or descriptions of how a library converted their print collections to digital collec-tions are excluded.
- A wide variety of research methods are covered (including surveys, transaction log analysis, experimental). Because different kinds of research methods allow different types of conclusions to be drawn, this report describes the research method used in stud-ies and what types of conclusions made by the researchers are valid in accordance with the method.
- Studies are restricted to those conducted Since, 1995, or a post-Web world. Some studies compare recent findings with past studies (for example, the Tenopir and King studies), so they may address how usage patterns have changed with the advent of electronic resources, but the main focus remains user behaviour in an increas-ingly digital age.
- Poorly conducted research from which valid conclusions cannot be drawn is excluded.

Applying the foregoing parameters resulted in a pool of more than 200 individual research publications. Some publications de-scribe different phases or parts of large, and often ongoing, research projects. A further distinction was made to separate these large or ongoing studies from the more limited studies and to describe each major study as a whole, rather than as separate publication parts. This led to a distinction between "Tier 1" and "Tier 2" studies. Tier 1 studies are those major studies that have many publica-tions, sometimes by many different authors.

The studies involve hundreds or thousands of subjects over multiple workplaces, work roles, or subject disciplines. Many important conclusions can be drawn from each of these studies and they are typically widely re-ported and discussed in the library community. Each Tier 1 study is actually a group of studies conducted by a research team. Tier 1 stud-ies are discussed in the greatest detail Since, they may use multiple methods and provide, at times, complex findings. The designation as a Tier 1 study was intentionally highly se-lective. Only eight user studies (actually, groups of studies) were designated as Tier 1 studies, but they represent nearly 100 individual articles or reports.

Additionally, nearly that many other publications are designated Tier 2 studies. Tier 2 studies are not of lesser quality than Tier 1 studies; they are just typically smaller in scale or are one-time projects. Tier 2 studies may involve only dozens or hundreds of subjects. They may focus on a single workplace (for example, a single college campus).

They provide valuable insights into library user behaviour, but are best taken together as a whole to reach general conclusions. In addition to Tier 1 and Tier 2 studies, selected related materials are briefly described and are included in the bibliography. These in-clude bibliographies of writings about users of digital library materi-als and several important methods papers.

TIER 1 STUDIES

Eight groups of studies were identified as "Tier 1" or major recent research studies on how people use electronic library resources.

Tier 1 studies are (in no particular order):

- SuperJournal
- Digital Library Federation/Council on Library and Information Resources/Outsell (DLF/CLIR/Outsell)

- HighWire/eJUSt
- Pew Internet and American Life (with comparison to OCLC/Harris and Urban Libraries Council)
- OhioLINK
- Tenopir and King studies
- LibQUAL+™
- JSTOR studies

A synopsis of each is given first, followed by an analysis of the methods used, participants included, levels of conclusions, and find-ings for each group. In the bibliography, all of the publications that report on each study are listed together by the study group name.

SuperJournal

The SuperJournal project is a group of studies of e-journal use that began in 1995 in the United Kingdom in response to the information explosion and limited budgets. The researchers use a variety of research methods, including log file analysis, surveys, interviews, and focus groups, to study how academic users interact with e-journals and what features they value. Academic scientists and social scientists were studied, including both faculty and students in British universities.

Digital Library Federation/Council on Library and Information Resources/Outsell (DLF/CLIR/Outsell)

Outsell, Inc., conducted a survey of information use for the Digital Library Federation and Council on Library and Information Resources in the fall of 2001 and early winter of 2002.

Some 3,234 faculty, graduate students, and undergraduate students across seven subject disciplines at private and public doctoral research universities and leading liberal arts colleges were interviewed over the telephone. They were asked about their use and preferences for both print and electronic resources from the library.

HighWire/eJUSt

The Stanford E-Journal Users Study (e-JUSt), published by HighWire Press, used a variety of methods to gain insights into the use of electronic journals, including qualitative user surveys, transaction log analysis, and an ethnographic study of scholarly e-journal usage. The qualitative user surveys were done online with participants taken from subscribers to HighWire's medical and scientific journal Table of Contents service. The participants included graduate students, faculty members, and clinicians from universities, hospitals, and government and academic research institutes from 99 countries.

Pew Internet and American Life (also OCLC/Harris, and Urban Libraries Council)

The Pew Internet and American Life Project conducted two studies about how students use the Internet. In the "Internet Goes to College," 2,054 college students at two- and four-year public and private colleges completed surveys. In addition, graduate student researchers observed the behaviour of college students at Chicago area colleges and universities. In the other Pew Internet and American Life Project, "The Digital Disconnect: The Widening Gap between Internet Savvy Students and their Schools," middle and high school students were studied between November 2001 and March 2002. About 200 students wrote essays in which they expressed how they and their friends used the Internet for school and how they might use it in the future. Both these studies included how the students view the library.

OCLC/Harris and the Urban Libraries Council conducted similar surveys comparing library and Internet use by students and the public respectively. In the OCLC/Harris study, 1,050 participants were surveyed between December 11, 2001, and January 1, 2002. In the Urban Libraries Council study, 3,097 participants were surveyed by telephone between March and April 2000.

OhioLINK

The Ohio Library and Information Network is a consortium of Ohio's college and university libraries and the State Library of Ohio. The consortium serves in excess of 500,000 students, faculty, and staff at more than 80 institutions of higher learning. OhioLINK's Electronic Journal Center makes electronic articles and journals available to OhioLINK members. Transaction log analysis is used to measure the number of articles users download from the Electronic Journal Center. This programme, begun in April 1998, is ongoing.

Tenopir and King Studies

The Tenopir and King research studies are a series of surveys of more than 16,000 scientists, engineers, medical professionals, and social scientists in university and Non-university research settings. The surveys measure reading and authorship patterns of these subject experts through critical incident, demographic, and usage questions. Information-seeking behaviours, amount of reading, purposes of reading, and source of readings are all measured. Recent studies have focused on how reading patterns have changed over time with the adoption of e-journals and what role library-provided journals play in overall reading patterns. These ongoing experiments began in 1977.

LibQUAL+™

LibQUAL+™, conducted by the Association of Research Libraries (ARL) in conjunction with Texas A & M University, surveyed students, faculty, and staff at various community colleges, four-year colleges, and health science schools in the United States as well as the New York Public Library and Smithsonian Institution during the spring of 2002. More than 70,000 faculty, staff, and students related how often they used the physical and electronic libraries. Furthermore, they answered questions about their library's level of service that they found minimally acceptable, the level they perceived, and the level they desired.

The results are presented by status of respondent and type of institution. Only those few questions that focus on desired levels for print and electronic collections and services are relevant and reported here.

JSTOR

The JSTOR system provides electronic archives of back issues of scholarly journals. JSTOR uses log analysis of both viewed and printed articles to characterise use of its materials. In addition, some JSTOR subscribing libraries have analysed their use of the JSTOR journals within their specific library environment.

In the fall of 2000, JSTOR surveyed more than 4,000 academic users of the collection in humanities, social sciences, and economics to discover usage patterns and preferences of university faculty.

PARTICIPANTS

Each of the eight Tier 1 studies examined a variety of participants, with college and university students and faculty members the most often studied, followed by practitioners and other subject experts in science, engineering, health, and social sciences. Table summarises the main participants included in each study.

Table.6.1 Tier 1: Participants

Study	Participants
SuperJournal	Students and faculty
DLF/CLIR/Outsell	Students and faculty
HighWire/eJUSt	Scholars and clinicians
Pew/OCLC-Harris/Urban Libraries Council	Middle, high, and college students/ general public
OhioLINK	OhioLINK users
Tenopir and King	Scientists and social scientists (academic and Non-academic)
LibQUAL+™ higher education	Library users at institutions of (students and faculty)
JSTOR	JSTOR users (mostly faculty)

METHODS

The method or methods used in a research study determine what types of conclusions can be drawn about the sampled participants and what findings can be generalised to the population as a whole.

Wang provides an overview of methods for user behavioural research. An extension of her categorisation of methods is used here to describe Tier 1 studies. Tier 1 studies use one or more of the following methods:

- Surveying users
- Interviewing users (including focus groups)
- Observing users through experiments
- Observing users in natural settings (including keeping journals)
- Transaction log analysis

Covey also categorises usage studies to help librarians design the most appropriate studies for the type of information they hope to gather.

Covey's categories of research studies are similar to Wang's and include the following:

- Surveys (questionnaires)
- Focus groups
- User protocols (experiments and observations are both included here)
- Other (heuristic evaluations, paper prototypes and scenarios, and card-sorting tests)
- Transaction log analysis

Table summarises the methods used by the Tier 1 studies. Several use multiple methods for different phases of their projects; others rely on a single method.

Table.6.2. Tier 1: Methods Used.

Study	Methods
SuperJournal	Logs/surveys/focus groups/ interviews
DLF/CLIR/Outsell	Interviews
HighWire/eJUSt	Surveys/interviews/logs
Pew/OCLC-Harris/Urban Libraries Council	Surveys/observation/focus groups/ journal keeping
OhioLINK	Logs
Tenopir and King	Surveys/critical incident
LibQUAL+™	Surveys
JSTOR	Logs

Surveys of users are typically done by sending a

questionnaire by e-mail, the Web, or paper mail to a randomly selected percentage of the population under study. Tenopir and King, for example, survey samples of university faculty, members of professional organisations such as the American Astronomical Society, and scientists in companies and government laboratories. LibQUAL+™ libraries survey students and faculty within their own university community for comparison with other LibQUAL+™ libraries. Conclusions based on the responses are generalised to the whole using appropriate statistical tests. Care in selecting samples and a reasonable return rate are necessary to draw valid conclusions.

Almost all of the studies reported here that use surveys follow these basic precepts of sampling and analysis, but the types of conclusions that can be drawn vary by the types of questions that are asked. Among the Tier 1 studies that use surveys, the main distinctions in types of questions asked can be characterised as follows:

- Preference (focusing on what people want or think about a particular service; *e.g.*, LibQUAL+™, Pew)
- Reported behaviour (focusing on what people say they do in general; *e.g.*, DLF/CLIR/Outsell, HighWire/eJUSt)
- Critical incident questions (focusing on what people say they do in regard to a specific instance or reading; *e.g.*, Tenopir and King).

Table shows methods in more depth by looking at what types of questions were asked.

Table.6.3. Tier 1: Types of Questions

Study	Type of Questions
SuperJournal	Preference and reported behaviour
DLF/CLIR/Outsell	Preference and reported behaviour
HighWire/eJUSt	Preference and reported behaviour
Pew/OCLC-Harris/Urban Libraries Council	Preference and behaviour-reported and observed
OhioLINK	Log analysis
Tenopir and King	Critical incident, preference and reported behaviour

Table Countd...

LibQUAL+™	Preference and reported behaviour
JSTOR	Preference and reported behaviour and log analysis

Together, the categories of participants and the methods used determine at which of three levels valid conclusions can be drawn:

- The "user level," that is, what do individuals or groups of individuals such as social science faculty say they do or prefer;
- The "group level," that is, what do groups of users at an institution do, without demographic differentiation; or
- The "readings or incident level," that is, what do specific users or groups of users do or prefer about a specific type of information or reading.

Table.6.4 Tier 1: Conclusion Level.

Study	Conclusions
SuperJournal	User level
DLF/CLIR/Outsell	User level
Study	**Conclusions**
HighWire/eJUSt	User level
Pew/OCLC-Harris/Urban Libraries Council	User level
OhioLINK	Group level
Tenopir and King	User and reading levels
LibQUAL+™	User level
JSTOR	User and group level

SuperJournal, for example, uses transaction logs, surveys with questions about preferences and behaviour, focus groups, and interviews to study faculty and graduate students. Demographic information is known for each user. These multiple methods allow conclusions to be drawn at the user level for both behaviour and preferences (what specific types of users do and what they prefer). JSTOR uses transaction logs separate from survey questions. DLF/CLIR/Outsell used interviews to gather information on what users say they prefer and say they do in general. Demographic information is known about each user.

This allows conclusions to be drawn at the user level as well. Tenopir and King use critical incident questions in their surveys, which ask users to focus on the last article read. Together with demographic data, this allows conclusions to be made at the readings level (characteristics of the total amount of readings done by individuals and groups of individuals). Each of these methods has advantages and disadvantages.

According to Covey, problems or concerns with surveys include the following:

- General surveys are time-consuming and expensive to prepare, conduct, and interpret.
- Unless follow-ups are sent so longitudinal analysis can track changing patterns of use, surveys provide no baseline data.
- People receive many surveys, and it is difficult to motivate them to complete and return surveys.
- The usage information gathered in general surveys might better be gathered by transactional logs.
- Specific surveys are more beneficial, but must be repeated over time.
- User satisfaction surveys may not provide enough information to solve the problem, and service "gap" surveys are more difficult to administer and analyse.
- A survey is only as good as the wording of the questions and the response rate.

Problems or concerns with focus groups, according to Covey, include the following:

- A skilled moderator needs to direct the groups to keep discussions on track.
- An unskilled observer may fail to take adequate notes.
- The qualitative data gathered in focus groups can be time consuming and difficult to interpret.

Problems or concerns with experiments or observations (called user protocols by Covey), include the following:

- Librarians, if observing, have a difficult time not assisting the subjects.
- Librarians may not be trained to interpret and analyse the data from user protocols.

- Recruiting subjects, in particular subjects who are comfortable with the process of thinking aloud, is difficult.

Problems with transaction log analysis, according to Covey, in-clude the following:

- Deciding on the right and most useful usage statistics
- Collecting the right usage statistics
- Getting the right and consistent usage statistics from vendors
- Analysing and interpreting data (it can be time consuming and difficult)
- Presenting the data in a meaningful way.

In summary, the conclusions that can be drawn from each of the Tier 1 and Tier 2 studies depends on the methods used, including the overall method(s), types of questions asked, level of questions, and participants studied. It may be tempting for a researcher to draw broader conclusions than his or her methods justify—a failing that was found in more than one study examined. Only those findings that are justified by each study's methods are reported here. In general, the following types of conclusions can be drawn from each technique:

- *Transaction logs*: What groups do in general; for example, what the college or university libraries in the OhioLINK system do in general. Transaction logs do not show preferences; rather, they show action from which preferences are often inferred. Demographic data from individuals are usually not gathered because of privacy concerns. Instead usage is identified by IP address, location, or library, so conclusions about differences in work fields or status of user cannot be drawn. Transaction logs that result from an experimental design allow more finely tuned conclusions.
- *Interviews or surveys: preference questions*: Preference questions, or questions about what people want, show what people say they prefer or value. Demographic information is almost always asked, allowing conclusions to be made about groups. (For example, in HighWire/eJUSt, most science faculty members say

their favorite e-journal feature is linking.) Preferences may or may not predict actual or future behaviour.

- *Interviews or surveys*: behavioural questions: Questions about behav-ior in general (for example, "Do you use the library's electronic journals?") show what people do at least some of the time. Demographic information is almost always gathered as well, allowing conclusions to be drawn about individuals or groups of individuals. (For example, the DLF/CLIR/Outsell study shows that most humanities fac-ulty members use the print collection for at least part of their work.)
- *Interviews or surveys*: critical incident questions: Respondents are asked to focus on a specific incident; for example, the last article they read or the last article they authored. Specific questions about that incident are then asked. Demographic information is also collected. This allows conclusions to be made about the total amount of reading or for specific characteristics of users or readings. (For example, Tenopir report that 80 per cent of the articles astronomers read in a year are from electronic sources.)
- *Focus groups*: Focus group participants are not randomly selected; instead, individuals who can express opinions about a service or issue are invited to participate. Therefore, preferences and behaviors observed in focus groups must not be overly generalised to the population as a whole, nor interpreted as the only possibilities. (For example, from SuperJournal, faculty members report a variety of uses for electronic journals, including keeping current in their areas of research, gathering background information, and preparing for a specific event.) Focus groups are helpful as a first step or in conjunction with other research methods.
- *Observation*: experimental: Controlled experiments gather both quantitative and qualitative data on how users behave in a controlled environment, such as searching on a specific online system, and why they behave in a certain way. Demographic data are

gathered, along with other data about individual differences, such as from controlled tests. Conclusions depend on the experimental treatment. (For example, log analysis in conjunction with experimental observation in the SuperJournal study shows that social scientists browse differently than scientists.)

- *Observation in natural setting*: journal keeping: Participants are asked to record their interactions with information systems or their research process. Conclusions can be drawn about types of behaviour, and models of behaviour can be derived. (For example, in the Pew Studies, students recorded using electronic resources more than print resources and felt they knew more about the Internet than do their teachers.)

TIER 2 ANALYSIS

How people use electronic resources or their preferences for print and electronic library services have been the focus of dozens of in-dividual research studies in the last few years. Surveys are by far the most popular method, with academic faculty and students the most popular participants.

Although participants include a variety of subject experts, scientists of various sorts have been studied most frequently. Not every study will be discussed in detail in this analysis, but both common threads and unique findings of the studies will be highlighted. Summary analyses of the methods used and groups studied are shown in figures.

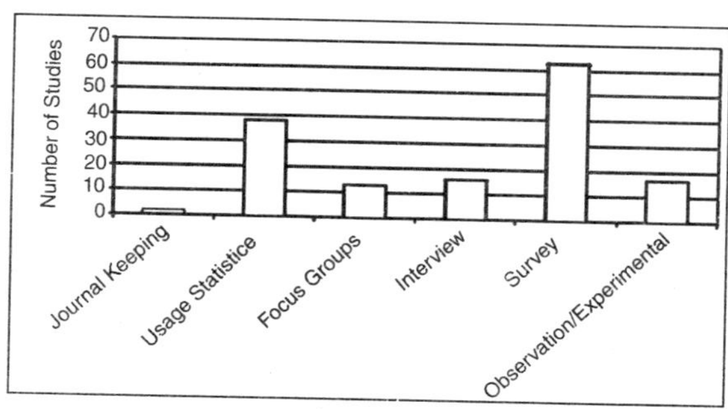

Fig. 6.1. Methods Used in Tier 2 Studies.

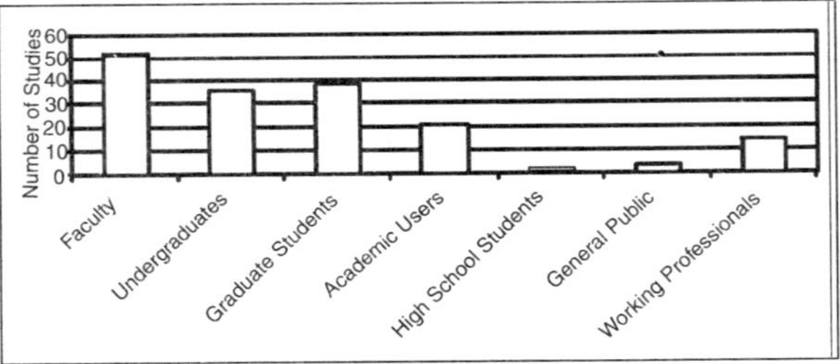

Fig. 6.2. Participants Studied in Tier 2 Studies.

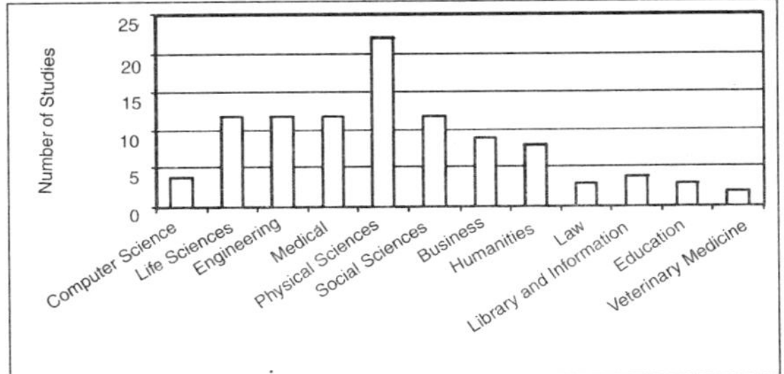

Fig. 6.3. Workfields of Participants Studied in Tier 2 Studies.

The Tier 2 studies echo many of the findings of the larger Tier 1 studies, allowing some consistent conclusions to be drawn about user behaviour. This section is arranged by general themes that are found in many studies, and then further organised by specific themes, some of which emerge in only some of the studies, others that emerge consistently, but with contradictory results.

The general themes and specific sub-themes are as follows:

- Differences in behaviour or preferences that can be explained by differences among users. Differences include:
  - Differences by subject discipline
  - Differences by user status or workplace
  - Differences by task
  - Differences by age or gender
- Information-seeking behaviour and preferences, including differences between print and electronic resources:
  - Browsing versus searching
  - Preferences for print or electronic resources
  - Awareness of electronic resources

  - Search strategies
  - Reasons for using the resources
  - Sources of information about resources
  - Self-evaluation of system navigation
- Perceived advantages of electronic resources and preferences, in-cluding:
  - How electronic resources improve workflow or save time
  - Preferred features of electronic information systems
  - Currency and timeliness of sources
- Perceived disadvantages or concerns about electronic resources, including:
  - Technological or service problems
  - Archiving
  - Problems or confusion with information systems
  - Preferred formats for reading
  - Electronic versus print resources
- Library policy and financial issues:
  - Willingness to pay for electronic information
  - Willingness to cancel print journals in favour of electronic
  - Other library budgetary issues that affect users

Differences in Behaviour or Preferences that can be Explained by Differences Among Users

The concept of a single typical "user" of information systems is clearly a fallacy. Scientists seek and use information differently than do social scientists or humanists; undergraduate students behave differently than do graduate students or faculty; searching for information for personal use is different from searching for work-related tasks.

Numerous studies have reached these conclusions. Faculty members and other professionals in the sciences, math, and medicine fields were early adopters of electronic journals and other digital library resources and remain the heaviest and most enthusiastic users. Lenares found as early as the late 1990s that 90 per cent of the physical science faculty used electronic journals at least part of the time, compared with 61 per cent of all faculty users in ARL universities.

The percentage of faculty using electronic journals for at least some of their readings increased from 1998 to 1999 and has continued to increase each year. By 2002 at the University of Maryland, more faculty members used electronic journals daily or weekly than they did print journals. This corresponds to the decrease in physical visits to the library by graduate students and faculty, especially in health sciences, science, and engineering. Enthusiasm for electronic journals and patterns of use vary even among fields of science. Chemists and physicists use them frequently, while earth scientists and mathematicians see fewer advantages.

Medical school users rely on fewer electronic journal titles for their downloads and readings than do other library users. These variations are also reported by Tenopir and King, who found physicists and astronomers to be among the most enthusiastic users of electronic articles, partly because the digital e-print archives, the Astrophysics Data System (ADS), and e-journals of the American Astronomical Society were designed specifically to facilitate their natural work patterns. Business school faculty members were also early adopters. Business school faculty reported the highest use, while Palmer and Sandler found economics faculty to be the most enthusiastic users of electronic journals. Speier and Hahn found that among business faculty, finance and management information systems faculty were more aware of electronic journals than those in other fields. Faculty members in history, education, and the arts have been slower to adopt electronic journals.

Among corporate users, investment and banking companies or departments spend a higher per cent of their budgets on electronic products than do other types of businesses such as pharmaceutical firms, legal services, food services, or telecommunications. Although high percentages of faculty members use electronic journals, they still use a variety of sources, including print, for their readings. In 1999, Lenares found that although 90 per cent of physical sciences faculty respondents at ARL libraries used electronic journals, half reported that they read articles from electronic journals infrequently.

Undergraduates in the life science disciplines were found by Whitmire to engage in more information-seeking activities than were students in other disciplines, including using the online catalog, asking librarians for help, using indexes, and browsing the stacks. Engineers engaged in the fewest information-seeking behaviours. Variations in information-seeking behaviour by individual groups make the task of designing an e-journal, user interface, or electronic library a challenge. One attempt to meet this challenge is to provide a "MyLibrary" feature on a library's home page. This allows users to customise their view of the electronic library and highlight the resources they use most often. Another solution is to maintain a balance between print and electronic collections, depending on the preferences of the main user groups.

Librarians must gauge their systems, collection development deci-sions, and instruction with user differences firmly in mind. No single solution will be best for everyone and the totally digital library is a long way in the future in many subject disciplines. Publishers also must design electronic resources that facilitate the work patterns of their target audiences. Differences in motivation or task also cause variations in information seeking and use. Nelson in a study of faculty and students at the University of West England, found that the greatest predictor of electronic use was whether or not the person was engaged in research. Researchers and academic staff were more likely to use electronic journals than were administrative staff. King and Mont-gomery found that more than half of the readings by faculty and doctoral students are done while conducting primary research. Faculty who publish more and those who had served on promotion and tenure committees were found to be more likely to be aware of electronic journals, and faculty with tenure are more likely to submit articles to electronic journals.

Scientists who win awards read more on average. Graduate students, particularly Ph.D. students, are often found to be heavy users of electronic journals, most likely in their role as researchers. As found in the SuperJournal projects, graduate students may be "binge" users, consulting electronic journals extensively for a short period when they are writing a thesis or dissertation. There are some exceptions—undergraduates were the most frequent users in an experimental study conducted by the American Chemical Society. Different workplaces or types of institutions have varying use patterns as well. Davis examined electronic journal user logs in libraries of the NorthEast Research Library Consortium and found that each institution has a unique pattern of use—medical institution users had higher use of a smaller number of journals, while users at large universities and smaller colleges downloaded articles from a greater variety of journal titles. Other differences are more controversial or less conclusive.

Some studies found differences in preferences or behaviour based on the age of the user. In the late-1990s, Researchers found that younger ARL university business faculty members reported that they read from electronic journals more often and were more aware of electronic journals than were older faculty. In a study done in 1996 and 1997, more than half of the faculty members under the age of 40 reported using electronic journals, as compared with only 14 per cent of those over 40, although more than 80 per cent of the total respondents indicated they would consider using electronic journals in the future. Antoir found that older people preferred print articles; Monopoli found that users between 21 and 34 used electronic journals most frequently. Older University of Michigan social sciences faculty members tended to prefer print more often than did younger faculty. Age made a difference in how faculty members, staff, and students at Colorado State University rated their computer skills, with more respondents under 30 rating their skills as good.

Differences in electronic journal use may be attributed to age, status, or rank. Tenner and Yang found that assistant professors are most likely to have used electronic journals (44.7 per cent), followed by full professors (34.5 per cent), and associate professors (34.2 per cent). Researchers found that undergraduates, medical students, and residents prefer electronic journals, while clinical and research faculty members prefer print. Researchers in other studies found no relationship between age and searching skills, although the researchers observed that younger users are more likely to browse on the computer, while older users prefer print journals for browsing. Researchers found no relationship between age and reading patterns among astronomers. Age differences should be studied more, at least for the next generation, Since, most college students now are computer literate and report that they use the Web frequently. This does not necessarily correlate with effective use, however. An experimental study found that faculty performed tasks requiring retrieval and use of journal and newspaper articles significantly better than undergraduates.

Researcher found that students had more confidence in their searching skills than did their faculty. Although lower division undergraduate students used the Web and Web search engines frequently, students are mostly unaware of the distinctions between material on the Web and peer-reviewed journals. Freshman psychology students with higher self-efficacy scores are more motivated to learn about electronic journals and find electronic journals easier to use, but they also visit the library more often. Gender differences are even more inconclusive. Only a few studies have examined gender as a factor in information use, beyond studies of recreational Internet use.

In teaching, men report significantly more use of a search engine to access e-journals than do women who access e-journals. Some individual differences may be a factor only in early adoption and, as electronic resources become familiar and ubiquitous through the library, these differences may cease to be important. Other factors, such as the way different disciplines do their work, may be more pervasive.

Researchers for example, found that biologists rely on print because of deeply ingrained work habits, and earth scientists fail to see work advantages of electronic journals. Part of the hesitancy of some may be a discomfort with technology, unavailability of technology, or insufficient knowledge of electronic journals, all of which are already changing. Physicists embrace preprints and have adopted e-print servers enthusiastically in part because their research tends to be highly collaborative and is conducted in large research institutions that have internal peer review.

INFORMATION-SEEKING BEHAVIOUR AND PREFERENCES

Students, faculty, and Non-university professionals now use a variety of sources for articles, including electronic journals, print journals, Web sites of professional organisations, author's Web sites, e-mail from colleagues, and e-print servers. Print remains important for at least some information for all subject disciplines and as part of the research process for undergraduates.

Even as early as 1996, academic users expressed dissatisfaction with library collections of printed journals, books, and conference proceedings. Both current and older materials remain important, as many of the Tier 1 studies found. At the University of California, Berkeley, 93 per cent of faculty members and 87 per cent of graduate students across academic disciplines reported that they use materials older than five years "sometimes" or "often." Most preferred electronic resources and often use the library from their desktops.

Faculty and other subject experts make a distinction between core journal titles and Non-core journals. At the University of Maryland, 70 per cent of the faculty want core journals in both print and electronic form, but the same number wanted Non-core journals only in electronic form. Although both browsing and searching remain important information seeking strategies, electronic journals are causing a decrease in browsing titles, while searching by topic has increased. Browsing of core journals by tables of contents remains important, but searching by topic for additional journals and articles is increasingly popular, particularly in large, mixed-journal title databases. Most libraries offer a combination of these large full-text databases, which facilitate searching, and journal systems from publishers, which facilitate browsing. In systems restricted to journals from a single publisher, browsing through tables of contents remains important.

There was a dramatic increase in the number of articles viewed or downloaded between 1999 and 2001, but PDF remained a more popular format than HTML. Worlock found that articles recommended by colleagues were more often in print than in electronic format. Contradictory results were obtained by the researchers, who discovered that e-mail and listservs make it easier to share recommended articles with colleagues. University faculty members reported the ability to send articles to their colleagues instantly as being one of the major advan-tages of electronic journals. Use of online indexes and abstracts seems to have increased, particularly when there are links to full texts.

More than 80 per cent of veterinary medicine students at Iowa State University used online indexes in 1997, compared with only 16 per cent a decade earlier indicating a major shift to electronic resources during that decade. More than half of the medical faculty, residents, and students at a regional site of the University of Illinois report that they search MEDLINE at least weekly and much of their identification of journals comes from MEDLINE.

Awareness and use of other abstracting and indexing services or full text databases is low, however. The Pew studies and Graham clearly show that high school students, in particular, and undergraduate students prefer to search the Internet first for school-related tasks. When given a specific research task, only 2 per cent of undergraduates at Wellesley College's "Computers and the Internet" class included Non-Internet resources in their answers.

The students have extraordinary faith in their favorite search engine, even though they are unclear how it works. A nationwide survey of students and academics in the Neth-erlands found that 60 per cent of respondents in the humanities, 78 per cent of respondents in the social sciences, and 82 per cent of respondents in the sciences used the Internet for study or work and nearly all believed they had Internet skills. Still, when rating the importance of different means of searching, more than 88 per cent believed that subject searching of tables of contents databases was important or very important, followed by searching the OPAC, citations, and asking colleagues.

Nearly two-thirds believed searching the Internet or the Web were important or very important, and most perceived that their Web searches yielded enough or more than enough information. A vast majority reported they were self-taught

Internet searchers, who rely on trial and error. Assistance from colleagues was the second most frequently cited means of acquiring searching skills; gaining the skills through library courses was far less commonly cited. Ninety-seven per cent of freshmen psychology students reported that they access the Internet at least weekly, about 44 per cent of the time for educational information. More than three-quarters say they begin their research through the Internet, and two-thirds say they find most of their information through the Internet. Still, two-thirds also report that they visit the physical library at least weekly, most often for studying.

The role of the library as a place to study and socialise was more important than as a place to get information. Half of the students access the library's electronic resources from home, and only a quarter said that use of the electronic resources was a reason to visit the library. Dilevko and Gottlieb report efforts to attract undergraduates to the physical library. Since, most undergraduates report that they turn first to online sources, and Since, turnstile counts were going down at the University of Toronto library, they surveyed students to find what role print materials still play for undergraduates. About 47 per cent of undergraduates reported that they began their assignments with online sources 90 per cent of the time, but printed journals and, especially, print books remain important in their research, particularly for humanities students. The authors conclude that print books are still vital and are associated with high-quality work. They recommend that librarians stress the value of printed materials in addition to online materials for the successful completion of assignments.

A teacher's or librarian's recommendation of specific sources, such as a library full-text database or a specific Web site, is reported to influence a student's choice of sources. At the University of California, Berkeley, the groups of faculty and graduate students that report the heaviest use of electronic resources also recommend the need for more library reference and instructional services.

Use of electronic books is also clearly course driven—books with the highest usage are those required in a class, and most users come to an electronic book collec-tion to use a single title.

Researchers also found that most un-dergraduates in a composition class were always or almost always likely to use a recommended full-text database provided by the library as a first stop for information; the next largest group went first to the Web, and the smallest group went first to print.

When searching on a mixed full-text/bibliographic database, many said they always restricted their search to full text. Most students did not limit their research to a single source of information, but of those who did, the Web was the most popular single source for information, followed by a full-text database. Faculty members and librarians can influence students' choices of electronic resources, although faculty may not always be familiar with the range of sources available to them through the library.

Library instruction, with time for practice, increases college students' efficacy in online searching. Researcher found that students who had a more positive attitude Towards learning electronic information search skills had fewer negative emotions about electronic searching and performed better in assignments. Librarians should stress the importance of all library materials, including print and electronic resources, since, undergraduate students value recommendations.

The most effective way for students to learn about important resources in academic libraries seems to be for librarians to work directly with faculty to bring relevant electronic resources into the classroom. Students bring web searching habits to their use of electronic scholarly materials and seem to have difficulty adapting to different types of information resources, interfaces, or search systems. In a controlled study of 49 undergraduates, graduates, and faculty members, Researchers found that few undergraduates took time to read explanations or help screens, and that they give up easily and are not selective.

These findings are similar to the many Web use studies beyond the scope of this report that show Web users in general tend to enter only a single search term and seldom look beyond the first screen. Students claim to use evaluation methods for Web sites.

However, researcher found that students were susceptible to advertising claims on Web sites, government misinformation, and propaganda and could not consistently differentiate between advertising and fact.

Only a few students in this experiment double-checked the information they found on the Web. There is some evidence also that college students have a low tolerance for system features that don't work or are too difficult. Bishop conducted user tests at the University of Illinois and found that if an abstract was missing when a student clicked on the abstract button, the student never again clicked on the button for abstracts.

Researcher concluded that one small system failure might have a long-term impact on student searching behaviour. Some college students report that they receive at least some training in evaluating library sources, but a sizable minority do not. Those with no training show a slight preference for the Internet over the library for research.

More than half of the undergraduate and graduate students from 97 different majors in a medium-sized Western university reported they use both the library and the Internet for research, while 21 per cent use the library exclusively, 21 per cent use the Internet exclusively, and 6 per cent use neither. Although this report does not attempt to cover the many studies of Internet-only use and Internet searching behaviour, these studies can provide some insights into the Web search patterns of children and adults who use the Web for both recreational and work-related purposes. To locate many of these studies.

PERCEIVED ADVANTAGES OF ELECTRONIC RESOURCES AND PREFERENCES

Users perceive electronic resources—in particular electronic journals and, for students, the Internet—to hold many advantages. Faculty members at ARL institutions cited convenience, timeliness, and the ability to search text as the most important factors in choosing electronic journals over print. Least important to them was animation of graphics, although others sometimes mention that as an important advantage.

In other surveys, graduate students said the top reasons for using electronic journals were the ability to link to additional information, the ability to search, and the currency of materials.

The ability to search across a wide range of journal articles, search within an article, and interact with multiple levels of information objects were listed as the top three significant features sought in future electronic journals.Many studies have found that users believe the main advantage of electronic journals is convenience of accessing articles any time from their desktop computer. Experienced users also liked the ease of skimming and searching, the possibility of downloading or printing the desired document or segment, the currency of information, the speed of access, and the ability to send articles to their colleagues instantly.

Storing articles electronically, then printing out a portable print copy, appeals to frequent e-journal users. Convenience and speed of access are mentioned or implied repeatedly. Students reported the top three ways that access to electronic resources has improved their academic careers: access to a wider range of information, faster access to information, and easier access to information. In England, Tilburg University faculty members cite timely availability, easy access, full text searching, and access from home as factors that promote the use of electronic journals. Focus groups of engineering faculty members and students wanted to search electronic journals quickly and easily, but they desired interfaces that could be customised and the ability to create personal collections, while economics students and faculty want the addition of data sets.

The TULIP project, an early electronic journals study was a cooperative undertaking between several university libraries and Elsevier. It attempted to predict the potential use of electronic journals through log analysis, focus groups, and interviews, while making sample collections available to faculty members and graduate students.

The lessons from TULIP are incorporated into later commercial products, and the conclusions agree with later studies. Even in the early 1990s, faculty members and graduate students wanted electronic journal systems that are as intuitive as possible, preferably using a familiar interface, with access to all information from one source. They wanted high processing speed for downloading and printing, timely information, good image quality, many journal titles and sufficient dates covered, and linking.

Graduate students used the system more often than faculty members. At this early date, TULIP researchers noticed an emotional tie to paper and the library—something that has diminished fairly rapidly with today's convenience of electronic journals. Still, users liked the convenience of desktop access, but, consistent with almost all studies today, they preferred to print out a hard copy for reading. Promotion and training were both found to be crucial to develop a base of regular users. Familiarity, in the case of electronic journals, has bred continued use.

PROBLEMS OR CONCERNS WITH ELECTRONIC RESOURCES

Although the advantages are outweighing the perceived problems or concerns as use increases and more resources are available, users still express some concerns about the disadvantages of electronic library collections. Participants in several studies expressed the desire for more online materials, including additional journal titles, a wider variety of special or out-of-the mainstream materials, and complete volumes or back files of existing journals. Print is a proven archival format. Even those who prefer electronic access to journals, prefer that books remain in print format.

The most common complaint found in many studies is the dis-comfort of reading from the screen or poor graphic quality. Respondents consistently report that they prefer to print out articles for reading and do most of their reading from the paper printout. They prefer PDF format for printing, although the HTML format is better for skimming.Faculty members from ARL institutions said that the most im-portant characteristics that would lead them to choose print over electronic were ability to browse, portability, physical comfort, and convenience. In citing the chief reasons for preferring print over electronic journals, Vanderbilt University medical faculty and students said that print is an easier to read format, of better graphic quality, easier to browse, and easier to access.

Access to adequate technology may still be a problem for some; 22 per cent of science faculty respondents at the University of Michigan requested that procedural or technological barriers to access be removed. When asked to identify problems, only a small percentage of respondents to most interviews or surveys agree to the same ones. The response rate for any one concern or problem is rarely more than 20 per cent and "top problems" are usually expressed by less than 10 per cent of the respondents. Students at one university were asked how "access to electronic resources has hindered your academic career." Although not nearly as many agreed to hindrances as they did to improvements, the top three hindrances mentioned were that online access is time consuming (16.4 per cent), it detracts from doing work (13.5 per cent), and lack of information technology knowledge hinders effective use (11.1 per cent). The top category for disadvantages among faculty members and graduate students at Ohio State University was "don't know"; an additional 8 per cent of faculty and 6 per cent of graduate students saw no disadvantages.

A continuing problem is that users may be unaware of relevant resources in the library collection. In a survey at the University of Maryland, 31 per cent of the faculty members reported never using electronic journals; the reasons cited were unfamiliarity with how to access the journals and a lack of need because of personal subscriptions.In a study of computer engineering undergraduate students in Nanyang Technological University in Singapore, researchers discovered that more than one-third of the respondents had never accessed computer engineering databases available through the library and of those, half had never heard of them. Lower-division undergraduates in focus groups at the University of Tennessee report that they know the Web and major search engines such as Google, but unless a library resource is specifically named (and required) in a class, they are unaware of its usefulness. Although French research scientists are using electronic journals more often, librarians still need to promote the resources because scientists hesitate to use electronic sources when they feel they have insufficient knowledge of them. The perception that electronic journals are of lower quality than print is another problem that may be diminishing as a high percentage of peer-reviewed journals are digitised.

In the late-1990s, business school faculty members surveyed at ARL institutions reported that they did not perceive electronic journals to be of as high quality as paper counterparts; their responses changed, however, when they were asked to evaluate a well-respected print journal evolving to electronic format.

While more than 70 per cent of the faculty members in a British university believe the quality of articles in electronic journals is the same as in print journals, this same group of respondents cited the top disadvantage of electronic journals as being the impression that electronic publication is not "real" publication. On the other hand, faculty members at the University of West England reported that they believed electronic journal content generally to be of good quality, and in some cases, to have added value. They said that they would use more electronic journals as more were made available in their area of interest and would recommend them to students. Texas A&M faculty members also reported that they have no objections to students using peer-reviewed elec-tronic journals and that they would recommend electronic journals to students. The proliferation of sources for articles and the sheer amount of information now available may be confusing to some users. Retrieving too much information is a problem mentioned by some, as is getting lost on a tangent and not knowing when to quit searching.

The distinction between the "article" and the "journal" in full-text databases was unclear to faculty members and undergraduates surveyed in the Decomate study, although at Columbia University researchers found that students clearly understood the difference between electronic databases and Web sites.

In focus groups at the University of Tennessee, Tenopir found that students understand that information found on the Web is different from the resources provided by the library, but many are not fully aware of what resources the library offers.

LIBRARY POLICIES AND FINANCIAL CONCERNS

Decisions that libraries make based on financial concerns, such as pay per use, may have unintended consequences on user behaviour. Electronic journal collections in libraries are growing steadily and some libraries are formulating collection development policies that encourage lease of electronic journals over purchase of print journals.

Even as early as 1999, 29 per cent of ARL and 33.5 per cent of Non-ARL academic libraries reported cancellations of print journals in favour of electronic access, and more said they would cancel print in the future. There has been a steady increase in the percentage of acquisitions dollars spent on electronic resources in ARL libraries.

On average, ARL libraries spent 13.2 per cent of their acquisitions budget on electronic resources in 1999-2000, and several libraries reported spending more than 20 per cent. By 2000–2001 the average had grown to 16 per cent and some special libraries spend a far greater percentage. Investment banking and brokerage firms are reported to spend 40-100 per cent of their information budgets on online products, by far the highest of any type of company. Library policies that favour electronic journals over print are having an effect on user behaviour. Users are increasingly positive about electronic collections and visits to the physical library by faculty and graduate students are down in many libraries, replaced by visits to the virtual library.

At the University of Washington, between 1998 and 2001 graduate students and faculty in the health sciences, sciences, and engineering reported the most pronounced decline in visits to the physical library. The primary use of the library by undergraduates tends to be as a workplace, although science and engineering students say they visited the library most often to find journals. Libraries that report a decline in visits to the physical library as a decrease in library usage do themselves a disservice. Users enjoy the convenience and other benefits of electronic access and are adjusting their behaviour as encouraged by library collection development policies.

Total library use—physical plus virtual—is likely actually up in most institutions. Virtual library users are less likely to ask for help or communicate with librarians unless the library offers special virtual reference services. University faculty members report that an increase in their electronic journal usage is accompanied by a decrease in the frequency of their use of print journals. Surveys of Ohio State University users from 1998 to 2000 found a steady increase in acceptance of electronic journals and their reported use.

By 2000, almost two-thirds of faculty members and graduate students said it was important for OSU libraries to replace their print subscriptions with electronic journal subscriptions when permanent electronic storage is available. Users of the University of Southern California Norris Medical Library viewed approximately 28,000 electronic full-text articles in a six-month period, as compared with 1,800 uses of the corresponding print volumes.

Even considering that users might have read more than one article per print volume, the electronic viewings far outnumbered the print. Part of this may be explained by the availability of new titles in electronic form, but use of both print and electronic titles was concentrated on a small number of the most popular titles—just 20 of the titles accounted for 60 per cent of the total usage and the top 25 titles were common to both print and electronic.The most requested electronic titles at the Elektronishche Zeitschriftenbibliothek in Germany are major journals whose print editions are also heavily used.

Use is also higher for electronic versions of books at Columbia University compared with the same titles available in print, although the University of Pittsburgh Health Sciences library found that use of both print journal titles and electronic journal titles covered by the Ovid online system increased at a similar rate. This pattern of a small number of titles accounting for a large percentage of use is, of course, not new to electronic resources.

The so-called 80/20 rule has been well documented in library collections, where a large percentage of use is concentrated in a small percentage of the collection. Usage logs make the calculations of use much easier with electronic resources, and this 80/20 phenomenon is reported by many studies that use transaction log analysis. Interestingly, this rule may also hold true for users—a small per cent of total library users is responsible for most electronic journal use.

This is similar to the phenomenon of "binge" users in the SuperJournal project. Davis and Solla found that a vast majority of users of American Chemical Society journals at Cornell University download few articles and consult few journals.

They conclude that a small number of heavy users can have a great effect on the number of total downloads. Still, as the OhioLINK studies have shown, many of the remaining 80 or so per cent of the journals in an electronic collection will get some usage. In addition, Day found that at least one article was downloaded from 92 per cent of the journals available to users at the University of Manchester Institute of Science and Technology.

In his examination of NERL usage logs, however, Davis found that no institution uses every available title and some journal titles are used infrequently by all institutions. Overall, 90 per cent of the downloads came from 40 per cent of the collection. Faculty and graduate students say 24-hour availability is a prime advantage of electronic journals, but even with 24/7 availability of the virtual library, most academic use follows the normal rhythms of the workweek and academic calendar. Just as turnstile counts mark the use of physical academic libraries, log data of virtual collections show peak use in March, November, and April and Monday through Thursday mid-morning to late afternoons, with a huge drop-off on Friday afternoons.

Although a user's institution pays for subscriptions or access to electronic journals, this cost is hidden from the user. Any overt charge or obvious pay perview has an impact on user behaviour. The "Pricing Electronic Access to Knowledge" (PEAK) project in the late 1990s was a major experiment with 12 libraries of varying size and type and the Elsevier journal collection.

It measured not only use of electronic journals by journal title and type of library, but also measured use under two different payment models for articles. Users of the subject libraries were provided with both "unmetered" access and "metered" access to journal articles. Although use increased from the first to the second year in the experiment, 60 per cent of accesses were for "unmetered" content, most of which was more than one year old.

The study concluded that the "user cost of access, consisting of both monetary payments and time or effort, has a significant effect on the number of articles that readers access".

Pay per-view or pay per-use creates a barrier that affects the frequency of online access and downloads. Nicolas and Huntington found that users who entered an online journals system from a subscribing institution visited the collection more often than Non-subscribers.

Subscribers also spent more time viewing each article, viewed articles from more journals, and used a wider variety of journal titles and subjects than did non-subscribers. Although seven students studied at Central Connecticut State University found the enduser system Questia easy to use, only one of the seven thought "it is worth it to subscribe" on their own. Some users may be willing to pay for electronic articles, at least part of the time. Worlock surveyed 252 working scientists and social scientists in the United Kingdom to find out if they ever pay for articles. Nearly two-thirds of the respondents reported that, on average, they pay for between one and five articles per week beyond regular subscriptions. Still, two-thirds said they felt the articles were too expensive. Passwords can be another barrier to use, in particular different passwords for different databases or collections. Users want free access, without having to remember multiple passwords or logon protocols. In eliminating special access requirements, however, libraries may create a problem for themselves.

There is evidence that many faculty members and students do not realise that the numerous electronic journals they can reach from their office, dormitory, or home computer through their university user name or identification are actually paid for and provided by the library. If users are not aware what the library provides, they will be less inclined to advocate for the library at budget time. Users can help libraries set collection and service priorities, with no one best solution for all types of libraries, types of users, or all subject disciplines. They can help make decisions about licensing choices and be made familiar with relative costs and tradeoffs.

When asked to make choices about what they were willing to forego to get more electronic access, researchers from the Max Planck Society felt there were certain services or materials they could do without, including binding of journals, journals with low impact factors, and print versions of journals readily available electronically. Science, engineering, and health sciences faculty at the University of Washington favored canceling print journals in favour of electronic only, while humanities and social sciences faculty opposed this idea and responded that maintaining the quality of the print collection is their highest priority.

REVIEWS OF THE LITERATURE AND METHODS

Although this report summarises conclusions from recent research studies and highlights some conclusions about how people use electronic collections, there are individual and library-specific differ-ences that make it beneficial for many libraries to collect their own data. The last section of the bibliography in this report lists selected resources to help with this process and to identify additional usage studies. For several years, Charles Bailey at the University of Houston has maintained a comprehensive literature review of all types of articles about scholarly electronic publishing.

This monumental piece of work is the first place to look to identify articles on any aspect of the topic, including research and user studies. Since, the review is updated regularly, bibliographic information about new studies appears there frequently. Literature reviews by Kling and Callahan and Giangrande supplement Bailey; also, the Annual Review of Information Science and Technology occasionally publishes review articles that focus on electronic publishing or research techniques. Several recent relevant chapters from ARIST are listed in the bibliography.

ARIST typically is published every autumn, but the topics vary from year to year. Beyond general textbooks of research methods, several recent publications focus on research methods for library and Web usage studies. The ARIST chapter by Wang formed the basis for the categorisation of research methods in this repor. This method provides a richness in interview or survey data beyond opinions or reports of estimated behaviour by asking respondents to focus on details of a specific incident of research or reading. The Tenopir and King studies also use critical incident technique to draw conclusions about readings. Experimental tests are less often used in the library environment, perhaps because they are time-consuming and must use relatively small groups of participants. Usability tests allow specific system design features to be compared and measured and are particularly useful for testing library catalog and Web site design.

Think-aloud or verbal protocols provide information on why subjects pursue certain courses of action and how they react to systems at the time of use. Covey explains in detail when to use and how to design studies that gather data from surveys focus groups, user protocols transaction log analysis, and other research methods. In addition to excellent advice on conducting user studies, researcher presents a selected bibliography covering general research methods and specific articles through 2001 on each of the research methods she describes.

CONCLUSIONS

Although there are some contradictions in the findings of the many recent research studies on user behaviour with electronic library collections, some clear messages emerge. By examining the wide variety of methods, participants, and workplaces in these 200-plus studies we do know some things that library users are telling us about their use of electronic resources in the past, present, and future. Although there is no one typical user for whom a single system design or collection decisions can be made, users can be segmented into groups that display similar preferences and patterns of use. Behavior differs based on the following:

- *Status*: High school students and undergraduate students, for ex-ample, turn first to the Web for research but will change behaviours if they are given a specific assignment or are asked to use a particular resource. Graduate students are heavy and cyclical users of electronic journals, especially for research. Faculty members and professionals will use electronic journals if they are convenient and support their natural work patterns. Peer reviewed journals that are considered to be core to a researcher's work will be sought regardless of convenience.

- *Subject discipline, for subject experts*: Scientists and business faculty members were early adopters of electronic journals and read from a variety of full-text databases and e-journals; some fields of science use many sources to get articles, including e-print servers. Social scientists and humanists use both electronic resources and print and rely more on books than other fields.
- *Task*: Most high school and undergraduate students turn first to the Internet for class assignments and feel they are expert searchers. The heaviest use of electronic resources is for research, followed by preparing for teaching and gaining current awareness.
- *Type of institution or workplace*: Academic faculty and graduate students read the most, and they readily use electronic journals accessible from their office or home, but scientists in government laboratories and companies also rely on electronic and paper journals for research. Students prefer to access electronic resources through the library from home. Users in medical libraries read from fewer journal titles than do general university or college users.
- *Age*: There is some evidence that younger users are more enthusiastic adopters of electronic resources than are older users. Younger users rely on electronic resources more heavily and rate themselves more expert in using them than do older users.
- *Gender*: There is little evidence that gender in most cultures makes a difference in use of electronic resources, although in the DLF/CLIR/Outsell studies, women report more use of electronic jour-nals and men use Web search engines more often to locate journals.

In terms of information seeking, today's researcher seems to be comfortable with using a wide variety of sources for information. Internet search engines, e-print servers, author Web sites, full-text databases, electronic journals, and print resources are all used to some degree by most users. The relative amounts of use and enthusiasm for use vary, but today's users are mostly flexible and adaptable. Both browsing and searching remain important information-seeking behaviours, but there is some evidence that the amount of searching is going up when users have access to multi-title, full-text databases. Browsing through journal issues is done in print issues or in electronic journals for core journal titles. Articles from Non-core journals are most often located through searching. Students are highly responsive to recommendations of specific resources by their teachers, friends, or a librarian. Educating both high school and college students in the best resources, how to evalu-ate Web resources, and search strategies is important. Convenience remains the single most important factor for information use—all types of users prefer electronic journals only if they make their work easier and give them the information they need. Desktop access, speed of access, and the ability to download, print, and send articles are top advantages of electronic journals for all groups. Almost universally, users report that they print out relevant articles for detailed reading. This means that both viewer-friendly formats, such as HTML, and printer-friendly formats, such as PDF, are important features in electronic journals. Some concerns remain, such as worries that electronic journal collections may not be complete or long-lived. Concerns over the quality of e-journals seem to be diminishing as most mainstream peer-reviewed journals are digitised. Still, concerns remain over the quality of Web resources, particularly among faculty and librarians who fear students use the Web indiscriminately. There is still confusion over the variety and relative quality of e-resources, in particular among novice users or students. Archiving has been expressed as a concern in some studies. When high-quality electronic collections are made available, people use them. Use of electronic journals increases every year. Among faculty members, graduate students, and other professionals, higher use of electronic journals is accompanied by a decrease in visits to the physical library.

Access to back files and many journal titles is important to many users, although the 80/20 rule has been shown to apply to electronic journal titles. Most readings will come from a relatively small percentage of the collection, but users will read from a greater variety of titles when they are made freely and easily accessible to them. Both Tier 1 and Tier 2 studies show that library policies have intentional and unintentional effects on user behaviour. Unfettered access to electronic collections will result in an increasing use and reliance on electronic resources, although a certain percentage of use in many disciplines will continue to come from print resources for some time to come. Virtual reference services are needed to accompany this shift, as are better ways to count and report virtual library use.

7

Web Search Engines and Search Strategies

INTRODUCTION

Imagine Internet as a huge library with no catalogue and no staff to assist. To access a site/source on the Internet, one should know its URL (Uniform Resource Locator) or Web address. It is not possible to remember the addresses of all the required sites/sources. Since, information retrieval becomes a major problem a number of search tools or services have been developed. Search engines were originally described as automated programmes that compiled and updated databases without human intervention. An Internet novice is often told to "search" when looking for details pertaining to a particular topic. Search Engines are useful because the Internet is made up of literally millions of web sites containing various forms of information and products. Search Engines are Internet companies that collect information about all other web sites. The information is then listed by category and description to expedite the process of finding available web sites in a desired category.

WHAT IS SEARCH ENGINE

Any arbitrary method of Internet searching is called a "search service" (the most general term). A manually administered database is called a "catalog" or a "directory" (or in simple cases a "list"). An automatic robot, which indexes

Internet data mainly by itself, is called a "search engine". Search engine is a programme ("robot" or "spider") that indexes other Web pages. The name Search Engine is an intriguing term. Just as a car engine, a search engine has many parts to it. The first element is often called the SPIDER or the CRAWLER, which visits web pages and reads the information found. Next comes the INDEX part, which is also often referred to as the catalog. This is like a giant book, which contains a copy of every page on the web that the SPIDER has found.

A search engine is a collection of software programmes that collect information from the Web, index it, and put it in a database so it can be searched. Search Engine is automated keyword searching tools, it use piece of software, usually known as a 'spider' or 'crawler' to gather the information from web and other servers and generate indexes. Search engine crawl the networks continuously to update their databases. It usually indexes the full-text of web page and holds lot of information in the databases. They are quite comprehensive and freely available but not complete. Search Engine is a specialised programme that facilitates information retrieval from large segments of the Internet. Search engines attempt to help a user locate desired information or resources by seeking matches to user-specified key words. The usual method for finding and isolating this information is to compile and maintain an index of Web resources that can be queried for the key words or concepts entered by the user.

The indices are often built from specific resource lists, and may also be created from the output of Web crawlers, wanderers, robots, spiders, or worms. The indices are usually compiled during times of minimum network traffic. Different engines are appropriate for different kinds of searches, and most can be optimised for specified results. It allows you to enter words and phrases about what we are looking for and then tries to find the closest match in its database. Some common search engines are AltaVista, Excite, Google, Infoseek and Yahoo. The search engine performs keyword searches against the database and retrieves a set of Web Pages matching the query. A search engine is a giant database of many Web sites on the Internet. A search engine generally returns the result of a search ranked by 'that search engines' indexing criteria. This formula varies widely between search engines.

COMPONENT OF A SEARCH ENGINE

Internet search engines operate in a manner similar to information retrieval systems. The main components of a search engine are *Gatherer* (A Spider), *Indexer* and the *Search Interface.*

Gatherer

Gatherer or Crawler or Spider gathers content descriptors from the document collection, which continuously traverses the Web and picks up the newly added WebPages/documents.

- Spiders or Crawlers or Robots travel from site to site, looking for new WWW pages
- Gatherer or Crawler or Spider gathers content descriptors from the document collection, which continuously traverses the Web and picks up the newly added WebPages/documents.
- Some spiders only go to the "What's New" or the "What's Hot" pages

Indexer

Indexes the web pages gathered by the spider and build the database.

- Some search engines do full text indexing. e.g. AltaVista and Open Text
- Some search engines do keyword indexing, e.g. Lycos and Excite
- Yahoo and Magellan are two of the few examples of human indexing.
- While indexing, types of Web sites indexed may be– HTTP, Gopher, Telnet, FTP, and Usenet Groups.
- Single type of source Indexing. e.g. Dejanews indexes only Usenet group postings
- Types of files indexing: HTML files, Audio, Video, Images, etc.

Search Interface

- It is an interface between User and Database
- Interface has been designed using HTML and CGI
- It collects query (Keywords) from the user, submit to the Database and display results based on the matching and relevance.

CHRONOLOGICAL DEVELOPMENT OF SEARCH ENGINES

Table. 7.1

Year Search	Engine Name
• 1990	Archie
• 1991	Gopher
• 1992	Veronica
• 1993	Jughead
• 1993	World Wide Web Wanderer
• 1994	Galaxy
• 1994	Yahoo!
• 1994	WebCrawler
• 1994	Lycos
• 1995	Infoseek
• 1995	MetaCrawler
• 1995	Excite
• 1995	AltaVista
• 1995	Search Savvy Meta search engine.
• 1996	Inktomi
• 1996	HotBot
• 1996	LookSmart
• 1997	Ask Jeeves
• 1997	GoTo
• 1997	Northern Light
• 1998	Open Directory Project
• 1998	Google
• 1998	MSN
• 1998	Direct Hit
• 1999	InfoSeek

Contd...

Year Search	Engine Name
• 1999	NBC
• 1999	FAST Search
• 2000	Teoma
• 2001	Ask Jeeves acquires the Teoma search property
• 2001	Lycos search Discontinued
• 2001	AltaVista switches to Yahoo!
• 2002	LookSmart bought the WiseNut search engine.
• 2002	Froogle search engine
• 2003	Google released a contextual based ad programme by the name of AdSense
• 2003	Overture purchased AllTheWeb and AltaVista. Yahoo gobbled up Intomi and Overture.
• 2004	Yahoo in 2004 dumped Google in favour of its own in house search engine. Yahoo! Slurp is believed to be collecting data to make a new database separate from the Inktomi database. The new Yahoo! Database replaced both AltaVista and
AllTheWeb	in March 2004

CATEGORIES OF SEARCH ENGINE

Search engines fall into five categories they are:

- Robotic Internet search engines uses a Web robot to retrieve a significant number of documents from the World Wide Web.
- Mega-indexes have links to the robotic search engines
- Simultaneous mega-indexes access the robotic search engines simultaneously
- Subject directories are manually-maintained collections of Web sites organised by topic and
- Robotic specialised search engines focus on a small or specialised segment of the Internet.

TYPES OF SEARCH ENGINE

There are five types of search engines:

- Free-Text Search Engines

- Index or Directory-based Search Engines
- Multi or Meta-Search Engines
- Natural-Language Search Engines
- Resource or site specific Search Engines

FREE-TEXT SEARCH ENGINE

Free-text Search Engines are just one way of finding the information that we need on the net. These types of search engine are very easy and useful if we know exactly what we are looking for. Simply search for any single word, a number of word or in some cases a phrase. e.g. AltaVista, Lycos, HotBot and Northern Light etc.

Free-text Search Engines will:

- Accept any terms the user wishes to search for,
- Can search for terms in any combination,
- Can search for phrase as well as single words,
- Allow users considerable flexibility in choosing how to search.

INDEX OR DIRECTORY-BASED SEARCH ENGINES

Index–based search engines are less useful if we require a broad overview of a subject or unfamiliar with a subject and its technical jargon. e.g. Yahoo, Magellan, Excite Index–based search engines are;

- Arrange data in a structured fashion,
- Make use of heading and subheading–general to specific,
- Web authors (human made) to submit pages to the engine,
- Depend on their category structure for their success,
- Generally quite simple to use, and appeal to novice searches,
- Useful if we want a broad approach to a subject,
- Useful if we are unsure of keywords to use in a search.

MULTI OR META-SEARCH ENGINES

An automat that scans search engines in parallel and merges the results is called a *"meta-search engine"*. If this automat is running as a client on the user PC it is *"client-based"* meta-search engine. If this automat is running as a server, answering queries of many users, it's a *"server-based"* meta-search engine. They are also called Meta Crawlers or multi search engines and they do not crawl the web compiling their own searchable databases. They search the databases of multiple sets of individual search engines simultaneously from a single site using the same interface. They function as intermediary and present the results of their searches in two ways:-one is single lists (merged and duplicates removed) and Multiple Lists (not collated, displayed specially, duplicates may appear).

Three Main Factors Determine the Usefulness of any Meta-search Engine

The search engines: the search terms send to (size, content, number of search engines, ability to choose the search engines) all of them search subject directories as well as search engines and intermixed results from all. How the search terms and search syntax are handled (Boolean operators, phrases, and defaults imposed) How results are displayed (ranking; aggregated into one list, or with each search engine's results reported separately)

What does this Meta Engine do?

- Translates the search request.
- Queries all relevant search engines intelligently for you.
- Processes the results.
- Presents you with the best possible sites.

Unlike the individual search engines and directories, meta-search engines do not have their own databases; they do not collect web pages; they do not accept URL additions; and they do not classify or review web sites. Instead, they send queries simultaneously to multiple Web search engines and/or Web directories. Many of the meta-search engines integrate search results: duplicate findings are merged into one entry; some rank the results according to various criteria; some allow selection of search engines to be searched. Meta search engines don't crawl the web themselves to build databases. Instead, they allow searches to be sent to several search engines all at once. The results are then blended together onto one page. Successful use of a meta-search engine depends on the status of each of the individual search engines used. Some may be heavily loaded at the time; some may be unreachable. The added features require further resources from the meta-search engines, resulting in slower response time, a serious problem with many of the meta-search engines. Many of them, therefore, have a timeout period, so that attempts to work with a particular search engine can be abandoned if no response comes from it within a set period of time

Seven Steps can Describe the Principle of a Meta-search Engine

- Accept a user query,
- Convert the query into the correct syntax for every underlying search engine,
- Launch the multiple queries,
- Wait for the results, and in parallel do some searching on a local database (Quick Tips),
- Analyse the results, eliminate duplicates, do a ranking,
- Merge the results,
- Deliver the post-processed results to the user's client.

Limitations of Meta-Search Engines

How do you know if your search terms will "work"? Anyone who does Internet searching knows, search protocol (the way you enter search keywords) is far from standardised. Almost all accept "" as causing a *phrase.* A few accept *Boolean* AND, OR, and NOT. Fewer accept ( ) to group terms. Some only accept + or -. Some default to OR, some to AND. Some take * to *truncate.* Other *stem* automatically and so on.

NATURAL-LANGUAGE SEARCH ENGINES

Some support natural language queries - accepts queries like 'What is the height of Mount Everest' or 'Why is the sky blue'. A recent development in the field of search engine technology is the introduction of what may be termed natural-language search engines that is a search engine which not only understand the request that has been made, but is able to interrupt the question and come up with answers about the subject that are not entirely based on the words or phrases used by the questioner. They can be very useful if you have real problem finding information. e.g. AskJeeves, Albert.

RESOURCE OR SITE SPECIFIC SEARCH ENGINES

This type of search engines are perhaps the largest but paradoxically the least used, probably as a result of their diversity. e.g. search a particular resource, such as Bible, a Dictionary, and Encyclopaedia.

GENERAL TIPS FOR SEARCHING THE WEB

SEARCH OPTIONS

- Natural Language Processing
- Boolean Operators
- Vectors
- Fuzzy Matching
- Phrase Searching
- Proximity Matching
- Concept Browsing and Automatic Matching
- Thesaurus
- Query By Example
- Stemming and Substitutions
- Non-English character matching
- Special features (price-range searching, for example)
- Spelling error tolerance.

CATEGORIES OF SEARCH TOOLS

Information:

- Directories
- Search engines
- Meta search engines
- Subject gateways and virtual libraries

People:

- Online directory service
- E-mail and phone directories on institutional web sites

- Mailing list memberships
- Directories of people using Usenet news

Resource/Tools for Searching... Software:

- Searchable database of software service
- Anonymous FTP archives
- Archie

BOOLEAN OPERATORS

Boolean logic takes its name from British mathematician George Boole (1815-1864), who wrote about a system of logic designed to produce better search results by formulating precise queries. Broad or general terms will return thousands of possible sites.

Try to use terms that are more specific to your topic. To narrow your terms, look at sites that you already have found and that are relevant to your topic. Identify possible search terms from those sites. You also can combine terms, using Boolean Operators. Particular words called Boolean operators: AND, OR, NOT can be used in searching to help specify the information to be located.

How they work?

- AND Search will reveal only profiles containing both words.
- OR Search will reveal profiles with entire word.

* NOT That word will not appear in the results

Wildcards and other operations:

- NEAR Result will have the linked words within number of words of each other
- FAR The linked words will appear within some number of words apart at least once in result.
- BEFORE Words appear in specific order but not necessarily near each other.
- ADJ The words will appear next to each other.
- BUT NOT That word will not appear in the search results.
- NEAR/# Result will have the linked words within the specific number (#) words of ach other.
- O Directly before another operation (OADJ) will force result to be in order to specify.

- /# Use directly after ADJ, NEAR and FAR to specify the # of words allowed between search words.
- () Group words together so you can search for a couple of different options at a time.
- NEAR# Result will have the linked words within the specific number # words of each other.
- * Substitute for any string of characters.
- ? Substitute for one letter.
- ^ Substitute for any string of characters
- | Narrow by placing between a broad-category search word and a narrowcategory search word.
- URL Search for link to a URL
- U Search word will appear in URL
- T Search word will appear in Title
- Site Search for pages at a particular web site.
- {} Search words in brackets will appear within some number words of one another.
- + Requires following search word to appear in each search result.
- - Requires following search word to be absent in each search result.
- "" Place around any number of word you want searched for as a phrase.

SEARCH TIPS

Some Search Engine allows searching of both the web and many Usenet Newsgroups. It allows control of the result lists in a standard, compact, and detailed format. It provides both simple and advanced searches.

Advanced searches include all the features of simple ones, and also allow the use of Boolean and proximity operators, grouping of terms by parentheses, and results ranking by keyword.

- *Case Sensitivity*: Search terms entered in lower case letters are case insensitive. The use of capitalised terms (or accented letters) makes the term case sensitive. HotDog finds only the terms spelled exactly with that capitalisation; hotdog finds all occurrences of the term, regardless of capitalisation. López only finds a word spelled exactly that way.

- *Phrases*: To group search terms into phrases, include them in double quotes. "Abraham Lincoln" finds occurrences of the name Abraham Lincoln, capitalised in just that way.
- *Required Terms*: To require that one of your terms be included in the document being indexed, preface (the formal term is prepend) it with a + symbol
- *Prohibited Terms*: To prohibit the inclusion of a term from a document for which you are searching, prepped it with a–symbol
- *Wildcards*: With simple queries you are allowed to enter a wildcard character at the end of phrases, which will substitute for any combination of letters. The asterisk (*) is AltaVista's wildcard character
- *Rankings*: AltaVista will assign a confidence ranking to the hits it returns based on the following:
- The query terms are found in the first few words of the document (especially the title of web pages).
- The query terms are found in close proximity to one another in the document.
- The document contains more of the search terms than other documents.

SEARCH ENGINES AND INFORMATION PROFESSIONALS

HOW TO USE SEARCH ENGINE?

- Simply enter relevant words in to a search form
- Set the appropriate options
- Search terms will then be compared to the index/ database and any matching results returned
- Results are displayed as per the relevance (ranking)

WHEN TO USE SEARCH ENGINE

- If we need lots of information

- If we have a fairly specific information need
- If we are searching for organisations or people

GOOD FOR SIMPLE SEARCHES

Meta-Search engines are useful if the user looking for a unique term or phrase (enclose phrases in quotes " "); or simply want to test run a couple of keywords to see if they get. For such straight-forward searches, the unique ranking algorithm used by Google (based on how many other sites link to a site) often finds exactly what they want, better than any meta-search engine.

FOR MORE DIFFICULT SEARCHES

we recommend a search engine where you can search within results on a term or phrase you specify. We recommend learning Alta Vista Advanced Search and Northern Light Power Search and possibly Info seek whenever you retrieve a huge result and want to focus on some aspect, some other approach. Please consult our recommended search strategy based on what you know and want to know. As suggested, learn when to consult Subject Directories, how to look for expert guides and specialised databases-all of which have a valuable place in the repertoire of searching skills for the experienced searcher.

USE META-SEARCH ENGINES-BUT USE THEM CAUTIOUSLY

Most meta-search engines only spend a short time in each database and often retrieve only 10 per cent of any of the results in any of the databases queried. This makes their searches usually "quick and dirty," but often good enough to find what you want. Most meta-searchers simply pass your search terms along, and if your search contains more than one or two words or very complex logic, most of that will be lost. It will only make sense to the few search engines that support such logic. Quantity in results does not equal satisfaction. If you get more results than you want, try refining the results by going directly to AltaVista Advanced Search, Northern Light, or Infoseek by clicking on their link in the results. Choose meta-search engines that offer some of these as options. Look for meta-search engines that also send your terms to selective or odd databases like WebCrawler, Thunderstone, Direct Hit, and WhatUSeek. One of the advantages of a meta-searcher is that you might overlook databases like these which may have sites missed by the big boys.

A WORD ON PORTALS

The trend is for many search sites to offer not only searching and links to resources by subject, but also many other services (stock quotes, airline tickets, shopping malls, news links, games, chat rooms, free e-mail, and much more). The goal seems to be to lure as many users to the site and keep them there as long as possible, probably because the site's advertisers may benefit.

Advantages

- Best suited for complex/interdisciplinary search topics
- Searches can be limited to a period of time
- Currency of information: Web spiders traverse the Web almost everyday, so the latest additions to the Web can be retrieved
- Exhaustive information is retrieved on a particular topic

Disadvantages

- The search is time consuming: The search normally results in too many hits and this contains a lot of irrelevant documents
- The searcher should be familiar with the search techniques
- Search engines vary from each other
- The retrieved set may contain dead links

CONCLUSION

URL guessing can help in finding pages for URLs that no longer work and links that lead to dead ends. Try chopping off parts of the URL starting on the right-hand side and stopping at every. Subject directories select and classify resources into subject categories and subcategories. Some include reviews and/or ratings. Access is by keyword search or by Search Engines attempt to find and index as many sites as possible. Search features vary greatly, as does the actual scope, size, and accuracy of the databases. Unique Keywords, Combinations of unique keywords, Field searching and limiting and Pages buried deep in a web site are the main points. Searching information on the Internet is a complex process and tools that use in locating are directories, search engines, meta-search engines, subject gateways/virtual libraries etc. Keeping up-to-date with the developments in the area is necessary and as information on the net grows, more and more search tools will be designed. There is a greater need for organising these resources using skills of librarianship.

8

Framework and Application

CONVERGENCE AND DIVERGENCE AMONG DIGITAL LIBRARIES AND THE PUBLISHING INDUSTRY

The Internet's dynamic impact on society, industries and individuals has been studied intensively across a broad number of academic disciplines. Digital media are spurring both creativity and dislocation in every field of study, as well as the workplace. These forces have also triggered sweeping changes in how traditional players in the creation of knowledge and scholarship operate and interact with each other. "Digital convergence," as it is widely known, invites not only creativity and enterprise, but also new and energetic competition in nearly every line of work.

The evolving roles of the traditional publisher and the research library in the United States are particularly illuminating as indicators of the ferment that the digital era is producing. These two groups have long enjoyed ties of mutual benefit, but now face radical forces of change, and find themselves in competition with each other—as digital publishers. Indeed, it is now possible for each agent to assume the characteristics of the other: librarians can act as digital publishers, and publishers can add new roles as preservàtionists and guarantors of long term access to content. Innovators in each group are already experimenting with expanded services in large and small ways. Ventures may involve wholly new services, or more basic experiments that gauge their audience's interest. The opportunity to assume much - enlarged professional roles and offer services with good prospects for success places publishers and digital librarians in a new relationship, and is causing fundamental shifts in each field. Can digital libraries act as full-service publishers? If so, should they undertake such a path? Likewise, when the lifespan of a work of literature or scholarship is measured in its entirety, publishers can scarcely miss synergistic opportunities that add new functions and skills to their historical areas of expertise.

Indeed, other "content creators" of every stripe frequently assume custodial and interpretive roles— much like library-services - acting as repository managers, purveyors of social media and online conversationalists. Should publishers assume any of these roles? These questions go to the heart of both the library and the publishing professions. How each group decides to answer them will have a significant impact on the future of scholarship, education and entertainment, as well as the form and function of digital libraries themselves. This article will explore the recent history and pivotal experiences of U.S. publishers and research libraries, and the prospects for competition or collaboration between the two groups. The crux of this analysis will lie not on industry studies, but rather on an evaluation of the "professional cultures" of publishing and digital libraries.

Although commercial publishers and digital libraries are not identical types of organisations, they share many values and their necessary skills hold many similarities. Indeed, the underpinnings of their respective skill sets are closely related. Therefore even though outright competition is a viable strategy, so also is a future based on strategic alliances of mutual benefit. Whatever course history takes, the outcome will have an important impact on both of these information-handling groups as well as the social and technological architectures of knowledge resources. Sociology provides us with solid theories that evaluate the dynamics of competition and strategic collaboration, and such theories have grown in importance during the digital era. Andrew Abbott has argued persuasively that professions that handle related areas of expertise will take advantage of new opportunities to advance their status, whether by adding skills into existing portfolios or by forming new levels of licensure, standards, or international oversight. At the same time, there is also a growing perception that all kinds of digital production occur on a continuum of activity, involving many phases and a diversity of players, reinforcing the need for traditional players such as publishers and digital librarians to look beyond traditional spheres of authority for new opportunities. What is more, theories about competitive motives and their interplay with digital convergence are not limited to sociology; similar theories now appear in business literature, as well cultural debates about the future of scholarship.

This is little doubt that the technological hurdles to assuming the role of digital publisher have never been lower; the remaining barriers are of an organisational nature, such as the urge to hold onto prevailing beliefs about functional roles and workflows, not to mention pre-conceived notions of how markets or services "should" operate. The present turmoil is both energising and destabilising for all established players in the information professions, and conditions are so dynamic that 2011 may bring a host of new challenges for both groups. With these factors in mind, the following review of the cultures and recent histories of these two crucial players in knowledge creation may provoke insights about the future strategies—and prospects—of both groups, whether they may compete or collaborate, and what impact their choices may have on the future development of digital libraries.

COMPETING PROFESSIONS: THE NEW LANDSCAPE

Digital technology has been rewriting professional roles for many years. This process is dynamic and stressful for the affected groups. Understanding how professions compete for dominance has gained new importance in the digital era, because each affected group must come to terms with the possibility that their own native area of expertise-whether it is publishing, distributing or archiving, for example - may be taken over by a competing group with a better idea.

The current ferment in all professional groups that manage information is one of the best examples of competition for new roles in the digital era. For a long time, publishers and libraries in particular have enjoyed stable perceptions of their roles, but those days are gone and not likely to return.

Instead, these two groups are deeply involved not only in re-imagining what their core services are, but also what roles they may be able to "poach" from others in the overall process of knowledge creation. Abbott's broad analysis of the U,S.,. system of professions sheds considerable light on the relationship between expert labour, technology and organisational design, and offers some explanations for patterns of competition between different professions.

Professionals have standing in society to evaluate the important matters of our lives, ranging from medicine through law; they "diagnose" and "treat" conditions and are regulated by organised bodies of their peers. Expert status depends upon sound and irrefutable "abstract knowledge": a set of skills that is controlled by the profession and applied to practical problems.

The use of specialised language is one example of how abstract knowledge retains power; engineers or doctors utilise sophisticated terminologies to retain authority over their practice areas.Also with respect to medicine, physician associations aggressively protect the meaning and definition of "practicing medicine," fending off efforts by other practitioners such as acupuncturists to gain higher levels of recognition for their treatments. Professions that lose control of their system of abstract knowledge risk the loss of prestige and status.

The height of professional power is determined by licensure by state- or national-level licensing bodies, which confer the official status to practice a profession. This is the case with accountancy, law, medicine and other fields. Professions and occupations that are not universally licensed by government—such as publishing and libraries—are at greater risk of competition from others who may seek to offer their own expert solutions.

Treatment Substitution

Digital technology has created numerous opportunities for the expansion of prestige. Competing groups, such as librarians, publishers or technology managers, may attempt to take over new areas of responsibility, in essence by offering a better treatment than their competitors. As technology influences working life, professional status may rise or fall depending on the vitality of abstract knowledge. New types of abstract knowledge, such as the ability to understand how people use technology and information resources, or how to structure metadata for a digital future, are potential sources of new professional power.

Treatment substitution holds three important lessons for the information professions. First, power, or the standing to diagnose and treat, is best maintained by the strategic preservation of abstract knowledge. Second, constant self-evaluation publicly exposes weaknesses in the abstract underpinnings of professional expertise, which can invite competition. Third, digital media offer new groups the chance to expand their zones of influence, if their practitioner skills provide them with new abstract knowledge. Because of these factors, all of the information professions are using digital technology to gain political leverage and to take new roles in knowledge creation.

The Knowledge Creation Continuum

Abbott's study of the professions was originally conducted before the most explosive years of Internet growth began rewriting the rules for scholarly activity and publishing. Subsequent research about the impact of new technologies on the creative and intellectual processes of scholarship strengthens his theories about competition among the professions. During the early days of the Internet era, the Getty Information Institute established useful models for understanding what was happening to the traditional information industries. Researchers at the Getty Information Institute identified the "knowledge creation continuum" as a means for understanding scholarly communications. Under this model, all of the various players in the creation of knowledge operate upon this continuum, bumping into each other as they find new opportunities during the digital era.

Each player dominates a "zone of progressive release" of knowledge, as creative work finds its way from author to reader.

This dynamic process defines much of the action underway at the present time, as authors, publishers, media outlets and repositories such as digital libraries redefine their roles. Organisation studies researchers, university leaders, and information professionals have also found the metaphor of the continuum to be useful.

Tian recast the continuum as a "data-information-knowledge spiral," lending the visual image of upward movement. Ellison and Eatman, who wrote a major policy document about the American tenure system, identify a "continuum of scholarship" that encompasses not only the faculty but every contributor to the knowledge creation process. Fister undertook a study of trade publishing to explore the changing roles of all of the industry's contributors on a continuum of actions, seen with an information professional's perspective.

As the continuum evolves, zones of added value may collapse into one another. This trend is also widely studied, and is well described by Marcus Banks, in his analysis of the shifting distinctions between "grey" and "Non-grey" literature. The application of abstract knowledge governs strategic action; therefore an assessment of the comparative robustness of abstract knowledge among various groups may provide a useful indicator of future success. It may also reveal who is most likely to compete with each other, and which zones of progressive release they will move into.

Publishers and Libraries Face Blurring Boundaries

The abstract knowledge bases of publishers and digital librarians contain many similarities, but they are also distinct in how they perceive special skill. For publishers, the skills of discovering, editing, preparing and selling books for consumers or for academics is a wellunderstood chain of actions; as a result publishers historically have viewed themselves as indispensable players on the knowledge creation continuum.

For librarians, collection, categorisation, interpretation and preservation of vast repositories of literature likewise define the core expertise of the profession. However, digital technology has blurred the distinct boundaries for just where each zone of expertise begins and ends.

New technologies, beginning with desktop publishing programmes and moving onward through an avalanche of electronic devices and networked information, now make it possible for other skilful groups to offer competing publishing solutions.

For example, digital librarians may choose to enter the publishing zone, or publishers may launch new programmes as archivists or preservationists of the knowledge they create. The "open source" movement is another example, with universities offering a full-scale publishing alternative to commercial journals.

Open source journals are free of charge and compete directly with expensive and respected scholarly journals—a classic example of treatment substitution. Likewise, much of the struggle between publishers and libraries over the past 20 years has focused on price control or access to markets, with publishers advocating for greater pricing authority over knowledge resources and librarians advocating for expansive access, within the reasonable constraints of the "first sale" principle that underlies the book market.

If information can be managed in new and flexible ways, traditional perceptions of both publishers and digital libraries are also more fluid than they once were in the eyes of other groups.

For example, information technologists have competed with numerous strategies to manage information, including search engines, database services, large-scale archiving and records management. These forays into the traditional role of publisher or librarian have been sustained for as long as computers have been in existence.

New Media, New Competition

The digital era presents many opportunities for enterprising individuals to reinvent publishing practices. As a result, most information-handling professionals are evaluating their options, using models such as the knowledge creation continuum to understand what moves to make. It is a dangerous and exciting time to be in the publishing industry, and also in the library field;

virtually all of a sudden, new agents that range from software developers to authors are able to style themselves as a publisher to varying degrees, or as managers of repositories of information. In such a tumultuous environment, success comes from possession of abstract knowledge that can make sense of the new and unknown.

In this regard, the creation and evolution of digital libraries is much influenced by what goes on in the publishing sector, as well as in the library sphere. As publishers and digital librarians confront competition from new agents on the knowledge creation continuum, their responses to the turmoil are instructive for assessing how digital libraries will grow. As conditions change, the traditional beliefs of entrenched players such as publishers and librarians can either help or hinder efforts to protect their traditional roles. With that in mind, an overview of recent history and the professional dialogues of publishing and librarianship, as a preface to analysing each group's challenges and their prospects for collaborating or competing with each other.

DYSTOPIA AND DISTRESS: PUBLISHING'S PROFESSIONAL DIALOGUE

As the disruptive power of technology creates a diversity of opinion about what will come next, established players typically respond to new challenges by drawing on their known areas of expertise. For example, publishers have responded to the digital era by analysing the shifting terrain through the lens of market analysis and the benchmarking of sales goals. This approach made good sense, as it served the industry well prior to the digital era. Indeed, recently, the U.S. publishing industry's total revenue was in excess of 100 billion dollars, with a substantial percentage of revenue generated by book publishing. Reporting on the book industry in that same year, Datamonitor, a market analysis firm, opined that the "online publishing industry" had not yet materialised, and forecast even higher revenue in 2010. The U.S. publishing industry had revenue of slightly more than 50 billion dollars, e-books and e-readers had gained wider acceptance, and industry analysts lowered their revenue forecasts.

In the face of such alarming figures, the publishing industry interpreted the emergence of a digital marketplace as a threat to revenue. This initial perception influenced much of the industry's professional dialogue about what would follow. Notably, a market-based system of perception and strategic thinking is based on viewing readers as consumers who purchase books; certainly this is a valid assessment, but as a paradigm, it excludes viewing readers as members of "community" who have many interests in addition to purchasing books, such as social interaction with publishers and authors. The general tendency to view readers as consumers has been a strategic "Achilles heel" for publishing and has persisted for years, but is beginning to break down.

A History of Embattlement

Publishers have perceived their industry as embattled for decades, due to a series of destabilising events that predated the emergence of the Internet. It is important to understand the impact of this long-running and alarmist professional dialogue, decades old as it is, on the current strategic thinking of publishers. Throughout the 1970s and 1980s, the dominance of the mass-market paperback threatened the profitability of trade publishers.

Thomas Whiteside describes this threat as part of the "blockbuster complex": new rules pushed ever-increasing resources to the production of high-volume bestsellers at the expense of "mid-list" books of interest and value. The massmarket crisis period was quickly followed by bookseller consolidation, as Barnes and Noble and the now-defunct Waldenbooks expanded and began exerting heavy influence through their buying patterns. As the Internet and the World Wide Web made all-digital publishing a serious option, Webbased reading alternatives began to grow very rapidly, causing consternation and even panic for publishers. High-powered online distribution services such as Amazon seemed to gain even more influence than their predecessors of the print-only era over what readers would choose to buy.

The invention of "digital ink" and the e-book seemed to pose further threats to publisher profits. With sales and market development as analytical paradigms, publishers entered the digital era without adequate strategic preparation for technological change. Consequently, they retained a sense of embattlement, as new agents who possessed innovative abstract knowledge began to emerge - once again demonstrating the process of treatment substitution.

With much narrower margins and downward pressure on budgets, traditional publishing's internal dialogue reached new rhetorical heights of anxiety after the turn of the century. *The New Yorker* magazine launched a Weblog called "Publisher Death Watch," which kept track of downsising businesses, including individual posts from demoralised staff. Jason Epstein, long-time Publisher at Random House and a major thinker of the publishing profession, responded to the growing anxiety with a variety of new business models, including on-demand print publishing, as well as passionate philosophical manifestos meant to renew and uplift. Epstein has been joined by other prominent figures such as Peter Jovanovich, offering a series of roadmaps for survival, focusing on adaptation to new technology and digital rights management. Yet even as new ideas began to flow, publishing staff morale reached new lows. Debate at publisher association meetings often reflected the grim business environment.

At the 2008 Association of American University Presses meeting in Montreal, incoming president Alex Holzman declared that "We meet under darkening clouds," referring to lightning-fast technological change, the open access publishing movement, new competitors, economic downturns and more. At the same time, independent booksellers - key partners to the publishing industry - had also suffered severe losses in market share, complicating traditional revenue streams. Booksellers have long enjoyed close relationships with publishers, and therefore publishers possessed keen understanding of bookstores as their key sales outlet. However Since, 1985, independent booksellers have been shrinking in number, although some robust bookstores continue to thrive.

New super-stores such as Borders and Barnes and Noble entered the vacuum left by disappearing independents, bringing different business patterns for sales and returns of merchandise with them. With fewer and larger retailers, the unique process of returning unsold books to publishers for credit has had far greater impact on sales cycles and profits. Under such conditions, reverberations of distress flowing from the bookselling industry carry heavy impact for publishers. When Barnes and Noble, which dominates U.S. bookselling, announced that it may put itself up for sale in 2010 or 2011, the announcement created fresh alarm for publishers.

Core Competencies Face New Realities

The sheer drama of the publishing industry's waves of consolidation, downsising and new ventures helped to focus the profession's attention on the meaning and value of its core skills and roles. These skills and roles are typically boiled down to four principal functions, although they can vary in name. These roles are Agents; Editors; Design and Marketing; and Sales staff. Publishing work begins with authors via agency, and proceeds to add value by editing and preparing an author's work for sale. Each of the functions along this path to market is labour-intensive, requiring large investments of time and resources, and each is also widely held to be an essential, value-added service that no other group can offer at a higher standard.

Of the four roles, editing is held as the most durable service that publishers offer. The curricula of graduate programmes that grant degrees or certificates in publishing reflect several of the trends underway in the marketplace. For example, the *New York Times* Knowledge Network co-hosts an ePublishing certificate programme with Rosemont College, and the introductory description for the programme is telling as a gauge of uncertainty. It states: *"The world of publishing is changing rapidly, due to one little letter:*

"e." The advent of ePublishing has launched an era of rapid change, growth and turmoil in the publishing industry. What are these new technologies and how do they work? How will they continue to develop and be used? What will the industry look like in five years, in six months, next week? And what skills are needed to survive and succeed in the publishing workplace?"

Just as this description articulates the widespread uncertainty, a closer review of the 36 unit master's degree at Rosemont College illustrates how transferrable the core skills of publishing have become. Over the course of study students learn the principles of editing, marketing, production and more; yet the same curriculum could easily appear as coursework for a career in Web administration, journalism or information science. The ease with which digital publishing skills may transfer to other fields accentuates how publishing expertise is much more widespread than it was just 15 years ago, and that other groups can now learn these skills and experiment with publishing strategies.

Tipping Towards Innovation

The professional dialogue of publishers is intriguing, given the industry's continued existence despite its many challenges. The blockbuster mentality produced much alarm, but also yielded impressive revenue streams for publishers who could respond with strong bestselling lists.

It has also made many authors into multi-millionaires. Mass-market books did not "kill" publishers; instead, they revolutionised marketing strategies. The success of mass market paperbacks spawned the larger-format, higher-profit "trade paperback," which was conceived as a business builder and a permanent artifact for library collections. Big distributors during the print-only era and the print-plus-digital era have also contributed some positive impacts on sales, by creating unexpected top selling titles.

E-books, while they are growing in use, still constitute just a few percentage points of total book sales—and book sales, although they have been shrinking Since, 2004, Non-etheless generated more than 25 billion dollars in 2009. Moreover, 2010 appears to be the year that acceptance of e-book devices and electronic text reading will accelerate in popularity.

By the end of 2010, 10.3 million people are forecast to own an e-reader, and will buy as many as 100 million e-books. With such rapid trends underway, the influential Book Industry Study Group has devoted considerable energy and resources to study the whole of the industry, with a close focus on electronic products.

Publishers have also have released content in aggregated and topical "libraries" such as Wiley Custom Select, which offers a coursereader solution to professors. In short, the business environment, though fraught with challenges, continues to be functional, and publisher strategies have been evolving at a faster pace. Although new ideas are being actively studied, staff morale continues to suffer.

Attention to the publisher "death watch" and a "rallying the troops" rhetorical style continue to dominate the tenor of publishing's professional dialogue. In 2010, the Book Industry Study Group conducted an important survey of publishing staff, to gauge their perspectives and sentiments regarding new media and e-books.

When asked when they expected to see fundamental change in their own functional work area, 31 per cent of respondents replied that it had "already happened", and 45 per cent said it was "happening now". At the same time, enterprising digital publishers such as O'Reilly Media have countered with comprehensive business models that draw on the full array of social media, creating interactive user experiences that go beyond the book format. By 2008, the full force of experimentation and pursuit of innovation had gripped the publishing industry, creating a sense of making up for lost time.

DIGITAL LIBRARIANS: PRESERVING THE PAST, LOOKING FORWARD

Throughout the same eras of upheaval and change, librarians faced similarly daunting challenges. Researcher calls heralding the imminent demise of a proud profession crowded the professional literature of every specialised sector of librarianship for decades. In response, various innovators have explored a mulitiplicity of strategies. Nancy Lemon argues that rethinking traditional roles enables librarians to climb organisational "value chains;" Researchers review the plight of news media libraries and see a history of cyclical renewal, in which existing jobs give way to new opportunities in new locations.

Among corporate libraries, a wide variety of bareknuckle strategies have been put forward, urging librarians to find a competitive edge by offering services that can be demonstrated to boost profits. In the public libary sphere, despite straitened civic budgets and the shock of new media, libraries have achieved a degree of success in staying relevant. Circulation, library card membership and on-site use of services are at an all-time high, countering the idea that community libraries are outdated during the digital era. On the contrary, they are more popular than ever. Therefore even as pessimism about the future became a standard feature in the professional literature, a parallel stream of daring and innovative thinking has run concurrently among a wide spectrum of library specialists.

The resulting intellectual ferment has produced new paradigms and new energy for rethinking library goals in light of the emergence of digital technology. Rather than wait to see what would happen, librarians repeatedly took initiative with new media. They staked an early claim on the crucial issue of intellectual property and copyright, working both with and against publishers as needed to preserve the library's public service mission. As part of this process, librarians became more deeply aware of the publishing industry's travails with digital media. This awareness led to greater strategic knowledge about the marketplace.

Spanning "Online" Eras

Librarians were shaken by the rapid emergence of Web-based information resources, because they had been important players in the previous "online" economy that was dominated by firms like LEXIS/NEXIS and Dialog Information Services. This first "online" era gave librarians the opportunity to cast themselves as experts who conducted mediated searches on behalf of users such as attorneys, scientists and business leaders. As the initial "online" era faded and the Internet exploded into growth, librarians joined the first wave of Internet e-mail "conversationalists", Web content users, Web site producers, and aggregators of high quality information.

They also grasped the importance of creating stable and robust Web portals, which organised and "branded" library-hosted aggregations of databases; such activist strategies stretched scarce budgets while formalising a Web-based library presence. Similarly, the economic upheaval caused by the skyrocketing price of scholarly journals generated energetic responses on the part of research libraries, including formation of the Scholarly Publishing and Academic Resources Coalition (SPARC), as well as active congressional lobbying to protect copyright and "fair use" principles from a runaway marketplace.

The same upheaval also sparked a sustained outreach to faculty, in search of much stronger partnerships with the academy's principle content creators. In general, digital librarians have been agents for innovation over the past 15 years, and have participated in the sweeping process of rethinking scholarly communications. This lengthy process of trial and error has transformed digital librarians' self-perception. Rather than viewing digital media as a force of dislocation that would bring ruin to the profession, digital librarians have instead embraced it. Likewise, constant downward pressure on budgets forced innovative survival plans to the forefront, emphasising new technologies.

Metadata as Enhanced Competency

Perhaps the most significant advance on the part of digital librarians has been the profession's embrace of structured metadata and taxonomy as a reinvigorated core competency. Even as they faced the twin challenges of integrating new technologies and shrinking budgets, digital librarians participated in the formation of international metadata standards such as the Dublin Core.

Libraries became key institutional members of new groups such as the Coalition for Networked Information and the National Digital Library Federation. Academic librarians experimented with diverse forms of preservation, including digital repositories, e-journals, and increasingly, full-scale publishing initiatives that originate within the library. Many metadata platforms and languages have been explored, but Extensible Markup Language (XML) has become a dominant tool for managing digital assets.

XML is a "meta-language of languages," enabling developers to create taxonomies and metadata schema that are customisable, portable and attached to the "digital objects" they describe. The emergence of national and international standards for metadata, the ascendance of digital objects which are transferrable among collections, and a strong focus on systems interoperability have elevated the library profession to a technical status considerably higher than it enjoyed before the advent of the digital era. Although digital librarians are not the only XML developers - many computing firms and other academics are heavily involved—they have left an imprint on the development stream of XML.

XML-based systems have become accepted across many industries beyond the academy, and now play a crucial role in information management and data warehousing by large corporate firms. XML-based information architectures are essential tools for managing text, images and other artifacts, creating new workflows that are based on the principle of "one text, multiple outputs".This kind of workflow would transfer very effectively to the publishing world, yet the publishing industry has been slower to adopt XML workflows at a universal level. The opportunity to manage digital assets using XML is an important leap forward that publishers have not yet fully embraced, and forward-looking commentators have recognised this shortfall.

From Online Repository to Publishing Platform

The turmoil of the Internet's early years also produced solid initiatives to understand the digital library as a publisher in its own right. Thomas provides an early and comprehensive road map that offers large research libraries a template for launching high quality publishing services. She also describes the early emergence of online repositories as a new form of curated information resources. Online repositories grew quickly throughout the early years of the twenty-first century, taking much inspiration from the digital archiving efforts of the computer science and engineering fields.

Librarymanaged repositories also grew up with a strong bias for interoperability, which has led to more dialogue about the need for large-scale "federations" of digital libraries, even at the international level. As these repositories became more accepted, use skyrocted. The University of California's eScholarship repository experienced more than one million downloads in its first two years of operation. "Post prints" and research reports are now also collected in online repositories, and are frequently overseen by digital librarians, or at least coordinated by them.

In late 2009, eScholarship recast itself as a full-scale "publishing platform," which drew strength from the reputation of its source - the University of California system. Although this is not the only example of a library-sponsored publishing service with university imprimatur, it is certainly one of the most high profile experiments. The evolution of library-based online repositories and their current transformation into fullscale publishing platforms is a prime example of how contributors can expand their role and move into new "zones of progressive release". Digital librarians' publishing solutions are guided by two objectives: first, to empower authors, and second, to create robust, collaborative blocs of institutions that share expertise and improve access. These are new "treatments" that address the changing needs of academic publishing. Publishers are rushing to reinvigorate their relationships with authors, but to some degree they are playing a game of catch-up.

CONVERGENCE AND DIVERGENCE: STRATEGIES AND EXAMPLES

Recent events in these two fields reveal several interesting trends, not only in strategic planning but also in the underlying thinking of leading commentators. Although there is considerable ferment and thus many trends underway, there are four areas where publishers and digital librarians face similar challenges. The strategic decisions that each group makes in the coming years will have significant impact on their long-term futures. First, the hurdles to publishing a well-packaged text artifact are dropping rapidly. The result has been that authors, both in the academic and popular literature spheres, now have the option of creating their own digital artifacts without publishers' assistance.

Many already manage online presences and engage in dialogue with readers. In response publishers and digital librarians are testing strategies that reinforce their own roles. Second, the disruptive nature of digital media has forced publishers and digital librarians to evaluate their own native skill sets in a new light. The library profession's core competencies - collection development, information counselling, interpretation and preservation - involve in-depth analysis of information resources. Yet librarians already format, revise, copy-edit and even print bibliographies, scholarly e-journals, festschrift, and full-scale books in many cases.

As these content-intensive roles become more important, research libraries have responded by creating senior management positions with titles such as director of digital scholarly publishing, director of digital publishing, or director of built content. These positions carry responsibility for assessing new opportunities to publish, as well as assisting research faculty in doing so themselves. Publishers also have the opportunity to review what they do well, re-evaluating existing functions to include new services such content aggregation, developing much-enlarged Web presences, taking on custodial roles and offering services for long-term preservation of their own built content. The technological hurdles to adding new services of this nature are just as low for publishers as they are for librarians who are involved in digital publishing. Both groups are limited chiefly by imagination, by perceived commitments to doing "business as usual," and by the high cost of retraining their already-well-trained workforces to take on new tasks in addition to their existing workflows.

Third, both publishers and digital librarians are looking beyond the boundaries of their own fields of expertise for new ideas and strategies. For example, new social media have carried a heavy impact on the news industry, and both librarians and publishers have studied newspapers as a cautionary tale. News media were one of the first zones where readers began "talking back" to the press and contributing substantive new content. The Blogosphere has also attracted interest, although it increasingly produces voluminous and cyclical "blooms" of creative work that are followed by inactivity and the formation of "dead zones." This pattern suggests that new media are only as vibrant as the minds that are driving them forward. However, over time the Blogosphere has become firmly established as an effective platform for commentary, news, cultural critique and debate.

The Blogosphere's experience implies that longer-term value takes time to emerge as a new technology matures. Fourth, both groups have come to realise that as digital convergence has accelerated, bold action is required. As a consequence, the pace of intellectual thought that is devoted to innovation has also accelerated. There is also greater acceptance that bold actions may succeed or fail, yet they must be attempted to gain new knowledge and expertise. Both groups show evidence of complex responses to the necessity of taking bold action, because both groups believe that they must protect legacy print programmes, whether as book sales or print collections, even as they step into new digital futures. This is a difficult balancing act, because reader and user community loyalty may be challenged as risks are taken. These four trends illustrate the turmoil, and indeed, the excitement of the times for both publishers and librarians. They also illustrate how each group is operating on the knowledge creation continuum, and how they might choose convergent or divergent strategies when compared to each other.

Convergent Strategies

With respect to convergent strategies, publishers and digital librarians are aware that their core competencies must now include a robust and dynamic "conversation" with their readers, collaborators and user communities. Although this may seem obvious during the Internet era, it Nonetheless symbolises a major challenge for established players on the knowledge creation continuum.

New ideas and new technologies, commonly known as "Web 2.0", currently emphasize ubiquitous interaction in a wide variety of locations and via a long list of tools, ranging from desktop computers to "smartphones." Among publishers, this interactive paradigm and the tools it has spawned have caused a seismic shift in thinking.

A book's usefulness is no longer limited to the experience of reading it; it now has a lifespan that can take many forms, involve communities in addition to solo readers, and last for years. In response publishers have launched serious attempts to enter the Web 2.0 sphere. Likewise, digital librarians have seen their print-based mission expand exponentially to include not only the finished works of scholarship and literature, but also the artifacts created by the overall process of creating scholarship, from start to finish. Library responses also include innovative combinations of digital collections and community-building features, such as allowing commentary, running newsfeeds, and adding Wikis to facilitate dialogue. Publishers continue to focus on sales and profits, and they are experimenting with social media to increase revenue.

Two strategies dominate the landscape: narrowcasting and community-subscriber services. Narrowcasting refers to the strategy of discovering discrete markets or user communities who share strong interest in very specific literature, and then offering them targeted products that are based on market analysis. This approach is greatly assisted by "viral marketing," a common term in the Internet era, which describes how news of events or products can travel very quickly, even circumnavigating the globe in a matter of hours in some instances. Narrowcasting would be paired with general marketing strategies, just as print sales would be complemented by e-book sales, still a small revenue stream. Community-subscriber based strategies also make explicit publishers' new role as their own distribution outlets, joining bookstores, libraries and online firms such as Amazon in direct consumer outreach. Direct outreach is another example of treatment substitution, as it establishes a new zone of service on the knowledge creation continuum for publishers, shifting them further into the zone of distribution and perhaps even preservation.

Recent developments in textbook publishing provide evidence of innovative approaches by publishers and digital librarians, who are exploring classroom teaching aids. It is now possible to print textbooks or sections of them on demand, use e-readers to read them, or purchase printed readers, and the entire idea of how textbooks support teaching is rapidly evolving. Publishers are now perfecting "portal" style learning zones on the Web, which are based on textbooks but include many added features, including unbundled chapters, added teaching aids and accompanying training modules. Interestingly, 55 per cent of students still prefer to buy the textbook in print as part of their study plan.

Meanwhile, digital librarians are also involved in teaching portals, and they have been perfecting e-reserve systems and new formats for class e-readers. Finally, publishers are beginning to show interest in managing their backlists more along the lines of a repository or collection of resources. However, whether publishers will take up archiving and preserving content remains uncertain. Once again, networked information technologies have lowered the hurdles to creating online archives. But in practical terms, taking on an archival role would require publishing staff to learn new skills, or recruit new talent to join the firm. Early evidence suggests that publishers have not fully embraced the link between the process of acquiring, editing and selling books and the long-term value of archiving the material. This further suggests that publishers continue to regard themselves as facilitators of the early stages of a book's lifespan, but not as the custodians of its entire lifespan.

Divergent Strategies

There is a large common ground of shared strategies among publishers and digital librarians, derived primarily from the interactive nature of social media, and how it may be adapted for research or to enhance popular literature. However, the points of divergence between the two groups are pronounced. Divergent strategies flow directly from the history of each group. Digital librarians are working very hard to preserve and advance the role of managed knowledge resources, branded by the library, as part of the teaching process. In addition to experimentation with e-reserves and e-readers, they are now staking a large claim on the full-service teaching Web "portals." Open-source instructional portals now include a variety of added functions, including the ability at attach related files, images and simulations.

They also operate as eportfolios for students that follow them throughout their academic careers, and as information management tools for the faculty. Academic librarians perceive important new roles for information services in these learning spaces. Academic librarians are also brainstorming about ways to enhance "built" content that is created by the faculty—a key zone of knowledge creation where libraries may assume the role of digital publishers. The opportunities are vast, as pre-publication content creation encompasses the supporting information, texts and data sets that lead to finished work. Strategies to preserve this knowledge base are rapidly taking shape, and they are evidence of innovative thinking about librarian core competencies. What is more, the library profession's original core competencies—particularly collection development and classification—gain new relevance and importance as digital publishing moves to the forefront. Metadata schemes are vital tools for managing vast amounts of digital assets. The prevailing scheme, the Metadata Enhanced Technical Standard (METS), has seen heavy involvement by digital librarians; it ensures that metadata are portable and stay attached to a digital artifact, allowing the metadata and the object they describe to migrate over time. In contrast, publishers are in the early stages of harnessing XML to manage content more flexibly.

The most significant divergent characteristic between publishers and digital librarians has been librarians' willingness to enter into collaborative alliances, launching aggressive outreach to faculty authors, building political lobbying groups, and forming consortia that negotiate for better prices. They also have become software developers at their host universities, emphasising open-source computing. Ming-xing Huang envisions even more broad alliances, called "Digital Library Alliances"—which would enable academic libraries and their partners to enhance digitisation initiatives and search capabilities in ways that mimic large commercial firms such as Google. Digital librarians have also sought explicit partnerships with publishers themselves, when a shared goal could be seen. For example, the California Digital Library (CDL) entered into an early agreement with the Berkeley Electronic Press (BePress)—a full service journal publishing solution. Conversely, publishers' efforts to form large-scale collaborations have taken more measured steps.

With respect to libraries, collaborative efforts most often take the shape of advisory committees, which meet with editors and publishers once or twice per year. This has been a useful process, contributing to several significant joint efforts, such as the Wiley Online Library. Wiley's new "learning space" includes extensive links to library services for training and other assistance in using the aggregation of content. Digital librarians could afford to choose a collaborative stance, because they have been able to draw on strong relationships with their user communities. Historically, library patrons would visit a library in person, creating opportunities for a direct, personal relationship with welltrained professional staff. Armed with very good metrics on what library patrons actually need and how they prefer to gain access to resources, digital librarians are exploring how to create "user experiences" that reinforce a bond between the library and the user. Just as important, the library profession conceptualised the digital library as a matrix of content, services and human interactions from the earliest planning process.

In essence they have argued that a digital library is far more than a content platform; it is an entire community. For example, facilitating and teaching how to use of information services, whether print or online, is a measurable core competency for librarians. They have argued that technology should enhance human connectivity, rather than replace it, and they have backed up this claim with solid e-metrics showing how people are using libraries.

This assertion of the digital library as community is not nearly as evident in the professional literature of publishing. However, publishers are beginning to reach similar realisations about digital media, and are examining different approaches. As online publishing creates new synergies between print and electronic artifacts, the book gains a broader venue for discovery: the Web itself. Publishers continue to evaluate reader responses to books and related Web sites; and while print books will continue to exist, new zones are opening up for books to grow via Web sites, as e-books, and as subjects of reader forums. If indeed these trends follow their current course, the digital or Web version of a given book may eventually become the "master copy of record."

COLLABORATE, COMPETE, OR BOTH

Digital librarians possess all of the tools and expertise needed to compete directly with publishers. As universities accelerate their plans to create open-source journals and lend their imprimatur to them, digital librarians may take key leadership roles in managing the new archives and repositories, perhaps even the most central role of content owner. If so, they will be building upon existing relationships with the faculty; the two groups work in close proximity and in many cases share research interests.

Digital libraries also share the advantage of their host institution's imprimatur. This prestige enables them to expand their initiatives and to gain institutional support in doing so. This trend is already underway; if it accelerates, the trend would carry multiple benefits for digital librarians. First, it would cement and formalise their new role as a digital publisher within the academy. Second, the new status conferred by the role of digital publisher will provide digital librarians with a fresh opportunity to argue the value points of their longstanding core competencies.

Third, recognition of editorial work as a library skill will advance the professional status of digital librarians in the eyes of the research faculty and within the university administration. All of these enhancements to the status of digital librarians within the academy are excellent examples of "treatment substitution" as described by Abbott. Not only is the publisher role being offered by a competing group - digital librarians - it is also being used as a springboard to advance the status of the library profession as a whole.

Impetus for Collaboration

Even though digital libraries' enhanced imprimatur strengthens their chances of becoming effective digital publishers, evidence indicates that they remain quite receptive to collaboration, often proposing complimentary services in dialogue with publishers. This suggests that digital librarians could become partners in more ambitious alliances with publishers, structuring them to preserve revenue streams while advancing user access.Such a strategy would serve as a means for using digital media to find solutions to the longstanding problems of the former print-only era, with advantages for both parties. At present, digital librarians are exploring strategies to manage the entire lifespan of knowledge creation and the materials that lead to a finished work.

These include data sets, simulations, and Non--text artifacts of every sort. It is also increasingly common for research libraries to manage their own data functions and image collections, and work closely with other campus organisations that are involved in similar work. The role of data manager is being assumed by many innovators, not only at colleges and universities but also at the Library of Congress and other national-level collections. The digital librarian - as-data manager could be a very powerful ally for publishers who seek to transform their books into extended "dialogues" with readers, including related data resources and coherent and portable metadata management tools.

Collaboration as Revenue Protection

Much is made of the "scholarly journals crisis" and the imbroglios, both legal and rhetorical, that it has engendered; yet the crisis has also revealed how the best minds in both the publishing world and library profession view the economics associated with their mission.

As the difficult issues of pricing academic journals have been addressed, publishers have also learned more about how digital librarians view the future, and digital librarians have gained a much deeper understanding of the travails of publishing. This could lead to shared understandings and strategic alliances that bring both groups together, as they confront changing markets for academic and consumer-oriented publishing. Publisher-librarian collaborations will stimulate fresh perspectives about where value is being generated for both partners.

Revenue protection is vital for publishers, and need not come at the cost of fair use and related user benefits, which digital librarians seek to protect. Pricing models for electronic publishing vary dramatically, and have been the site of much tinkering over the years. It is unclear at this time which pricing models are going to be the most effective for publishers, as scholarly communications evolve, and consumer behaviour changes. A digital library perspective on value and pricing could be crucial for publishers as they attempt to create new markets and new revenue streams. Finally, evolving perceptions of how markets work in the digital era may encourage knowledge creators and providers to work together.

Long-standing beliefs about how to sell any type of consumer product are in flux, creating new opportunities to reframe markets for particular advantage to particular players. As a result, many thinkers who study organisations and markets are now exploring new models for understanding business practices.

The metaphor of the "supply chain" - which guides how goods or services move forward, from creation to the market - has limited ability to explain how business can operate in a networked and digital environment. In response, researchers are re-imagining the supply chain as a "web" of relationships, which spreads in many directions, and can create new revenue streams even as established revenue streams fade. The print publishing process is quite linear and so publishers continue to find the supply chain paradigm useful, but at the same time, the web of relationships is a useful means for studying the impact of new media. These competing paradigms may influence how each group forms strategies and views collaboration as opposed to competition.

Competition and its Consequences

There are compelling arguments for publishers and digital librarians to join forces in response to the digital era. But at the same time, modern society thrives on competition and the evolution of the Internet has been heavily influenced by innovation, as well as anticipation for the "next big thing."

On one side, a long-term, deeply rooted publisher-library coalition could save both parties considerable time and resources; yet on the other side, if either group devises a matrix of strategies for fully assuming the other's role while preserving its own, that group would gain a whole new level of prestige.

The shape and makeup of digital libraries would be heavily affected by such an outcome, no matter which group were to prevail. Library education provides an example of how core competencies can be repurposed to gain strategic advantage. A career in libraries requires an accredited master's degree, often accompanied by a second subject-area degree. This level of education is comparable to that of most editorial staff. Publishing practices are widely known, further easing the assumption of a publishing role.

Digital librarians who work in large institutions already edit newsletters, bibliographies and even book series. Moreover, digital librarians can partner with academics and administrators who have resources to underwrite publishing programmes at research universities, this trend is well underway. Publishers also may see advantage in taking on roles currently found in the sphere of libraries, for many of the same reasons.

The rigours of publishing require outreach, interpretation of markets, and management of large backlists. With low barriers to the creation of repositories and value-added "collections" of knowledge, it is reasonable to argue that digital librarians' role in collection development could shift to publishers, along with enhanced public service functions via the Internet. Since, publishers understand market dynamics and sales strategies, the arsenal of strategy at their disposal is significant.

INTEGRATED INFORMATION ACCESS TECHNOLOGY FOR DIGITAL LIBRARIES: ACCESS ACROSS LANGUAGES, PERIODS, AND CULTURES

Physical libraries store materials written in various languages, at various periods in history, and dealing with various cultures. As a result, large digital library projects such as Europeana, World Digital Library, HathiTrust, and Google Book Search have collections spanning different languages, periods, and cultures.

This diversity complicates information access, in part because the grammars, vocabularies, and scripts of languages usually change significantly over time. This chapter presents our approach to providing cross-language access that accounts for this evolution of languages over periods ranging from ancient to modern and even considers cultural differences. It also presents our method for providing integrated access to multiple digital libraries, archives, and museums by automatically mapping between different metadata schemas.

TRADITIONAL MONGOLIAN SCRIPT DIGITAL LIBRARY (TMSDL)

In recent years the importance of digital cultural heritage preservation has been increasing in the Asia-Pacific region as well as worldwide. This part provides a summary of the recent achievements of the Traditional Mongolian Script Digital Library (TMSDL), which aims to preserve over 800 years of historical records written in traditional Mongolian for future use and to make them available for public viewing. There are over 50,000 registered manuscripts and historical records written in traditional Mongolian script stored in the National Library of Mongolia.

About 21,100 of them are handwritten documents and over 9400 of those are related to the history of Mongolia. Despite the importance of keeping old historical materials in good conditions, the Mongolian environment for material storage is not suitable for keeping historical records for a long time.

An efficient and effective way to preserve and protect materials of historical importance while making them publicly available is to digitise them and create a digital library. Mongolian is spoken by most of the Mongolian population as well as by Inner Mongolians and other groups of people who live in several provinces of China and the Russian Federation. It is one of the many languages of the Mongol-Altaic family. Mongolians have used numerous writing systems, and traditional Mongolian script is the longest surviving script.

Although the Mongolian language has also been written in Chinese characters, Phags-pa script, Soyombo script, Horizontal square script, Latin, and Cyrillic script by the end of the 20th century the traditional Mongolian script had made an official, government-decreed return.At the result, modern Mongolian language has two distinct writing systems: Cyrillic and traditional Mongolian. The sounds of words changed as the Mongolian language evolved, but the spelling remained unchanged.

Thus was created a difference between written Mongolian and spoken Mongolian. However, in 1946 in Mongolia the Cyrillic script was adopted with two additional characters. At that time the spelling of modern Mongolian in the Cyrillic alphabet was based on the pronunciation of the dialect spoken by the Khalkha, a subgroup of the Mongols.

This was a radical change and alienated the Mongolian people from their culture and historical archives written in traditional Mongolian script.

Traditional Mongolian script preserves a more ancient language and reflects the Mongolian language spoken in the ancient period, while modern Mongolian reflects pronunciation differences in modern dialects. Traditional Mongolian is a distinct dialect with grammar different from that of modern Mongolian.The traditional Mongolian script is written vertically, from top to bottom, in columns advancing from left to right. This script is the writing system for the Mongolian language and has four derivative scripts: Todo, Manchu, Vaghintara, and Sibe (Xibe). The Todo script was used by the Oirats and Kalmyks, and the Manchu script was a writing system in the Qing dynasty. The Sibe script is used in Xinjiang, in the northwest of China.

The Vaghintara script was used by the Buryats. Like Arabic, traditional Mongolian is a contextual script where letters are cursively joined and have initial, medial, and final presentation forms for the same letter. In most cases the letters join together along a vertical stem, but in the case of certain consonants that lack a trailing vertical stem they may form a single ligature with a following vowel.

In addition to these cursive and positional forms, many letters also have variant forms used in accordance with spelling and grammatical rules. Using modern Mongolian to retrieve information from traditional Mongolian documents is not a simple task because the Mongolian language has changed substantially over time. The traditional Mongolian script digital library (TMSDL), which is based on Greenstone Digital Library Software (GSDL) and accepts modern Mongolian query input, will help the user access materials written in traditional Mongolian.

Ancient-to-Modern Information Retrieval

Thanks to advances in innovative information technologies and to the popularity of the Internet, many ancient historical documents are being digitised and made publicly available. We therefore want to offer an "ancient-to-modern information retrieval" method that considers language differences over time. We aimed to develop a retrieval system with which a user can access cross-period and crossscript ancient document databases by using a query in a modern language.

There has been little research on information retrieval techniques for historical documents, and almost none of the breakthroughs in research on information retrieval and information access have aimed at retrieving information in the native language from ancient, crossperiod and/or cross-script foreign language documents.Few approaches that could be considered a cross-period information retrieval have been proposed, and there has been little research on information retrieval techniques for historical documents. Focused on modern and archaic German and developed a retrieval method that considers the spelling differences and variations over time.

Considered the spelling and pronunciation differences between ancient and modern Dutch, while and considered the spelling differences and variations between modern and archaic German. Considered spelling variations of English and German historical texts. In general, the main challenge for historical European languages like Dutch, English, and German is the spelling variants. We applied an "ancient-to-modern information retrieval" method to ancient Mongolian historical collections written in traditional Mongolian script. Some ancient historical documents in traditional Mongolian script have recently been digitised and made publicly available, and text-display support for traditional Mongolian script and the input locale is enabled in Windows Vista and Windows 7.

The Uniscribe–Unicode Scripts Processor driver was updated to support OpenType advanced typographic functionality of complex text layouts, such as traditional Mongolian script. The situation for an ancient Mongolian language is a bit different because the Mongols have changed their writing systems several times and more than once have made language reforms that eliminate a difference between written and spoken language.

Proposed Approach

To cope with cross-period and cross-script Mongolian documents, we propose a simple model that retrieves traditional Mongolian documents using modern Mongolian query. The structure of the TMSDL, with the proposed "ancient-to-modern information retrieval" approach is shown in figure. We utilised the existing approach and improved the "retrieval technique with the modern Mongolian query on traditional Mongolian text" by integrating a dictionary. A prototype of the TMSDL, which could be considered a cross-period information retrieval system, has been developed.

The retrieval method of the TMSDL considers cross-period differences in the writing systems of the ancient and modern Mongolian languages.

Adding a dictionary-based query translation approach to the translation module was a major improvement that takes into account age differences in the writing systems of the ancient and modern Mongolian languages. We utilised the developing online version of Tsevel's concise Mongolian dictionary under the Creative Commons Attribution-Non-commercial-Share Alike 3.0 Unported license. Tsevel's dictionary was printed in 1966 and is one of two Mongolian dictionaries with definitions written in modern and traditional Mongolian available on the market. It includes over 30,000 words in Cyrillic and traditional Mongolian script.

To boost the quality of the translation, the "ancient-to-modern information retrieval" approach matches query terms to words in Tsevel's dictionary. If no exact match is found, the "retrieval technique with the modern Mongolian query on traditional Mongolian text", which is based on grammatical rules, is used.The proposed model allows the users to access documents written in an ancient language with a query input in a modern language.The query in modern Mongolian is translated into a query in traditional Mongolian script. The query in traditional Mongolian is then submitted as a retrieval query for traditional Mongolian script collections.

Chronological books of ancient Mongolian kings, Genghis Khan, and the Mongol Empire such as the Altan Tobci and the Story of Asragch etc, are available in the TMSDL with a modern Mongolian input interface. A database of such historical records with a modern language query input will help someone conducting research on the history of the High Middle Ages understand 13th-14th century history of Asia. The modern Mongolian input in the TMSDL is illustrated in figure.

Experimental Evaluation

In an experiment we conducted in order to check the correctness of translations from the modern language to the ancient one, we retrieved traditional Mongolian documents when using modern Mongolian query input in Cyrillic. Because of the large number of unfamiliar ancient proper nouns, terms, and their variants in ancient historical documents, we faced the challenge of measuring recall and precision as well as the challenge of defining relevant documents.

To check whether a queries in modern Mongolian were translated correctly, we selected queries the most frequently appearing words that are pronounced or written differently in modern and traditional Mongolian and compared their word counts in the search results with the corresponding word counts in "Qad-un undusun quriyangγui altan tobci - Textological Study". This textological study contains a detailed analysis of traditional Mongolian word frequencies in the Altan Tobci.

We compared the word count in the search results for two cases: one using only grammatical-rule-based translation, and the other additionally using a dictionary. The version with dictionary integration translated and retrieved 86 per cent of the input queries, whereas the grammatical-rule-based version retrieved only 61 per cent of the input queries. Even with the dictionary, however, 64 per cent of the input queries in modern Mongolian did not match with a word count that was less than or greater than the actual number because of possible errors of translation, grammatical inflection, and text digitisation, or limitations of the indexer and retrieval function. Comparisons of the retrieval results are illustrated in figure, and detailed retrieval results for sample query terms are shown in table along with modern and ancient forms, their meanings, and the word counts.

The TMSDL integrated with a dictionary translated and retrieved 86 per cent of the input queries, but only 22 per cent were retrieved without error.

Summary and Future Directions

In this part, we introduced the TMSDL that utilises cross-period and cross-script digital collections and that enables historical documents written in an ancient language to be accessed using a query in a modern language. The proposed system is suitable for full text searches on databases containing cross-period and cross-script documents.

Such research would involve extensive research in an ancient language that users and humanities researchers may or may not understand. It could apply to humanities researchers who are conducting research on ancient culture and looking for relevant historical materials written in that ancient language.

CROSS-PERIOD INFORMATION RETRIEVAL FROM ANCIENT JAPANESE HISTORICAL MATERIALS

Libraries, governments, and major internet providers have recently begun forming consortiums to preserve historical documents stored in libraries. This means that more and more old-text content will soon be accessible on the Internet.

The huge amount of knowledge in old documents is obviously as important as that in the recently created digital documents typically available on the web because old documents contain the wisdom of our ancestors.

Retrieving important information from old documents is not always easy, however, because languages and cultures change substantially over time. To access documents written in ancient Japanese by using a query in modern Japanese, for example, we need a cross-period information retrieval system based on a cross-period Japanese dictionary.

Construction of Ancient-modern Dictionary

Ancient documents in text form are being digitised, and the prevalence of search engines has made the retrieval of information from digital documents a familiar procedure. Current search engines, however, may be not able to acquire proper retrieval results for ancient Japanese documents because there is no ancient-modern Japanese dictionary with sufficient entries.

One reason for this is that the Japanese writing system has no term separation. That is, neither current nor ancient Japanese writing uses space or punctuation to separate words. A morphological analyser like ChaSen or MeCab, both of which need a modern term dictionary, is usually used to do term separation for modern Japanese, but there is no ancient-modern word dictionary with enough entries and there are no morphological analysers for ancient Japanese. This makes it difficult to do term separation for ancient Japanese.

We propose a method for constructing an ancient-modern Japanese dictionary by using a parallel corpus of ancient writings and their translations in modern Japanese. The parallel corpus thus consists of pairs of documents in the same language but in ancient and modern versions of that language. From this corpus we try to acquire pairs of equivalent archaic and modern words by analysing the frequencies of word occurrences in a sentence in ancient Japanese and its corresponding modern Japanese translation.

Related Work

Two methods for extracting pairs of equivalent words from a bilingual corpus in modern languages have already been proposed, one using a parallel corpus and the other using a Non--parallel corpus. In the method using a parallel corpus, equivalence is based on statistical correlation determined using co-occurrence frequency, contingency tables, etc.

In the method using a non-parallel corpus, equivalence is based on the context similarity of translation candidates.The method described here, however, identifies pairs of equivalent words not in two modern languages but in modern and archaic Japanese.

As there are few modern language translations of ancient writings, it is difficult to collect a parallel corpus of ancient writings and their translations in modern language.

Some famous ancient writings, though, have been translated into the modern forms of their languages. We therefore identify pairs of equivalent words in modern and archaic Japanese by using a parallel corpus comprising famous ancient Japanese writings and their translations in modern Japanese.

Proposed Method of Dictionary Construction

Many well-known ancient writings have modern-language translations, and some of these translations are digitised and open to the public. In a parallel corpus comprising writings in an ancient and modern language, one can usually determine which modern-language sentence corresponds to which ancient-language sentence.

A modern word equivalent to an archaic word in an ancient-language sentence is likely to appear in the modern-language translation of that sentence, and vice versa. Word pairs with high co-occurrence frequency in ancient and modern sentence pairs are thus likely to be translation equivalents.

In our method we detect similarities in the appearance tendencies of modern and archaic words in each sentence pair and then use these similarities to extract equivalent pairs of ancient and modern words.

One of the drawbacks of the N-gram approach is that there

will be many overlaps. On the other hand, an advantage of the N-gram approach is that it can divide the strings even if the language of the string, like ancient Japanese, does not have explicit delimiters between words. This is why we divide the archaic sentences into N-grams and treat those N-grams as words.

Word Extraction from Parallel Corpus

We use morphological analysis to extract words from the modern-language translations of the ancient writings, and because there is no morphological analyser for ancient Japanese. We divide the archaic sentences into N-grams and treat those N-grams as archaic words. An N-gram is a sequence of N characters from a given string. We first extract the first N characters from the target string and then shift one character and extract N characters from the target string. We repeat this shifting-and-extracting process until the Nth character in the N-gram is the last character of the target string. For example, the string "corpus" would be divided into the following four 3-grams: cor, orp, rpu, and pus.

Calculation of the Co-occurence of Modern and Archaic Words

This process is conducted for archaic and modern term pairs to appear in the equivalent sentences. In other words, the term pairs appearing in the equivalent sentences are considered as the co-occurring terms. In each sentence pair, the archaic and modern term pairs are created for every possible pairs of extracted modern terms and archaic N-grams. We count the occurrence frequency of each term pairs. This frequency is the co-occurrence frequency of archaic and modern term pairs.

Calculation of Similarity about Appearance of Tendency between Modern Term and Archaic Term

For parallel corpus composed two different languages documents such as Japanese and English, "mutual information" is proposed to use for the similarity between each two terms. Our method also adopts "mutual information" in order to calculate similarities about appearance of tendency between modern term and archaic term. The archaic and modern term pairs that have higher value of their mutual information is considered that appearance of tendency between modern term and archaic term is similar. These term pairs have higher possibility that the modern term is relation in translation for the archaic term. We extract term pairs that have higher similarities than some threshold, and consider that these pairs have relation in translation. The mutual information MI of a modern term *t* and an archaic N-gram *g* is given by the following formula.

$$\mathrm{MI}(t,g) = \mathrm{Log}\,\frac{P(t,g)}{P(t)P(g)}$$

Probability P(*t*, *g*) is the probability that the modern term *t* appears in the translation of the archaic sentence in which the archaic N-gram *g* appears, and it can be calculated from the co-occurrence frequency of archaic N-gram *g* and modern term *t*. Probabilities P(*t*) means the probability in the case that the modern term *t* appears in modern sentence.

Probabilities P(*g*) means the probability in the case that the archaic N-gram *g* appears in archaic sentence. Probabilities P(*g*) is able to be acquired from the term frequency of archaic N-gram *g*. The archaic and modern term pairs that have higher value of their mutual information are considered that appearance of tendency between modern term and archaic term is similar.

Extraction of Translation Pairs of Modern and Archaic Words

We extract archaic and modern term pairs that have higher possibilities of relation in translation. However, as the archaic terms of extracted pairs are represented by N-gram, these archaic terms are not always complete archaic term. Some archaic N-gram may be part of archaic term.

Another may be combined parts of some archaic terms. In these cases, we have to restore the archaic N-grams to original archaic terms. These archaic Ngrams are restored to original archaic terms by comparing spellings, term frequency and cooccurrence frequency between another archaic N-gram.

We consider that restored archaic and modern term pairs are related in translation. Finally, we collect these term pairs and construct ancient-modern term dictionary.

Future Directions

We proposed a method for constructing an ancient-modern Japanese dictionary by using a parallel corpus of ancient writings and their translations in modern Japanese.

If an ancientmodern Japanese dictionary with sufficient entries is constructed by the proposed method, we think that the techniques of natural language processing, for example morphological analysis, could be applied for ancient documents digitised in text form. We need to improve the term extracting process in order to reduce the number of unnecessary word pairs, to improve the calculation of similarities of the appearance tendencies of modern and archaic words, and to construct a practical ancient-modern Japanese dictionary.

Cross-period Information Retrieval System

There has been a lot of research on cross-language information retrieval in the last decade. Various approaches—including query translation, document translation, and the use of an intermediate language—has been studied, and adequate retrieval effectiveness has been achieved for some pairs of languages. There has, in contrast, been very little research on information retrieval methods for historical documents, and most of those methods are based on simple keyword matching. Some recently proposed approaches to accessing historical documents consider the evolution of languages and could be regarded as a kind of cross-age information retrieval.

We use the dictionary-based query translation approach because it is the one most effective for cross-language information retrieval. For dictionary-based methods to be effective we need to use precise and comprehensive dictionaries for both the modern and ancient language. We try to find relations between the entries in those dictionaries and to translate the query terms in the modern language into equivalent terms in the ancient language. For this translation process we propose the following method.

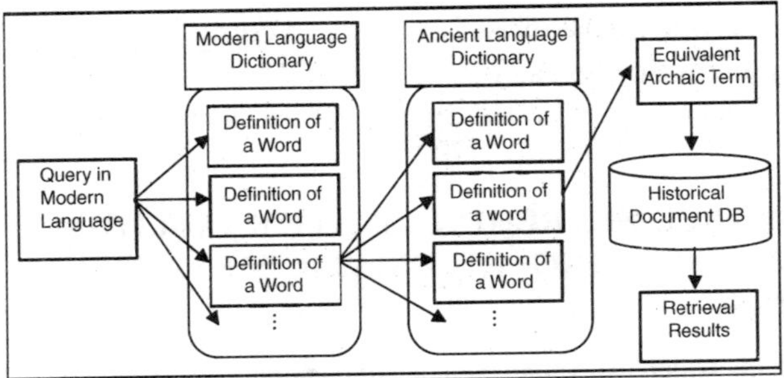

Overview of Proposed Method for Cross-period Information Retrieval.

- For each entry in the modern-language dictionary, we look for an equivalent entry in the ancient language dictionary by calculating the similarities between the definition of the modern word and all the definitions of the archaic words. We can do this using a standard text similarity measure based on the vector space model and the tf-idf term weighting scheme.
- We then take the most similar definition in the ancient language dictionary and regard the dictionary entry (headword) containing that definition as an equivalent of the modern word.
- If there is more than one equivalent entry, we find the one most nearly equivalent to the modern word by using a term association measure such as mutual information to disambiguate the candidate translations.

Implementation

We implemented a cross-period information retrieval system for the Japanese historical document called the *Hyohanki* diary. Written in late Heian era, it is a valuable resource for research on Japanese culture of that time. An example of its original copy is shown in figure. Part of the *Hyohanki* has deteriorated and is missing, but all of the existing pages have been digitised into text format. We need dictionaries in order to translate modern language query words into archaic words. In the case of the *Hyohanki* diary we can use some existing electronic dictionaries available on CD-ROMs. For modern Japanese we use *Kojien*, one of the most famous and comprehensive Japanese language dictionaries. For ancient Japanese we use *Kokugo-Daijiten*, which covers not only modern words but also archaic words.

FEDERATED SEARCHING SYSTEM FOR HUMANITIES DATABASES USING AUTOMATIC METADATA MAPPING

This section provides a summary of our approach to constructing a federated searching system for Japanese humanities databases using automatic metadata mapping.

The goals of our system are:

- To perform metadata mapping automatically for Japanese heterogeneous humanities databases and
- To let users access multiple humanities digital libraries by using only one query input.

This section also addresses the metadata-related challenges facing Japanese humanities databases. Metadata offers library and information science a solution to the problem of describing and managing the massive quantities of explosively increasing digital information. Various types of resources and humanities digital libraries coexist with heterogeneous metadata schemas nowadays, and many different metadata schemas are standardised by international standards organisations. How to deal with the diverse forms of metadata and interoperate is becoming a complex issue for research. There have been efforts to make heterogeneous standards interoperable and utilise multiple metadata standards. According to several different approaches were developed.

Reliable metadata interoperability has not been achieved yet because of the heterogeneity of metadata standards and because of the structural differences between standards. On the other hand, the use of metadata schemas and standards for Japanese humanities digital libraries is a bit tricky. Many metadata schemas of Japanese humanities digital libraries have been accepted in terms of their semantics and content but were developed before the international metadata standards or were developed without considering the international metadata standards and specific encoding methods. Most of the metadata schemas of Japanese humanities digital libraries were not derived from existing international metadata standards, and there is no explicit metadata framework, crosswalk, or metadata registry. It is necessary to understand the semantics of Japanese humanities digital libraries—such as elements, syntax, and structure—in order to perform automatic metadata mapping and achieve metadata interoperability. This section therefore addresses the metadata-related challenges to constructing a federated searching system for Japanese humanities databases.

Metadata Schemas for Japanese Humanities Digital Libraries and their Challenges

Humanities digital libraries and their metadata schemas are very heterogeneous because the humanities cover a variety of disciplines, such as literature, law, history, philosophy, religion, visual and performing arts, anthropology, cultural studies, and linguistics. Achieving metadata interoperability of humanities digital libraries is becoming more crucial in the current information environment, especially in the case of metadata schemas which were not derived from wellknown international metadata standards. One of the differences between western and Japanese databases that is relevant to people interested in constructing a federated searching system is the greater heterogeneity of the metadata schemas of Japanese humanities digital libraries. Many Japanese humanities databases developed metadata schemas based on their domain-specific semantics and content rather than adopt international metadata standards. Moreover, names or labels for metadata attributes/elements are written in Japanese, or labels in Japanese are used as the metadata elements.

The co-existence of nonstandard and heterogeneous metadata schemas makes automatic metadata mapping for Japanese humanities databases a rather challenging task. Another relevant difference is the Japanese writing system(s). Japanese is written in a mixture of three writing systems—one using ideographic symbols, or *kanji*, and the other two using the syllabary scripts *hiragana* and *katakana*—and it is written without explicit word boundaries. The absence of word delimiters makes word segmentation a critical problem in natural language processing for Japanese. Without knowing the boundaries of words in a sentence, any computer system will fail to perform tasks such as automatic metadata mapping. A single kanji can have many pronunciations and be used differently in words comprising two or more kanji. The situation will be much more difficult when collections contain ancient documents because a modern kanji is not always the same as its archaic equivalent. An archaic word written with a single kanji might be equivalent to a modern word written with more than a single modern kanji, or vice versa. Using a modern language query to find information in Japanese documents that are written in modern and archaic Japanese words is a rather challenging task.

Federated Searching System for Japanese Humanities Databases

The conceptual architecture of our proposed federated searching system is shown in figure given below.

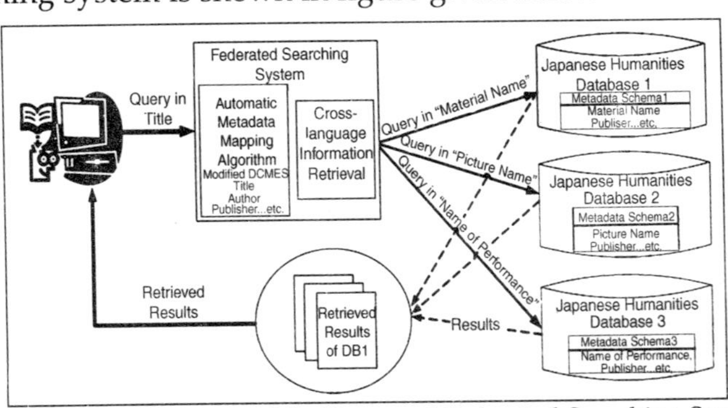

Conceptual Architecture of the Proposed Federated Searching System.

As illustrated above, if a user wants to find a humanities resource with the query word in the title, our system retrieves resources having the query word in the title or any metadata field that is similar to a title or could be treated as a title and retrieves these resources from heterogeneous humanities digital libraries even if those libraries do not provide metadata interoperability or crosswalk and do not support Z39.50 protocol, Search/Retrieve Web service/Search/Retrieve via URL, etc. We are developing a prototype federated searching system of Japanese humanities databases—including the image database of Japanese traditional fine art Ukiyo-e, donated Japanese books database, and old Japanese books database—that are freely accessible in Japanese at the Art Research Center of Ritsumeikan University. We utilised the automatic metadata mapping method of Kimura et al.. This prototype system also has a facility for cross-language searching between English and Japanese, which enables Englishspeaking users to search Japanese databases available only in Japanese.

Automatic Metadata Mapping

In our system the metadata attribute names of heterogeneous Japanese humanities collections in Japanese, the metadata schemas of which are unknown or do not conform to the international standards, are automatically mapped to our modified variant set of the Dublin Core metadata element set. Because CREATOR and CONTRIBUTOR are hard to distinguish in Japanese humanities collections, in the modified DCMES they are unified into the new element AUTHOR. When Japanese humanities metadata schemas are successfully mapped to the modified DCMES, our proposed system enables cross-domain metadata harvesting and federated searches as well as the exchange of metadata. Our automatic metadata mapping method consists of two preprocessing phases and four mapping phases.

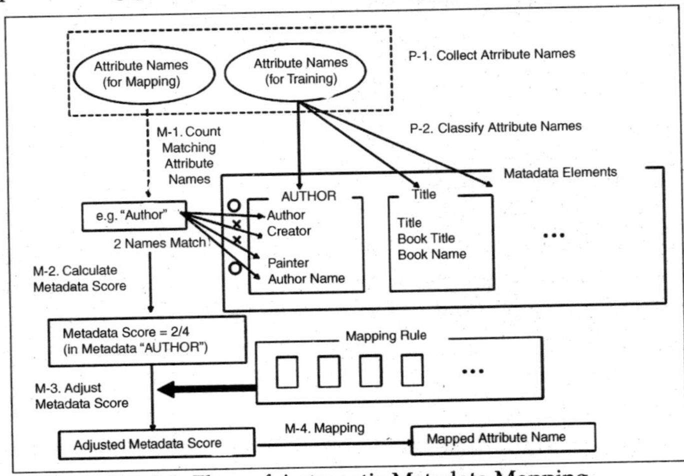

Fig. 8.1. Flow of Automatic Metadata Mapping.

The preprocessing consists of the following steps:

- P-1 Collect attribute names from humanities databases for training and mapping.
- P-2 Classify attribute names for training into appropriate metadata elements manually.

The automatic mapping phase consists of the following steps:

- M-1 Count the number of partial string matches between the attribute name for mapping and each metadata element.
- M-2 Calculate the *metadata score* of each metadata element by dividing the number of partial string matches by the number of attribute names in the metadata element.
- M-3 Adjust the metadata score for each metadata element, if the target attribute name matches one or more *mapping rules*, which consist of some kanji characters that are commonly used and known to be relevant to one or more particular metadata elements.
- M-4 Map the target attribute name to the metadata element that has the highest metadata score.

BRINGING THE DIGITAL LIBRARY DESIGN INTO THE REALM OF ENTERPRISE ARCHITECTURE

Previous digital library research and initiatives have conceptualised and proposed several frameworks for the design, development, evaluation and interaction of digital library systems. Levy and Marshall discussed a work-oriented perspective of digital library research that is based on the work people do, and how digital libraries assist in the completion of work related tasks. Their framework highlights three crucial characteristics of digital libraries: document, technology and work. Moen and McClure identified a framework of five interacting dimensions in digital library of Government Information Locator Service (GILS): policy, users, technology, contents, and standards. The evaluation framework also includes three perspectives, representing the "views" of the stakeholders in the GILS: users, agencies, and the government. Marchionini and Fox identified four dimensions of digital library development: community, technology, service and content. Researchers presented a framework, consisting seven levels, for examining digital libraries: social, institutional, individual, interface, engineering, processing and content. Another holistic framework is presented by Fuhr consisting four major dimensions, namely data/collection, system/technology, users and usage. Sandusky developed a list of six attributes in framing digital library usability research: audience, institution, access, content, services, and design and development. Soergel offered a digital library research framework consisting of three guiding principles and eleven specific themes for research and development.

Researcher introduced 5S and formalisms for Streams, Structures, Spaces, Scenarios, and Societies - as a framework for providing theoretical and practical unification of digital libraries. All these frameworks emphasise the importance of a holistic approach rather than examine digital libraries as a single view, which would be limited in their utility. However, the absence of common frameworks in the digital library development practices undermines the ability to develop and design digital library systems efficiently, to create large-scale collaborative activities, and to communicate the value of the systems to other communities.

Researcher wrote that the broad and deep requirements of digital libraries demand new frameworks and theories in order to understand better the complex interactions among their components. Supporting this claim, the summary report of the Joint NSF-European Union (EU) Working Groups on Future Directions of Digital 1 Libraries Research recommended that "new frameworks and theories be developed in order to understand the complex interactions between the various components in a globally distributed digital library". Formal frameworks are crucial to specify and understand clearly and unambiguously the characteristics, structure, and behaviour of complex information systems such as digital libraries.

The Digital Library Federation (DLF) in 2005 sponsored the formation of the Service Framework Group (SFG) to consider a more systematic, community-based approach to align the functions of digital libraries in fulfilling the needs of information environments. DLF envisaged that digital library functionalities be generated from the library business processes, considering the architectures as information systems with specific business requirements.

It is in this context, and in recognition of visions already underway to align digital library development with the emerging perspective of the Enterprise Architecture, the authors conducted a study that seeks to understand and model the digital library services adopting a framework that give preference to scopes, goal requirements and processes - those concepts already common in Enterprise Architecture processes Abdullah and Zainab regard a digital library as an enterprise that requires architecting.

An Enterprise Architecture for the digital library is a framework or blueprint which shows how the digital library organisation carries out an intended task and how the digital library will or can improve the processes.

It shows how a digital library represents a special workspace for the user community, not only for search and access but also for the process or workflow management, information creation, sharing and exchange, and distributed workgroup communication. In order to identify what is required of a digital library in a specific context, a sound methodology is needed to establish an understanding of the digital library entire structure.

A multi-faceted information services such as digital libraries may be examined along different dimensions and from different perspectives or views of the stakeholders. There is a need to identify potential users, their involvement and roles in the digital library, their attitude towards the technology, their perception of its potential use and how it fits within the digital library goals in general.

ENTERPRISE ARCHITECTURE

In general, Enterprise Architecture is a framework that describes how an organisation develops, manages and uses information technology to optimally support its business functions. Sometimes, the term refers to the group of people responsible for modeling and then documenting the information architecture; other times the term denotes the process of doing this work.

More commonly, Enterprise Architecture refers to the models, documents and reusable items that reflect the actual architecture. In the EA Community Enterprise Architecture is a framework or blueprint for how the organisation achieves the current and future business objectives.It examines business processes, information technology, software and hardware, local and wide area networks, people, operations and projects with an organisation's overall strategy. Each of these strategies has a separate architectural discipline and Enterprise Architecture is the "glue" that integrates each of these disciplines into a cohesive framework.

From these definitions, it is understood that Enterprise Architecture consists of the various structures and processes of an organisation. Following this understanding, it is known that an Enterprise Architecture model is a representation of those structures and processes. A good Enterprise Architecture model will depict the organisation both as it is today and as it is envisioned in the future, and will map the various views representing the architecture to one another.

These views include both business-oriented perspectives as well as technical perspectives. The blueprint or framework of the enterprise would reveal detailed statements and processes that characterised architectural drawings. The detail drawings would be in any form, such as rich pictures, structured charts, data flow diagrams, Unified Modelling Language (UML) activity diagrams, database tables and entity-relationship model.

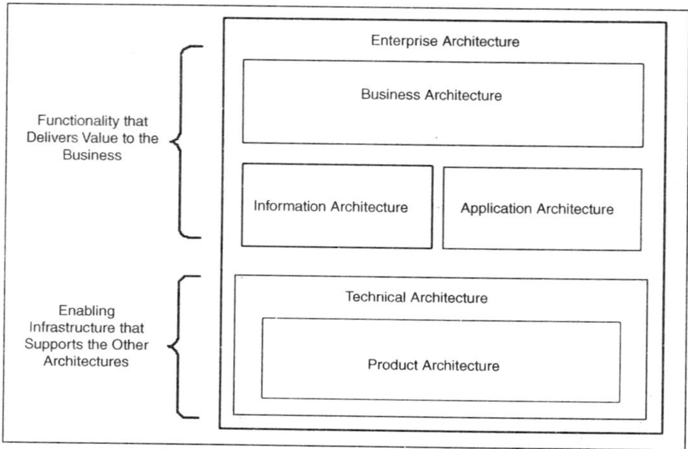

Fig. 8.2. Enterprise Architecture Relationship.

ZACHMAN FRAMEWORK FOR ENTERPRISE ARCHITECTURE

The Zachman Framework is a logical structure for classifying and organising the descriptive representations of the enterprise that are significant to the management of the enterprise, as well as to the development of the enterprise' systems.

The framework uses a grid model to provide a logical structure for classifying and organising the descriptive representation of an enterprise, in six different dimensions, and each dimension can be perceived in five different perspectives. In this framework, the architecture is described across two independent aspects, the rows represent the views of five different types of stakeholders and the columns represent six different aspects of the architecture.

The points of intersection between the rows and the columns form cells. Each of these cells holds important information of the enterprise that needs to be understood and explicitly declared. The Zachman Framework's enterprise design model is presented in figure.

The Zachman Framework for Enterprise Architecture is found suitable to investigate the initial requirements and define the digital library organisation, processes, technology and information flows, as well as ground the design of digital libraries for the following reasons:

- The framework helps to explicitly show the many perspectives that need to be addressed by the digital library. It requires the planner, owner and designer of the digital library to involve the stakeholders to ensure that it meets their needs and will be used. It holistically controls the approach to investigate the user requirements and guides the data gathering techniques.
- The framework requires the involvement of stakeholders, not just the enterprise architects and developers. and ideally this practice is what digital library designers and developers should follow. This aligns with the need to involve stakeholders in digital library design and development.
- The framework is robust enough. It explicitly shows and requires the designer to consider all aspects of the digital library design.
- The framework is generic in nature and can be applied perfectly to digital library organisation. As such it is a flexible framework and it does not impose a method or restrict any user to a set of pre-defined artifacts.

This chapter shows, through a case study, how the three tiers of Zachman Framework - the contextual or planner's perspectives, the conceptual or the owner's perspectives and the logical or the designer's perspectives– are used to design a digital library.

The first two rows or layers are referred to as the Business Architecture for they describe the functions a business performs and the information it uses. The third row refers to the information and the application architecture. The planner is concerned with positioning the digital library in the context of its environment.

This is when the planner enquires about the demographics of the stakeholders, ICT individual differences, their readiness to participate and collaborate, their awareness of the concept of digital libraries and their perception of the digital library initiative.

The owner is interested in the digital library's deliverable and how it will be used. The designer is concerned with how the digital library is to perform its functions.

This involves investigating the resources that are used, the user behaviour of seeking for resources, the experience of searching, the relevance perceived and the problems encountered.

The possible sets of constructs or artifacts to represent the cell content for each cell in the top three rows or layers of the Zachman Framework are presented in table.What How Where Who When Why SCOPE (Contextual) Planner List of things important to the business List of processes the business perform List of location in which the business operate List of people involved in the business List of events significant to the business List of business goals and objectives SCOPE (Contextual) Planner BUSINESS (Conceptual)

Owner Semantic Model Business Process Model Business Logistic Model Work flow model Master Schedule Business Plan BUSINESS (Conceptual) Owner SYSTEM (Logical) Designer Logical Data Model Application Architecture Distributed System Architecture Human Interface Architecture Processing Structure Business Data Model SYSTEM (Logical) Designer TECHNOLOGY (Physical) Builder DETAILED PRESENTA-TION (Out-of-context view) FUNCTIONING ENTERPRISE–The prototype Data Function Network People Time Motivation FUNCTIONING ENTERPRISE–The prototype table. Zachman Framework at the Contextual, Conceptual and Logical Systems Architecture

FORMULATION OF AN INTEGRATED FRAMEWORK FOR THE COLLABORATIVE DIGITAL LIBRARY

Collaborative digital libraries are constructed, collected and organised by a community of users and their functionalities support the information needs and uses of that community. Researchers viewed a digital library as a collaborative working and meeting space of people sharing common interests. Through a case study method, Zachman Framework is used as a basis to investigate the existing stakeholder's conditions and environment that would ensure the reception of a collaborative digital library for urban secondary schools use in Malaysia.

In this digital library environment, students collaboratively build the digital library resources, which indirectly allow members of the community to be aware and be actively involved in local content development.

The collaborative digital library would benefit both the students who would be the creator and publisher of digital project works and the teachers who would be given the experience of managing digital resources.

The multi-method approach used in the case study, to ensure the consideration of all the aspects (dimensions) of a digital library system and the relationship of these dimensions in the framework used, has been reported elsewhere.

Findings were used to populate the Zachman Framework with contextual, conceptual, logical and module diagrams at every intersection between the columns (why, what, who, how, where, when) and the rows (scope, business model, system model).

The framework abstracts the characteristics and features of the digital library based on the following six dimensions:

- Motivation factor, requiring the planner and owner to solicit answers to the "why" question, why there is need for the digital library? Why does the current business process need special handling such as those provided by the digital library?
- Data factor abstracts the "what" aspects of the digital library. What data that is currently handled by the stakeholders? What format would the data take in the digital library environment? What are the characteristics of the data used, processed, stored and presented or disseminated in terms of quality, accuracy, usability, description and organisation?
- People factor looks at the "who" questions or the roles of people in the digital project environment. Who will be instructing? Who will be handling the data? Who will be reporting the collated or processed data? Are the players in the digital library environment "ready" to

participate and contribute to the digital library initiative? Are they able to do so?

- Function or Process factor defines the "how" of the activities in the digital environment. How will users search for data, how will they store the data? How will students write, present and submit their project report? How will the teachers ensure that the students know what is required? How do they grade the reports? How will they keep the reports submitted for the specified time required by the Malaysian Ministry of Education? How can the school library or resource centre accommodate these reports?
- Place or Networks looks at the "where" factor. Where will the digital library be located? Where will it be accessed by the stakeholders?
- Time looks at the "when" aspects of the digital library. When will submission of reports take place? This is useful for designing schedules, the processing and control architecture and timing systems.

The next section illustrates the use of Zachman Framework in design of the digital library, focusing on all six dimensions of the framework from three perspectives. Each of these dimensions is investigated from the perspective of the planner, owner and designer of the digital library.

These perspectives help ensure that everything relevant to the digital library enterprise is covered. The columns, comprising the six dimensions, are arranged so that the most important column or the focus of attention is presented first. At the end, the outcome would be in the form of listings and diagrams depicting the scope, business and system model of the digital library. Rows 4, 5 and 6 are beyond the scope of this chapter.

CASE ANALYSIS OF ZACHMAN FRAMEWORK FOR THE COLLABORATIVE DIGITAL LIBRARY

Motivation: Why the Digital Library is Needed

Why (Motivation) column of Zachman Framework extracts the motivation of the people that support the realisation of the digital library. This reveals the reasons for creating the digital library, as well as the establishment of goals, objectives and business plan of the digital library. The authors felt motivation aspect (stakeholders' motivation) of the framework should be first populated and given the most importance. The case study revealed that the educational community is ready to collaboratively build the digital library as reflected by the following findings:

- Students are "Internet ready", as indicated by:
  - High home computer ownership as such they are ready to utilise the digital library;
  - High Internet penetration either at home, school, cyber cafes or friend's houses;
  - A high number of students either have 3-4 years or more than 5 years experience in computer usage;
  - Students regularly go online, between either every alternate days or everyday.
- Students are "digital ready" as indicated by their awareness, experience in using and preferring digital sources. The survey indicates that all students know how to word process; they know how to prepare slide presentations or draw using the computer, edit images, create multimedia and scan images, create web pages, database or undertake simple programming. This results show that they are aware and competent in handling digital resources, which is necessary when using digital library.
- Students are also moderately "Web ready" as they know how to use the web. Although most had no formal training, they learn how to use the Web by self-teaching, from books and people. The students also learn how to find sources on their own, from their parents and siblings or from their classmates and friends.
- Students are ready to collaboratively develop digital resources as they indicated sharing the resources they create or found with their friends either by e-mailing the URLs of web sites, informing others through chat room or social networks or creating links to web sites.

- Some students are "ready web publishers", as many of them either maintain a group web page, have their own personal web page or have been creating page pages for others. The results also show that the students have experience in creating digital resource over the Internet using webpage creator tools or HTML to develop their sites.
- Students do use the Internet for school related assignments or as a major source for their school project. Students sampled highly use the Internet resources to get information for the following subjects, History, Science and Geography. The results indicate that students believe that the Internet helps them with their school work.
- All students feel that there is a need for digital library of local information and feel that this would definitely benefit them. The results indicated very significant correlation between positive perception of the digital library with high Internet use, length of Internet experience, accessibility of Internet from home high self ratings of Internet skills.
- Teachers in the case study see the value of digital resources and online publishing for their students. They expressed the willingness to play the role as a facilitator in the digital library environment. They were keen on the digital library because students could contribute original works to be shared with other students, especially where some local contents are not available in textbooks. They believed students would be more careful in preparing their project report if they make it available to wider audience in the digital library environment.
- Teachers felt that a digital library would solve problem of storage and retrieval of reports submitted Since, project reports kept in resource room could only be retrieved by class name and level, and difficult to be retrieved by subject or topics of report or by specific student's name.

- The school's infrastructural facilities are ready to support a digital library as students can gain access to computers at self-accessed learning centres, especially for students and teachers who do not have computers or Internet access at their homes.

The findings indicated that the readiness factors serve as motivating indicators, goals and objectives that support the plan for developing the digital library.

Figure presents the motivating factors that support the plan of the collaborative digital library. The findings of the case study were plugged into the first three rows of the motivational aspect of Zachman Framework.

In Row 1, the Planner's goals and objectives are defined in the form of vision statement that provides the strategic direction for the digital library.The digital library will support secondary students' information needs in conducting research projects through project-based learning (PBL).

In PBL, students interpret, analyse, synthesise, generate, and evaluate information about a topic, collaborate with others, and produce a report.To support students in these types of activities, a full complement of tools is needed to meet the unique needs of learners, and Internet technologies such as digital libraries have the affordances to support students in these activities.

Based on this premise, as well as building from various illustrations of digital library initiatives' vision statement, the planner establishes the vision of the collaborative digital library to populate Row 1 of the Motivation column. The planner's vision of the digital library is as follows:

- "The collaborative digital library should enable secondary students conducting history1 school projects to access the information they need any time and any where, in a friendly, efficient and effective way, by overcoming the barriers o distance and language. The digital library should enable students to collaboratively contribute resources as the digital library is seen as a growing repository on Malaysian local history for education".

With the vision in mind, the planner establishes the following goals for developing and implementing the collaborative digital library:

- The development of local historical resources;
- Provision of resources for lifelong learning;
- Provision of round-the clock access; and
- Development of community of users.

In this capacity, it establishes "a digital library service environment" - that is, a networked, online information space in which students can discover, locate, acquire access to and, increasingly, use information.

School's Technical Readiness	Students' ICT Readiness	Students' Digital Readiness
* ICT Infrastructure is in Place * New Infrastructure is Planned * Awareness of ICT Support System * Implementation of ICT Mediated Learning	* High Computer Ownership * Ease of Internet Access * Home Access to Internet * Frequent Users * Technologically Skilled	* Could Use Digital Resources * Strong Preference for Digital Resources * Adequate Searching Skills * Familiar with Search Agents
Teacher's Ready to Collaborate	Motivating Factors	Acceptance of Digital Library
* Value of Integrating with Subject Learning * See the Value of Digital Resources * See the Value of Online Publishing	Strategic Readiness * Master Plan for ICT Integration * Budget Borne by Government and Parent-Teacher Association	* Perceive Digital Library as Useful * Willingness to Contribute Contents

Fig. 8.3. Motivating Factors that Support the Plan for Realization of the Digital Library.

The objective of the digital library is therefore to provide a learning environment and resources network for history education which is:

- Designed to meet the information needs of learners, in both individual and collaborative settings (enable the creation, organisation and maintaining of local history resources);
- Constructed to enable use of a broad array of materials for local history learning, primarily in digital format

submitted by the educational community themselves (they themselves become resource providers); and

- Managed actively to promote reliable access anytime-anywhere to quality collections and services (provided over the Internet), available both within and outside the network.

Row 2 of the figure of the Motivation column identifies the owners' business plan that is the approach to use the collaborative digital library. The digital library is modelled to focus on serving students information needs in conducting research projects. As such, in the implementation of this digital library project, the use of the online resources would be an integral part of history projects-based learning activities.

The digital library may move the student community towards an emerging digital resources and the submission of reports in the electronic form is therefore feasible. The implementation of the business plan is consistent with the Ministry of Education's implementation and evaluation of History project, which will make the accomplishment of the goals and objectives feasible.

The teachers on the other hand will be given the opportunity to validate the quality of submissions to maintain the quality of the digital library, grade the report online and add links to resources found on the Internet.

Row 3 spells out the the designer's perspectives which expressed the motivation of the digital library in the form of behavioural objectives.

The objectives of the collaborative DL from the designer's perspectives are to:

- Enable students to search and browse the digital library resources through various access points regarding the topics they are exploring
- Allow the students to sequence and organise their project reports in various styles, construct references and append digital objects or pictures to their report.
- Provide the students with the experience of publishing their project report, allow teachers grade and their friends to view the repot. The motivation for this is to

satisfy their innate need to share their work, so that their peers can give comments for improvements before the report is finally submitted.

- Allow teachers to check the suitability of submissions, maintain quality of contents of the digital library and grade the submissions.
- Allow teachers and students to provide metadata for resources submitted to the digital library. A metadata schema will be applied for this purpose.
- Enable students and user groups to register as members to login and submit and describe resources
- Allow users to submit feedback or submit useful links to other resources in the Internet.
- Guide and assist users in using the digital library functions and services.
- Allow authorised users to add, modify or delete submitted resources to the digital library.

These behavioural objectives of the digital library would assist the designer in developing the required digital library. The motivation and objective statements subsequently assist in the development of the user requirement and detailed definitions of the digital library services required in the Function column of the Framework.

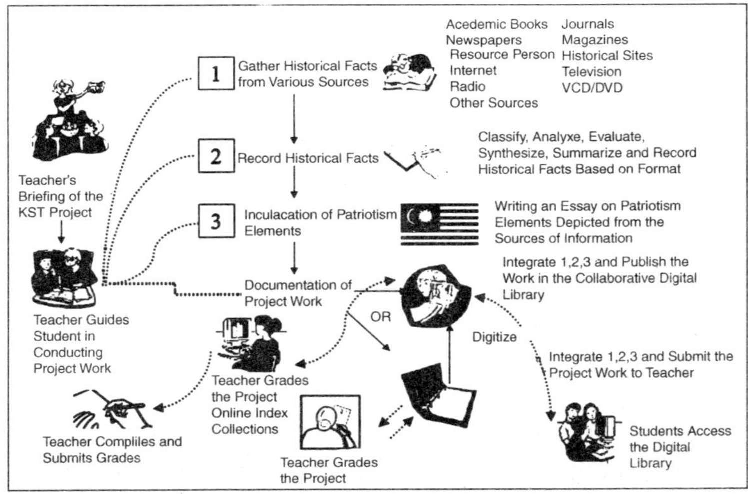

Fig. 8.4. The Business Plan to Use the Collaborative Digital Library.

Data: What Resources Constitute the Digital Library

What (Data) column of the Zachman Framework describes the digital library resources students used to fulfill their research needs. The data component, at the macro level identifies the information resources included or covered in the collaborative digital library, and at the micro level, concerned the collections, quality, accuracy, usability, description and organisation of the resources in the digital library.

Findings from the case study revealed that the students and teachers emphasised the needs for contents to be "clear, accurate, adequate, organised, valid, reliable, informative and resourceful" To cater for students' information needs, in Row 1, the planner describes the three main categories of resources, without policy-controlled access.

The types of resources are:

- Resources that are born digital;
- Digitised resources or digital proxies for physical items; and
- Links to other resources relevant to the domain focus of the digital libbrary.

The digital library collections incorporates not only digital resources in different media types such as text, images, web documents, audio and video, but also in different formats with different levels of content quality and metadata.

History has been chosen as the domain of the digital library test-bed based on the survey findings that indicated the students surveyed mainly use Internet resources to get information for their History project. Case findings revealed that the project reports are typically made available in the form of collections, which refers to groups of resources organised around three themes or topic namely prominent personalities, historical events and historical buildings.

Figure presents the semantic description of the domain focus, contents, content criteria and scope of the collaborative digital library, which populates the Data component of the Zachman Framework. The stakeholders' needs for contents to be "clear, accurate, adequate, organised, valid, reliable, informative and resourceful" are therefore used as a set of general guidelines or selection criteria of resources accepted for submission.

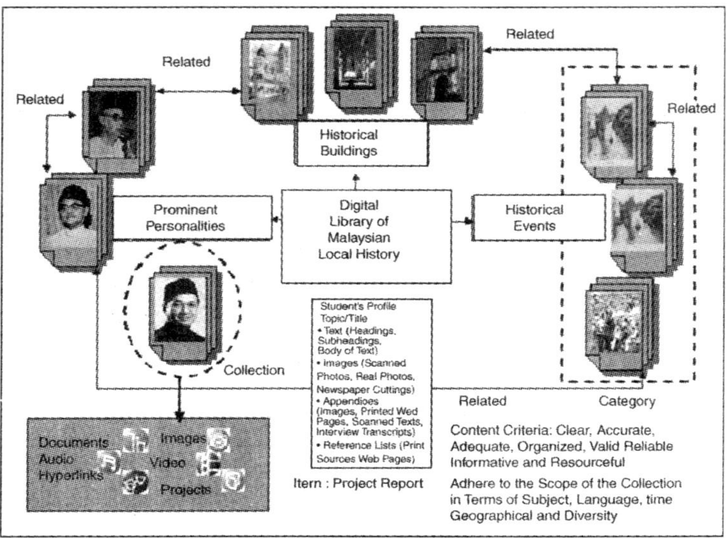

Fig. 8.5. Domain Focus, Contents, Content Criteria and Scope of the Collaborative Digital Library (Owner's View of Data).

From the designer's perspective, the data of the digital library is expressed as table definition for the digital library data (comprising digital objects data and metadata, user information, annotation and static information pages) and metadata profile for the digital object resource description (comprising administrative, technical and descriptive metadata). Administrative metadata is created by the author, technical metadata is automatically generated and descriptive metadata is assigned by the content access provider (human indexer).

The descriptive metadata schema used for the object data description is the Dublin Core (DC) Metadata.The digital library has altogether 16 metadata elements and incorporates DC's 14 out of 15 elements, namely title, creator, subject, description, publisher, contributor, date, type, format, identifier, language, relation, coverage and rights. The DC source metadata element is not used. Two other elements incorporated are Collection and Ranking metadata.

People: Who Interacts with/within the Digital Library

Who (People) column represents the stakeholders or the people within the digital library enterprise to which the digital library assigns responsibility for work. Thus, this component concerns the identification of the digital library users, their information needs, their usage of the Internet and online digital resources and their roles in the enterprise. The design of the enterprise has to do with the allocation of work and the structure of authority and responsibility.

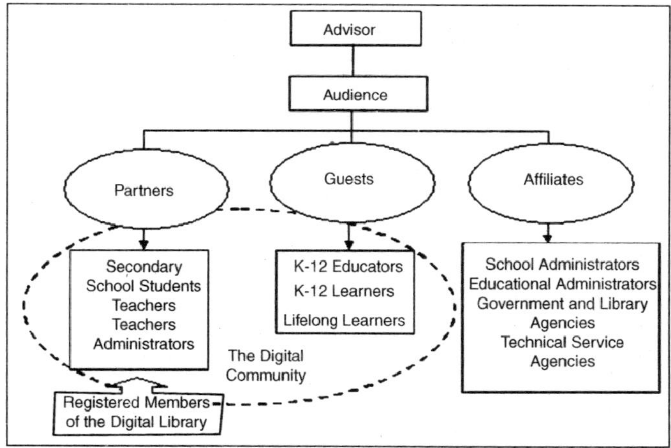

Fig. 8.6. The Digital Library Organisational Structure (Planner's View of People).

This column also deals with human-machine interfaces and relationships between the people and the work they perform. In Row 1, the planner identifies the audience and the digital library organisation. There are three types of audiences within the collaborative digital library enterprise, categorised as partners, guests and affiliate members. The planner identified these groups of people in the form of digital library organisational structure.

The digital community follows certain rules and their members play different roles, as consumers, content developers or providers, content access providers and content manager.

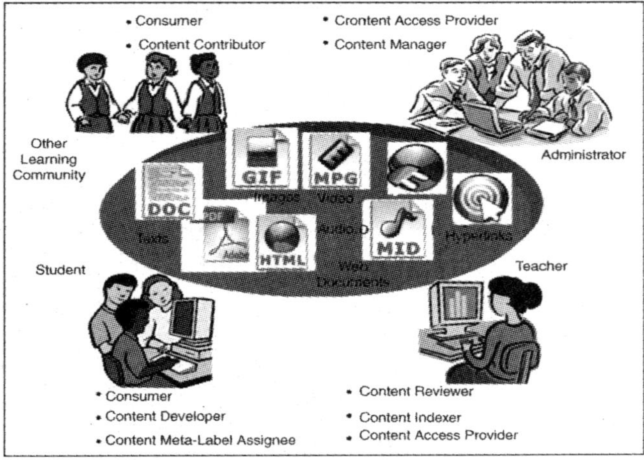

Fig. 8.7. The Digital Library Actor-Roles Diagram (Owner's View of People).

Here, the digital library community includes people as well as computers, agents, network connections, files and operating systems, user interfaces, communication links, and protocols, which either use or support the digital library services. The communities of autonomous agents and computers instantiate functions upon requests by the actors of the digital library.

To operate, these agents and computers need structures of vocabulary and protocols. They act by sending streams of queries and retrieving streams of results. The digital library system uses the three-tier client-server architecture.

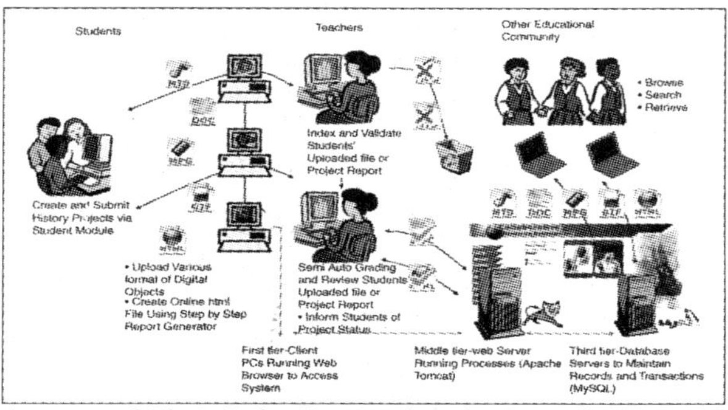

Fig. 8.8. Actors and Their Roles Depicted in the Digital Library Three-Tier Client-Server Architecture (Designer's View of People).

The client tier comprises computers with web browsers such as Internet Explorer, Netscape Navigator, Mozilla Firefox and Opera. User interfaces are provided for clients to process their application and manipulate their data. All application programmes reside in the middle-tier (web server). The web server processes the request from the client and then returns required result in web page format. It processes data request by linking to a database server (such as authenticating and validating users that login into the system). It is also linked to transaction server, especially when clients are uploading files to the web server. The third tier consists of the database server and transaction for maintaining data records.

Function: What Happens in the Digital Library

How (functions) defines the functions or activities the digital library enterprise is concerned about relative to each perspective. In Row 1, the planner describes the students' research activities that take place, which encompass the entire information seeking process (from recognising the need for information to finding, using and presenting it) and the submission and evaluation of the information in the form of project report. This is presented in the form of rich pictures. Basically, the students do solitary information seeking, have spontaneous interactions with other people such as parents, siblings and friends and ask for help, and work with information in a group. The description of the activities when conducting history projects are then transformed into the online activities the students and teachers would be able to perform in the collaborative digital library. Figure presents the workflows and processes the collaborative digital library enterprise should conduct. These processes are also in line with the owner's plan to use the digital library for school project. The function component refers to the activities students perform in their research, such as choosing topic, searching for information, organising resources, writing, presenting, submitting and teachers grading of project work.

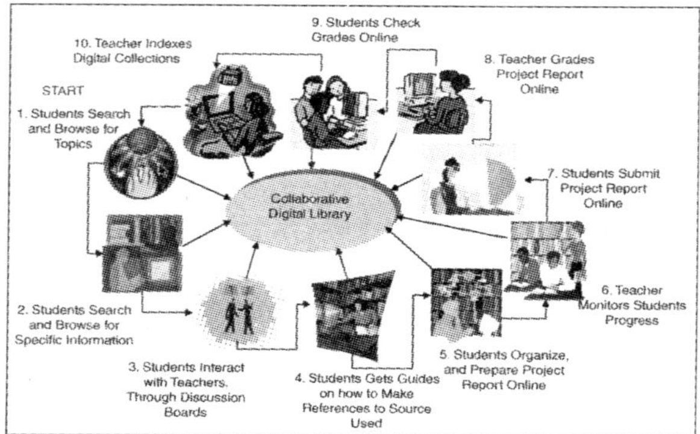

Fig. 8.9. Activities Performed in the Collaborative Digital Library.

Using data from analysis of the activities culled from the research, formulation of behavioural objectives of the digital library as well as from the analysis of digital library functional requirements, the planner develops the user requirement expressed in terms of functions and present it as services in a contiguous structured chart, The structured chart is comprehensible to the owner as the conceptual model of the digital library services. This structured chart populates Row 2 of the Function Column and describes the process of translating the objectives of the digital library enterprise into successively more detailed definitions of its services. Feedback from the stakeholders on the potential features of a service and digital library design implication derived from the analysis of the case study have helped to ascertain the main features required by the collaborative digital library.

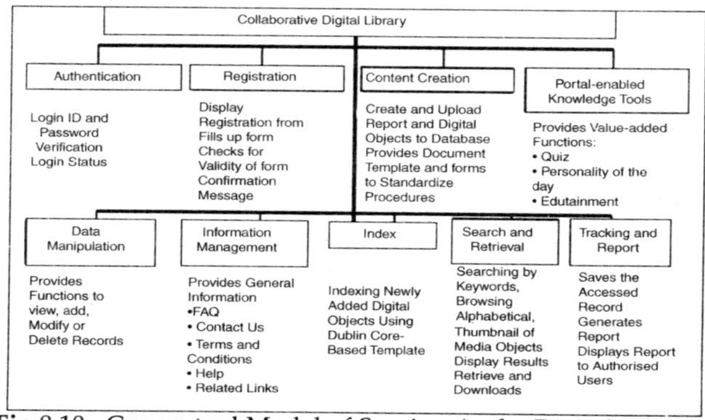

Fig.8.10. Conceptual Model of Services in the Digital Library.

In Row 3, the designer portrays the digital services in terms of data transforming processes, described exclusively in terms of definition of programme modules and how they interact with each other. The three system modules, namely administrators (including teachers), students and guests, provide different access types for different level of users. Along with this are specific definitions of security requirements, in terms of who (which role) is permitted access to what function, in the form of structured charts and detailed description of the modules menu.

Network: Where can one Access the Digital Library

Network (Where) shows the sites or geographical locations and the interconnections between activities within the digital library enterprise. It illustrates the network-related aspect of the digital libraries in terms of the physical locations of members in the digital library which spread over a geographical area. The planner provides the big picture of the digital library as a centralised system with the control for the whole structure at the Faculty of Computer Science and Information Technology University of Malaya (FCSIT UM) as the developer of the digital library system. FCSIT UM group manages the centralised database server. School A is the content collaborator and joint owner of the system and other potential future collaborators such as School B, Education Departments, Ministry of Education, as well as other repositories, would be able to utilise the application server running locally to fetch the required data from the database server.

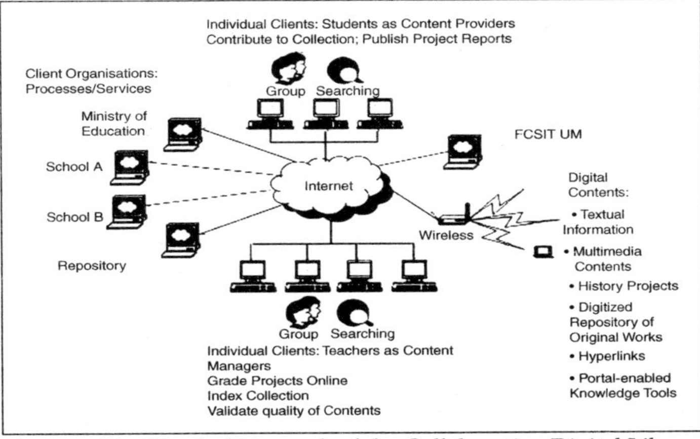

Fig. 8.11. The Physical Network of the Collaborative Digital Library

The owner is interested in the conceptual model of "Where" which includes the location of access and place where the primary stakeholders, namely the students and teachers use the digital library. It illustrates the collaborative digital library deployment expressed in term of location of access and computing facilities and network. The school community may access the collaborative digital library system from any 10 locations in the school, as all computers there are connected to the network.

From the designer's perspective, the Network Column presents the logical model of the network component of the collaborative digital library which depicts the types of systems facilities and controlling software at the nodes and lines such as processors/operating systems, database and lines/line operation systems.

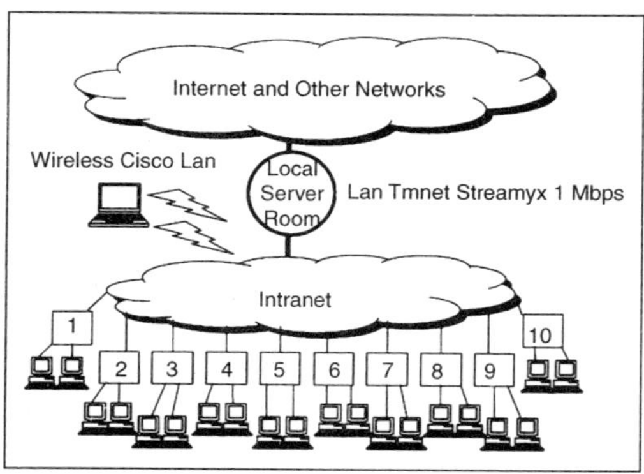

Fig. 8.12. The School's Network Diagram Positioning the Location of Access for the Digital Library

The notional distributed systems architecture shows servers supporting the digital library services served from the regional (FCSIT) and local data center environment to the school's three primary locations of access. It is referred to as a notional architecture Since, the extent of the ability to remotely serve specific applications in both the baseline state and the target state remains to be established.

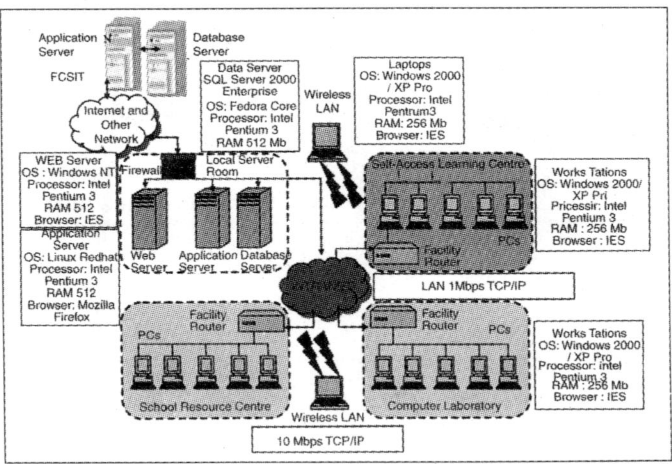

Fig. 8.13 The Digital Library Notional Distributed Systems Architecture.

Time: When can one use the Digital Library (When do things Happen)

The last column, "When" represents time, or the events to which the digital library responds in relation to time. This is useful for designing schedules, the processing architecture, the control architecture and timing systems. It is difficult to describe or address this column in isolation from the others, especially Column 2 (Process). At the strategic level, the planner describes Time as the business cycle and overall business events. As has been delineated in the digital library goals and objectives (Motivation Column), the digital library provides round-the-clock access. As the Internet is a 24/7 medium, the digital library is available 24 hours a day, 7 days a week. In the detailed model of owner's perspective, the Time Column defines when activities or processes are to happen.

Based on the findings of the case study regarding the school's approach in using the digital library, the chronology of events (such as teacher's notification and requirement of the project, students choose topic, gather information, create report, obtain teacher's feedback, edit and submit report) indicating the processes that take place in the digital library environment populates owner's view of the Time Column. The designer defines the business events or the processes in the digital library, which cause specific data transformations and entity state changes to take place. The business events populate the designer's view of the Time Column of the Zachman Framework used.

Table. 8.1. Business Events in the Digital Library.

The Process to take place.	Data transformations and entity state changes
Students register	Students receive automatically generated e-mail notifying membership of the digital library
Students create and submit report	Teachers and Administrators receive automatically generated e-mail notification indicating a new report has been submitted and ready to be viewed, graded or indexed.
Students create submit report	Students receive automatically generated e-and mail notification indicating that they have successfullysubmitted their project report.
Administrator	Teachers receive automatically generated e-mail registers teachers notification which indicates their User ID and Password.
Teacher evaluate and grade report	Students receive automatically generated e-mail notification indicating their projects have been evaluated.

INTEGRATING DISPARATE DIGITAL LIBRARIES USING THE WASSIT MEDIATION FRAMEWORK

Nowadays, there is a trend to integrate several digital libraries (DLs) to offer richer information. However, the following three characteristics of DLs make their integration a difficult task:

- *Distribution*: Geographical spread;
- *Heterogeneity*: Difference at both the technical level (*e.g.*, hardware platform, operating system, etc.) and conceptual level (*e.g.*, data model, query language, etc.);
- *Autonomy*: DLs are selfsufficient, as opposed to being delegated a role only as components in a larger system.

Therefore, challenges faced when integrating DLs include interoperability (among different DLs) and resource discovery (selection of the best sites to be integrated). There are two different types of interoperability for DLs integration: syntactic interoperability and semantic interoperability. Syntactic interoperability is the application-level interoperability that allows multiple software components to cooperate even though their data model, query language, interfaces, etc., are different. Semantic interoperability is the knowledge-level interoperability that allows digital libraries to be integrated, with the ability to bridge semantic conflicts arising from differences in implicit meanings, perspectives and assumptions, thus creating a semantically compatible information environment based on agreed-upon concepts. To deal with the interoperability problem, two solutions can be used: warehousing and mediation systems. In the warehouse approach, information is in some way periodically extracted from different sources, processed, merged with information from other sources, and then loaded into a centralised data store. Queries are posed against the local data without further interaction with the original sources. Modifications are filtered (e.g. for relevance or update-time) and propagated in some manner to upgrade the data warehouse. The main advantage of the warehousing approach is the performance of query processing. The main drawbacks are that the data may not be fresh and adding new data source requires reconsidering the warehouse schema. Thus, concerns about data quality and consistency must be addressed.

In mediation systems data remains at the sources and queries to the integrated system need to be translated, at run time, into a sequence of sub-queries to the underlying data sources. Data are not replicated and is guaranteed to be fresh at query time. However, a considerable performance penalty must be paid because sources are contacted for every query. Besides, in heterogeneous environments, especially in the context of DLs, sources may have diverse and limited query capabilities. Thus, not all of the translations are feasible.

Therefore, another challenge faced when integrating DLs is how to generate efficient and feasible query plans to retrieve data from DLs. Our solution for integrating disparate DLs is a mediation framework, called WASSIT *(frameWork d'intégrAtion de reSSources par la médIaTion)*. In this chapter, we describe the features of WASSIT. In particular, we present how DLs are selected and ranked according to the user quality requirements. Since, syntactic interoperability is treated implicitly in mediation systems (by using a common data model and wrappers), as suggested, focus on our solution for semantic interoperability. Generating feasible and efficient query plans, by WASSIT, is also part of this chapter.

HIGH-LEVEL ARCHITECTURE OF WASSIT

Our mediation framework WASSIT relies on the well-known mediator architecture. WASSIT defines an infrastructure which provides the generic structure and the behaviour of a set of reusable components in an information mediation context. Our framework is mainly made up of two principal components: Mediator and Wrappers. The Mediator, which is the query processing core of the framework WASSIT, has to decompose a user query into a set of sub-queries targeted to the sources. Each subquery is transmitted to the corresponding source via the associated wrapper.

The answers delivered by the wrappers are then combined to form the response to the initial query. The high level architecture of WASSIT is shown in figure. In this architecture, we distinguish three levels: the source level including the data sources and the wrappers, the mediation level containing the mediator, and finally the user level containing the user interface. In the mediation level, WASSIT is composed of six modules and a knowledge base.

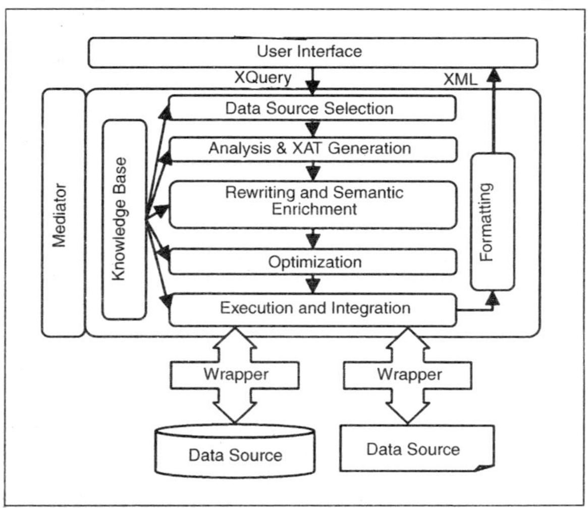

Fig. 8.14. High Level Architecture of WASSIT.

Our Technological Choices for WASSIT

DLs generally differ with respect to the structures they use to represent data. We use XML as a common data model in WASSIT to reconcile sources' heterogeneous data models because it provides a common format for expressing both data structures and contents.

Thus, it can integrate structured, semi-structured and unstructured data. XQuery is the query language we adopt in WASSIT Since, it is the W3C standard for querying XML documents. In order to achieve efficient query processing, we represent the queries according to an algebraic model. The one we have chosen is XAT. XAT algebra offers SQL operators such as union, join, etc. It offers also specific operators such as navigate, tagger, etc. Ontologies in WASSIT are used at two levels: to represent schema mappings and to capture the semantic of each source Since, we address semantic heterogeneity. We adopt OWL, the Ontology Web Language, to represent these ontologies.

Description of WASSIT's Components

WASSIT is made up of a user interface, a mediator which contains six modules and a knowledge base, and wrappers.

As suggested, present each entity of WASSIT.

- *User Interface:* It is a QBE (Query By Example) interface which frees the user from the knowledge of the XQuery language. In addition, this interface allows users to formulate their queries using the concepts of the global ontology. After the reception of a query by this interface, the corresponding XQuery query is generated. Moreover, the user interface allows users to express their preferences and needs through a user profile.
- *Data Source Selection module:* To select the most relevant sources, this module performs quality matching between a user's profile and sources' profiles. The selected sources are then integrated to get a personalised response that respects user's quality requirements.

- *Analysis and XAT Generation module*: This module has to analyse the user's queries. It rejects the syntactically incorrect ones. It eliminates also the queries that refer to unavailable concepts. This is achieved by using the knowledge base. User's queries are then transformed into XML algebra trees in order to be treated. Each node of a XAT tree is an algebraic operator.
- *Rewriting and Semantic Enrichment module*: Let's remind that our framework aims to access a set of heterogeneous information sources. Every source has its local schema that describes its structure in a data model. The query submitted to the framework is formulated in terms of mediated schema (global schema). To have the query executed, the framework must rewrite the user's query formulated in terms of mediated schema as a query execution plan (QEP). Each QEP is presented in the form of a tree, where leafs are sub-queries that will be sent to the wrappers, and nodes are reconstruction operators that will be used by the mediator to integrate the results. The *Rewriting* module generates a QEP through three steps; each step is processed by one sub-module. These sub-modules are described in the following.
- *Global views substitution module:* This module has two features. First it ensures global views substitution, which consists in replacing each global view reference by the definition of this view. Views definitions are retrieved from the mapping definition. Then global paths (used to define global query) are projected on local paths (used to define local views).
- *Union and join Operator ascending module:* Join and union operators, having distinct views from distinct data sources, can't be executed by a source. Thus, these operators have to be executed by the mediator. In order to schedule their execution, they are moved at the top of the algebra tree.
- *Bindings adjustment module*: Moving operators across the plan tree (previous step) makes parameters

inappropriate. Consequently, this module has to adjust binding operators' parameters.

Moreover, in this step, we enrich semantically each sub-query (when possible) with syNon-yms, hyperonyms and hyponyms.

- *Optimisation module*: The *Optimisation* module takes as input the QEP obtained after query rewriting. After extracting sub-queries from this QEP, the *Optimisation* module constructs a plan according to query capabilities of the underlying DLs.
- *Execution and integration module*: This module takes as input the sub-queries delivered by the *Optimisation* module and sends them to the appropriate wrappers using the localisation information given by the knowledge base. It is composed by three sub-modules, which are described in the following.
- *XQuery Query Generator module*: sub-queries are represented by a XAT tree. This module translates each XAT tree sub-query to a XQuery query.
- *Sub-queries Execution module*: this module ensures the actual execution of XQuery queries. It sends the XQuery queries to the right wrapper which translates the XQuery query to the underlying data source querying language.
- *XAT Table Generation module*: This module constructs a XAT table from the XML results returned by the wrappers. The resulting XAT tables are combined according to the optimised QEP to form the answer to the user query.
- *Formatting module*: In this module, the result returned by the *Execution and Integration* module is formatted in order to form the answer which will finally be returned to the end user.
- *The knowledge base*: The knowledge base is associated to the mediator, it stocks the general information used for query processing in the framework. It contains global ontology, local ontologies, users' profiles, sources' profiles, physical localisation of sources, source descriptions, localisation of wrappers, source capabilities, etc.

- *Wrappers*: At a given wrapper, a sub-query expressed in XQuery is translated into the source query language. The wrapper has also to format the results returned by the source in an XML format. In WASSIT, two wrappers are developed: an XQuery/SQL wrapper and an XQuery/SOAP wrapper.

DIGITAL LIBRARIES SELECTION IN WASSIT

Because of their increasing number and their heterogeneity, digital libraries may contain redundant information that differs by their quality characteristics. Since, WASSIT answers user's queries by combining responses from different DLs, the final response quality relies on the quality of the sources involved. The perception of quality differs also from a user to another. For example, user A may ask for actual data, when user B looks for historical one. To summarise, the concept of quality makes the difference between several DLs treating the same subject. It can be used to personalise the mediator's responses according to the user's preferences by selecting the most relevant DLs. The objective is to give a response that meets the user's quality requirements.

We present our solution for DLs selection according to user's quality requirements in WASSIT. Our approach consists in building a multi-dimensional user's profile which stores the knowledge about a given user, especially his identity and quality preferences. We also construct a source profile which contains source definition, content, location, and quality characteristics. Both user's profiles and source's profiles are stored in the knowledge base.

Related Works

Several systems have been developed to integrate disparate and heterogeneous DLs. The majority of them addresses the problem of source selection following two approaches. The first approach considers the source as a big document constructed via document concatenation, so the source selection becomes a simple problem of document retrieval. The most used source selection algorithm named CORI is based on this assumption, GIOSS and K-L divergence based algorithms belong also to this category.

The second approach considers the source as a repository of documents so the selected sources are those who are the most likely to return the maximum of relevant documents. ReDDE algorithm and the DTF give a source ranking by estimating the number of relevant documents for each query. The estimation is based on calculating a cost function which include quality and time factors. Both approaches require a source representation in their selection and ranking process. The source characteristics used are either given by the source, for example the protocol STARTS requires digital libraries to provide an accurate description of their content and quality, or discovered automatically through sampling queries.

Our source selection and ranking algorithm is inspired from the second approach. We estimate the quality of each source using sampling queries and we build a quality model to perform a personalised source selection. The main contribution is that the source selection and ranking is not based on user queries but on user's profiles. The selection is performed by matching user's preferences and sources' characteristics. So, for each user, the selected set of candidate sources meets the user's quality requirements and it is also independent from the queries. These sources are used later on in the rewriting process to give a personalised response.

The Quality Paradigm

Many researches have been conducted to define the quality paradigm in DLs, but no single definition or standard exists. Usually, the concept of quality is the aggregation of multiple criteria organised into dimensions or categories. These dimensions may concern the quality of software, the quality of web sites, the quality of services, the quality of documents and data, and the quality of sources. In the literature, there are a multitude of quality criteria depending on the domain and the application. Taxonomy of quality indicators is presented in.

The authors define quality using three factors:

- Utility, which measures the satisfaction of user's requirements;
- Cost, which reflects the payment given by the user and/or the system to satisfy the user's requirements;

- Time, which means how long the user waits to get an appropriate answer and how long the system takes to provide it.

Naumann and Leser present other parameters concerning especially the quality of data like viability, freshness, consistency and understandability. The quality of sources is measured in most cases using factors like popularity, completeness, freshness and extent. All these quality factors could be divided in two categories.

- Subjective quality factors, which depend on user's preferences, and vary according to the context of interaction. They are usually expressed explicitly with a score given by the user, or via a natural language using words like "good", "bad", "excellent", etc.
- Objective quality factors, which are considered as measurable metrics, collected implicitly through statistical and data mining algorithms. To sum up, the variety of existing quality indicators makes it difficult to build an appropriate quality model. First, we need to select the most useful quality indicators that WASSIT will use to select relevant sources. Then, we have to organise them into dimensions in order to facilitate their exploitation. In the next, we give our quality model based on two dimensions. We choose the corresponding metrics and explain how to get their values.

WASSIT Quality Model

To introduce our quality model, let us consider a user asking about children stories. The result may be different depending on the selected sources. If we select only a specialised source in Harry Potter editions, the result is clearly incomplete because we omit all other kid stories and novels. But if we select the most popular kids' digital library, this user may be satisfied about the completeness of the result.

The result differs also depending on the user preferences. For example, user A is more interested on old stories whereas user B prefers the last published ones. From these examples, we can say that defining a quality model in a digital library integration system depends on two dimensions, which are the user's quality preferences and the source's quality characteristics.

User's Quality Preferences

We define a preference as the desired level of quality that may satisfy the user's needs. User's quality preferences are related to the quality of retrieved documents, the quality of integrated sources and finally the quality of service depending on the retrieving process and the source capabilities. In the next, we study only the user's quality preferences related to the quality of sources Since, our objective is to select the most appropriate ones. We define a model where the user expresses his quality preferences in three steps.

First, he chooses his desired quality criteria from a global list available in the WASSIT's user interface. Second, he gives a ranking of these criteria from the most important one to the less using weights. Weighting quality criteria helps the system to emphasize the priority of the quality criterion to satisfy.

Third, he states his desired values for each criterion. Usually, user's preferences values are expressed using a numerical score in an appropriate scale, a percentage, words like "good", "bad", etc. or even a predicate. In this case, the user expresses his preference about the freshness of the source.

He considers that sources having only documents published before 2004 are not fresh enough. To simplify our model, we suppose that the user states required preferences via WASSIT's user interface either by putting a score directly or by a slider on an appropriate scale. The position of the slide gives the corresponding score.

Source's Quality Characteristics

We define the source's quality characteristics as the main quality criteria that make a significant difference between data sources. In our model, the source's quality characteristics are stored in source profile. In the next, we focus on four information quality metrics which are reputation, freshness, completeness and time of response.

Reputation

Reputation, also called popularity, means the degree to which a source is in high standing. Reputation of a source is related to several factors:

- The quality and quantity of information and documents in the source;
- The authority and credibility of the source's owner (*e.g.*, an official DL have a higher reputation than a wiki web site, a specialised DL in a given field such as computing science have a higher reputation than a DL treating all subjects);
- The quality of service including time of response, cost and security parameters.

Indeed, a source having a good response time and a lower cost is more appreciated by the users. Source's reputation depends on the user's judgement. It's a highly subjective criterion. For this reason, we consider that the reputation of a source S expressed by the user U is measured by a score from 1(bad reputation) to 5 (very high reputation). We denote this score by Reputation_Score(U,S). We need now to measure the reputation of a source S. For this purpose, we define a metric called Global_Reputation_Score which is the average of all Reputation_Scores expressed by a set of users U={U1, U2...Un}. The Global Reputation Score is computed using formula (1).

$$Global\_\mathrm{Re}\,putation\_Score(S)$$
$$= E\left[\sum_{i=1}^{n} \mathrm{Re}\,putation\_Score\left(Ui,S\right)/\,n\right]+1 \qquad (1)$$

Freshness

There are various definitions of source freshness in the literature, as well as different metrics to measure it. gives a state of the art of these definitions and presents taxonomy of metrics to measure it depending on the domain of application. For example, in data warehouse systems, one of the metrics used to measure source freshness is currency. Currency reflects the degree of change between data extracted and returned to the user and data stored in the source.

In our model, we consider that freshness refers to the age of information in the source and the update of its' content. To measure this factor, we use the Timeliness factor, which expresses how old is data in the source Since, its creation or update.

This factor is bounded with the update frequency of the source. We define a metric called Timeliness_Score which measures the time elapsed Since, data was updated. For example, a "Timeliness_Score=2 years" means that the source contains documents published after 2008. We also suppose that sources give the Timeliness_Score as a meta-data in their descriptions.

Completeness

Completeness is the extent to which data is not missing and are of sufficient breadth, depth, and scope for the task at hand. In other words, it expresses the degree to which all documents relevant to a domain have been recorded in the source. Completeness of a source is also called in the literature: coverage, scope, granularity, comprehensiveness and density. For example, a scientific digital library is more complete than a Non-specialised one. We measure completeness using sampling queries which estimate the coverage of a source regarding some specific topic. We define a metric called Completeness_Score which represent the percentage of relevant documents returned by the source S out of the size of this source. Completeness_Score is given by formula (2), Where Size(S) is the number of documents stored in S and Size(D) is the number of documents that answer the sample queries.

$$Completeness\_Score(S) = \left(\frac{Size(D)}{Size(S)} \right) * 100 \qquad (2)$$

Time of Response

Time of response is the time that a source takes to answer a given query. It is calculated in seconds. Time of response could be very high if the source is saturated or doesn't have the capability to answer the query. In this case, we use our *Optimisation* module to solve this problem. For the next, we suppose that the problem of source capabilities is resolved, so the time of response depends only on the communication process with the source. We use sample queries to determine this factor. Let SQ= {SQ1, SQ2,...,SQk} be the set of sample queries. For each sample query SQi, we measure the time of response denoted Query_Time_of_Response. The Time of Response of the source S is then computed as the maximum of all Query_Time_of_Responses using formula.

$$\text{Time\_of\_Response}(S) = \text{Max}_{i=1}^{k}(\text{Query\_Time\_of\_Response}(SQ_i)) \quad (3)$$

More quality factors could be found in the literature. For example, understandability, credibility, precision, correctness, etc. All these factors could be added in our model easily. The user then chooses those who meet his quality requirements. In this step of work, we think that the quality factors defined are sufficient for WASSIT to make a quality aware source selection and ranking. To attempt this goal, we need to make a compromise between all defined criteria. We face two major problems. First, the source quality scores are not homogenous: we have a percentage, a time, a number. So, we need to scale the scores to make them comparable. Second, users set their quality preferences by selecting quality criteria, then stating importance weightings for each selected criterion. Finally, they state preference values for each desired criterion. So we need to select the relevant sources according to the preference values. Then, we have to rank the selected sources using the preference weightings.

Source Selection and Ranking Algorithm

The quality of sources is measured with several criteria. Thus, source selection is a multiattribute decision making problem (MDMP). In the literature, several methods have been developed to resolve this problem such as SAW, TOPSIS and AHP. We choose to apply SAW (Simple Additive Weighting), because it's one of the most simple but nevertheless a good decision making procedure. SAW results are also usually close to more sophisticated methods.

The basic idea of SAW is to calculate a quality score for each source using a decision matrix and a vector of preference weights.

Although SAW solves the problem of the heterogeneity of quality criteria by scaling their values, this method ranks sources considering only the user's quality preferences weights. This ranking is based on the priority and importance of quality criterion but does not consider the preference's values. Consequently, we could not select the best sources unless the user defines a limit of the acceptable source's scores or a number of desired sources. To overcome these limitations, we develop a selection and ranking algorithm that respect both the user's quality preferences weights and values. The values defined by the user correspond to the criteria thresholds. Our algorithm is performed in two stages: source selection and source ranking using SAW method.

SEMANTIC INTEROPERABILITY IN WASSIT

Semantic interoperability in DLs means the capability of different information systems to communicate information consistent with the intended meaning. The NSF Post Digital Libraries Futures Workshop identified it as being of primary importance in digital library research. One of the well accepted mechanisms for achieving semantic interoperability is the utilisation of ontologies. Structure knowledge embedded in ontologies supports information retrieval and interoperability. Ontologies also help investigation of correspondences between elements of heterogeneous data sources. In WASSIT, we use ontologies to achieve semantic interoperability. Since, DLs are heterogeneous, they may have local schemas or ontologies expressed in various formalism degrees, going from the informal definitions up to Rigourously formal descriptions. However, the availability of a coherent formal ontology within the mediation system facilitates semantic query rewriting by enriching terms with semantically related ones.

Related Works

The most used approaches for constructing formal ontology in mediation systems are mapping and integration.

We present those approaches in the following:

- *Ontology mapping*: Mapping is a crucial process in schemas and ontologies integration as well as in semantic conflicts resolution between ontologies and between heterogeneous data sources. It is defined as being the set of operations permitting to define relationships between the elements of two schemas having a semantic correspondence. We distinguish two types of mapping: one-way and two-ways mapping. The first one consists in defining an expression of a destination ontology terms according to a source ontology terms, whereas the two-ways mapping operates in both directions. In our works, we are interested in the two-ways mapping, between schemas and local ontologies.

- *Ontology integration*: The integration process consists in creating a new ontology from two or more ontologies in order to replace or to unify and then to share their vocabulary. This can be achieved using operations such as union and intersection. The intersection approach consists in producing a reduced ontology based on the terms having common semantics. The advantage of this approach is that it makes possible to obtain, easily, a reduced shared vocabulary. However, its disadvantage lies in information loss that can result from this approach. This last is used in Observer where the intersection between the ontologies is measured by a percentage indicating information quantity loss during the query translation process between the different system nodes. The union approach is used when we want to get only one global ontology containing all the terms contained in these ontologies. This approach has the advantage to allow easy query rewriting Since, the necessary vocabulary is kept in the resulting global ontology without any information loss. It has the disadvantage to need a lot of efforts to elaborate the union task. Furthermore, adding or deleting ontologies is quite difficult. Several mediation systems use this approach. We can mention Picsel and SIMS.

We have adopted this last approach to build our knowledge base ontologies. But we extended it by using generalisation and specialisation operators. However, to palliate to its disadvantage, we propose a solution for semi-automatic integration of the local ontologies.

Building Ontologies in WASSIT

To resolve semantic conflicts, we adopt hybrid architecture for the knowledge base development. Our approach combines local data sources ontologies and a global ontology that provides a shared vocabulary. This architecture offers adaptability and extensibility for new sources addition Since, every source has its own local ontology. To build our ontologies, we follow the process represented in figure. The global ontology construction process takes place in two phases: the mapping of local schemas and ontologies, and the merging of local ontologies.

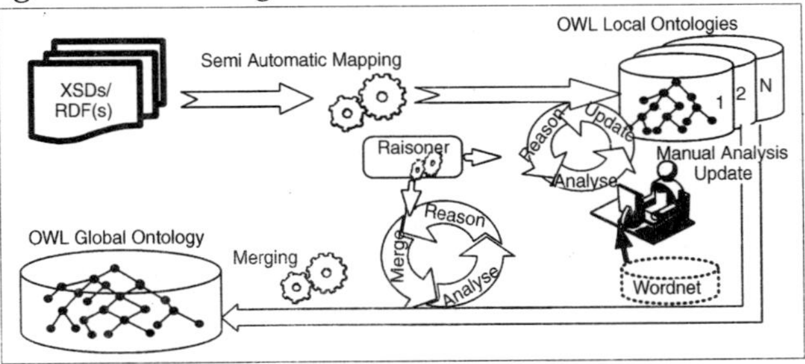

Fig. 8.15. The Construction Process of Local and Global Ontologies for WASSIT.

The mapping of the local schemas and ontologies of each local source in an OWL local ontology is achieved in order to permit a transparent and uniform merging of the local ontologies. At the end of this process, a mapping table is generated. It contains mapping information between local schemas and ontologies. The merging of all OWL local ontologies resulting from the first step is achieved to build the global ontology. During the merging process, the mapping table is updated by the correspondence information between local ontologies and the global one. To illustrate our approach, we take the example of the local schemas given in figures. Through this example, we present the three phases of our approach, which are: *Mapping local schemas to local ontologies, Merging local ontologies into the global ontology* and *Consistency checking.*

Mapping Local Schemas to Local Ontologies

Each source to be integrated is described by its local schema or its local ontology that we enrich by metadata, to add rich semantics about this data source, about its capacities and about its content. The construction of local ontologies is accomplished by mapping local schemas and ontologies that can be represented under various formats (XML schemas, DAML-OIL, etc.). In this chapter, we limit our study to the case of the local schemas described in XML schemas. As we adopted the OWL language for our knowledge base ontologies representation, a mapping between the XML schemas and OWL syntax is necessary. Several works for mapping between XML Schemas and OWL exist. We were inspired from the one introduced by Bohring and Auer.

Table. 8.2. Mapping between XML Schema and OWL Elements.

XSD	OWL
xsd:elements, containing other elements or attributes.	owl:Class, coupled with owl:ObjectProperties
xsd:elements, with neither sub-elements nor attributes	owl:DatatypeProperties
xsd:attribute	owl:DatatypeProperties
xsd:complexType	owl:Class
xsd:SimpleType	owl: Datatype Properties
xsd:minOccurs	owl:minCardinality
xsd:maxOccurs	owl:maxCardinality
xsd:choice	combination of owl: intersection Of, owl:unionOf and owl:complement Of
xsd:sequence, xsd:all	owl:intersection Of.

Moreover, the syntax mapping must be coupled with another one for concepts names contained in the local schemas to avoid ambiguousness that can be produced by this transformation. Indeed, an XML schema document has an ordered hierarchical structure that allows two elements to have the same identifier (name) so long as they are not in the same node. However, the order between these elements won't be taken in consideration after the mapping, because OWL doesn't define any order between properties. The OWL syntax components, rdfs:range and rdfs:domain, alone don't enable removing the generated ambiguity while transforming these elements and non-global attributes of the XML schemas towards OWL. The definition of Non-ambiguous identifiers to keep a two ways mapping between the local schemas and the local ontologies is essential to permit an applicable user's query resolution.

Therefore, we adopted the following process:

- The id of a local element is composed of the name of the complex type in which the element is declared +"." + its_local_name (*e.g.,* "Book_Type.Editor").
- The id of a local attribute is composed of the name of the complex type in which the attribute is declared +".$" + its_local_name (*e.g.,* "Book_Type.$ISBN").
- The id of a global attribute is composed of its namespace + "$"+ its_local_name.
- The id of an anonymous type is defined by the name of the element in which the definition of the type is declared +"."+ Anonymoustype (*e.g.,* "Book_ Type. author.anonymoustype").

Merging Local Ontologies into the Global Ontology

The goal of this phase is to generate a global ontology related to the mediated sources domain. As our objective is to achieve a virtual integration of distributed, autonomous and heterogeneous data sources, the user query must be expressed against the global ontology. Thus, this ontology must contain the whole domain concepts contained in the integrated data sources. To this end, we follow a hybrid integration of the ontologies by union completed by generalisation and specialisation operations. However, before performing this integration, a set of issues rises: What are the concepts and the classes to generate? What are the specialisations and/or generalisations to conceive? Do these generalisations also affect properties? To answer these questions, we took into account the following constraints:

- Equivalence degree must be maintained, Since, a pair of concepts considered equivalent can vary a lot semantically. For example, the merging process considers "member" in the University.XSD as semantically equivalent to "Author" in Publication. xsd, although Member can be more general than author. In general, a Member cannot be an Author.

- Semantic relationship that requires one-to-many mapping (and inversely many-to-one) must be expressed correctly. For example, member.name in University.XSD is semantically equivalent to the union of the two concepts Author.first-name and Author.last-name in the Publication.XSD.

Therefore, our approach is not reduced to a simple union of local ontologies, because we carry out specialisations and/or generalisations of the concepts and properties. We use the lexical ontology WorldNet for this purpose.

Consistency Checking

The reasoning mechanisms on ontologies allow to derive and to deduce new knowledge not described explicitly by the ontology. It can be achieved for OWL ontologies using a reasoner. The inferred information can be used to improve query resolution. In our system, we used these reasoning capacities to verify the consistency of the ontologies resulting from the mapping and merging procedures.

OPTIMISING QUERIES OVER DLS WITH LIMITED CAPABILITIES

In the context of digital libraries, sources may have diverse and limited query capabilities. For example, users of an online bookstore get information on books via forms. These forms allow several types of keyword based queries including search by title, subject, author, ISBN, price, etc. If we consider the web source Amazon.com <http://www.Amazon.com/>, this bookstore does not support any query that specifies conditions on the price attribute because this attribute is absent in the search form. Let us consider another web bookstore, Books.com <http://www.Books.com/>. This bookstore supports queries that specify the price attribute. However, it cannot support queries where the attribute publisher is mentioned. Consider now a third web bookstore Books-a-million.com <http://www.booksamillion.com/>. It does not offer search neither by price nor by publisher. DLs have diverse and limited query capabilities.

These restrictions have many reasons, including the concerns of efficiency of query processing, simplicity of the query interface and security. In such situation, DLs must inform the mediator which queries they can support, so that the mediator can construct query execution plans (QEPs) that contains only feasible sub-queries. This is known as the Capability-Based Rewriting (CBR) problem. In order to be able to perform capability-based rewriting, the mediator needs formal descriptions of the query capabilities of DLs. A capability-based rewriter takes as input these descriptions and the query, and it infers query plans for retrieving the required data that are compatible with the source query capabilities. Solving the CBR typically produces more than one candidate plans for the query. Choosing the optimal plan is done using a cost model. The problem we address in this section is how to generate efficient query plans that respect the limited and diverse capabilities of DLs in WASSIT. For this purpose, we model the source capabilities through *Capabilities Tables* and propose an algorithm to generate query plans respecting DLs capabilities.

Related Works

Few mediation systems have addressed the capability-based rewriting problem. Some of these systems use exhaustive search methods to construct the optimal query plan according to the adopted cost model. However, the exponential complexity of these search methods limits the number of integrated data sources. Other systems, like e-XMLMedia, verify the feasibility of the sub-queries after constructing the QEP. For each sub-query addressed to a source, the mediator checks its feasibility by consulting the source's capabilities. If a sub-query cannot be processed at a given source, the mediator attempts to download the entire source. Such an attempt is not only expensive but also may not be allowed by the source. Another category of mediation systems initially ignores the limited sources' capabilities to generate possible query plans. It then checks the query plans against the sources' capabilities and rejects those containing unsupported queries.

This strategy could be very expensive compared to capabilities-based rewriting as the latter ensures that the queries issued to the sources are answerable by these sources. While developing our solution, we took into account the disadvantages that we have just quoted. Since, the number of integrated DLs may be important, we use heuristic search algorithms. These algorithms construct QEPs that minimise as much as possible the cost of treatment, in a time less than that spent by the exhaustive search algorithms. In addition, the QEP generation process is based on sources capabilities descriptions. Thus, QEPs contains only feasible sub-queries. We present our solution for the capability-based rewriting problem.

Our Solution

A Running Example

Suppose that we have three sources S1, S2 and S3 and that each of them provides a local view. Let V1, V2 and V3 be their local views respectively, with: V1=(ISBN, Price, Subject), V2=(ISBN, Author) and V3=(ISBN, Publisher). Sources S1, S2 and S3 have limited capabilities for query processing. These capabilities are expressed as follows:

- Queries sent to S1 must either provide the Price or the Subject field. In both cases, the set of attributes returned by the source is {ISBN, Price, Subject};
- Queries sent to S2 must provide the ISBN field. The set of attributes returned by the source is {ISBN, Author};
- Queries sent to S3 must provide the ISBN field. The set of attributes returned by the source is {ISBN, Publisher}.

Let BooksGV(ISBN, Price, Subject, Author, Publisher) be a global view offered by WASSIT when integrating the three data sources. BooksGV is defined as follows: *((V1 JoinISBN V2) JoinISBN V3)*. Suppose we formulate a query (Q), at WASSIT's user interface, to find all books dealing with "Linux", whose author is "Radi" and whose publisher is "Elsevier". The condition attached to the query Q is: Subject = "Linux" $\wedge$ Author = "Radi" $\wedge$ Publisher = "Elsevier".

Describing Source Capabilities

To describe source capabilities, we use a table that we call *Capabilities Table.* A *Capabilities Table* of a source S enumerates the conditions expressions that can be evaluated by S, and the set of attributes returned by S after evaluating these expressions. For example, table describes capabilities of source S1. Each row in the table describes a condition expression C that S1 can evaluate, and the set of attributes returned by the source S1 when processing this condition expression. For example, row 1 states that S1 can evaluate condition expressions like (Subject= "XML") and returns the set {ISBN, Price, Subject}. *Capabilities Tables* of the integrated DLs are stored in the knowledge base of WASSIT.

Table. 8.3. Capabilities Table of Source S_1

	Evaluated_Attributes			Returned_Attributes		
Operator	ISBN	Price	Subject	ISBN	Price	Subject
∧	0	0	1	1	1	1
∧	0	1	0	1	1	1

We define a function called R_Attr(C) (for Returned_ Attributes) which returns the set of attributes returned by a source when evaluating a condition expression C. If a condition expression is not supported, then R_Attr(C) returns the empty set. For example, R_Attr (Price=P) = {ISBN, Price, Subject} and R_Attr (Subject=S ∧ Price =P) =Ø.

Our Cost Model

In order to obtain the cost of a plan, one must have statistics about the underlying data, such as sizes of relations and sizes of domains. It is also necessary to have a cost formula to calculate the processing cost for each implementation of each operator. Because data sources are autonomous, it may not be possible to have statistics about the sources or unreliable ones, preventing a direct application of cost models approaches developed for homogeneous systems.

Several approaches have been proposed for cost based query optimisation in mediation systems (DANG-NGOC, 2003). In this paper, we propose a simple cost model that we use while constructing query plans. In mediation systems, the cost of a plan may be approximated by the sum of communication cost, source query processing costs and mediator processing cost, as expressed in formula (4).

$$\text{Cost(Plan)} = \text{Communication\_cost} + \text{Mediator\_cost} + \text{Sources\_costs} \quad (4)$$

Furthermore, in the context of web data integration, communication cost dominates source query processing costs and mediator processing cost (DANG-NGOC, 2003). If the plan consists of N sub-queries (SQi) executed sequentially.

In this formula, Ri is the response corresponding to sub-query SQi. Minimizing the cost given in formula (5) involves reducing the number of sub-queries. This observation will be used while constructing QEPs

$$\text{Cost(Plan)} = \sum_{i=1}^{N} (\text{Communication\_cost(SQi)} + \text{Communication\_cost}(R_i)) \quad (5)$$

Constructing Query Plans

When a query is formulated at the WASSIT's interface, the corresponding XQuery query is generated. This query is processed by the *Analyse and XAT Generation* module and the *Rewriting and Semantic Enrichment* module.

The output of this second module is a QEP. As the global view is a join of the local sources views, the QEP generated, let be P1, consists in sending the sub-queries SQ1 (subject="Linux"), SQ2 (author="Radi") and SQ3 (Publisher="Elsevier") respectively to data sources S1, S2 and S3.

After retrieving results, a double join on the attribute ISBN is done at the mediator level Note that this plan is not feasible because sources S2 and S3 cannot answer SQ2 and SQ3 because of their limited query capabilities.

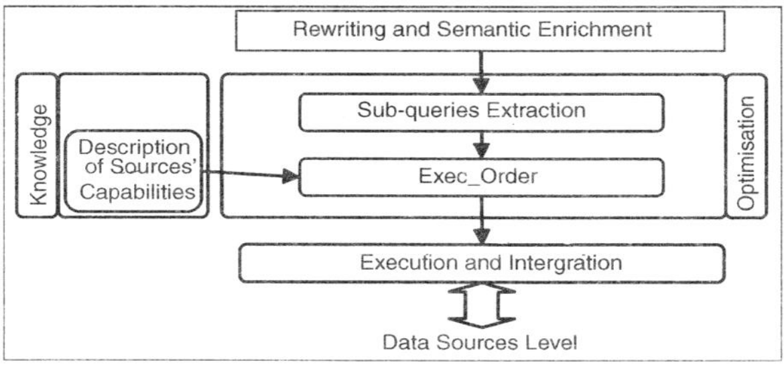

Fig. 8.16. Optimisation Module Architecture.

Since, the generated QEP contains sub-queries that are not feasible, the role of the *Optimisation* module is to construct a QEP with feasible sub-queries. To this end, the first operation performed by the *Optimisation* module, when receiving a QEP, is the extraction of its sub-queries. This operation is performed by the *Sub-queries Extraction* module. The extracted sub-queries are then processed by the *Exec_Order* module. The role of this module is to find an execution order of subqueries which takes into account the limited query capabilities of the integrated data sources and that minimizes the cost of the generated QEP. To illustrate this concept of execution order of sub-queries, consider a second QEP, let be P2. This plan consists on sending the subquery SQ1 (Subject = "Linux") to source S1. For each ISBNi returned, a sub-query SQ2 (ISBN= ISBNi) is sent to source S2. For each ISBNj returned satisfying the condition Author="Radi", a sub-query SQ3 (ISBN= ISBNj) is sent to S3. In plan P2, sub-queries are executed in chain. Each sub-query uses the results of the sub-query already executed. According to our cost model, minimizing the cost of a plan involves reducing the number of its sub-queries. Suppose that source S1 contains 30 books on "Linux" and that source S2 contains 3 books on "Linux" whose author is "Radi". For simplicity, we count the communication cost by calculating the number of sub-queries sent to a source. For each subquery sent to a source, we take a cost equal to 1. If we consider plan P2, the first sub-query executed is SQ1 (Subject="Linux"). Since, each sub-query has a cost equal to 1, the communication cost of SQ1 is equal to 1. For each ISBNi returned, the sub-query SQ2(ISBN=ISBNi) is sent to source S2. Since, S1 contains 30 books on "Linux", 30 sub-queries are sent to S2 with a cost equal to 30. For each ISBNj returned satisfying the condition Author="Radi", a sub-query SQ3 (ISBN= ISBNj) is sent to S3. Since, S2 contains 3 books on "Linux" whose author is "Radi", 3 sub-queries are sent to source S3 with a cost equal to 3. Thus, the communication cost of plan P2 is: 1+30+3 = 34. In the cost of plan P2, SQ1 has the minimal cost (1) because it is executed in block. Therefore, in our algorithm we seek all subqueries that can be executed in block. A join between these sub-queries constitute the first entity in the chain.

Algorithm for Constructing QEPs

Let SQ1, SQ2 and SQ3 be the sub-queries extracted from the plan generated by the *Rewriting* module. Let C be the condition attached to the user query. C is: Subject = "Linux" Λ author = "Radi" Λ Publisher = "Elsevier". Let Attr(C) be the set of attributes of the condition C. This set is noted A, where A = {Subject, Author, Publisher}. The algorithm developed is a greedy algorithm. Its idea is to find, at each iteration, a subquery that can be executed using the attributes of set A. After executing this sub-query, the function R_Attr() is used to get the returned attributes. These attributes are added to set A. This treatment is repeated until no more sub-queries can be executed. Thus, the execution plan constructed by this algorithm is a chain of sub-queries. However, the first sub-query constituting the chain may be either a simple query or a join between multiple sub-queries. In fact, seeking the first sub-query in the chain may lead to several sub-queries. Since, sub-queries at the beginning of the chain are executed in block, their execution reduces the communication cost. Therefore, these sub-queries must be executed simultaneously; a join on their results is performed at the mediator. This will constitute the first element of the chain.

To sum up, the algorithm consists of three stages:

- Stage 1. In this stage, the algorithm checks if all sub-queries can be executed using the attributes of set A. This test is based on *Capabilities Tables* of the integrated data sources. If so, the sub-queries are sent to data sources without any additional processing. If one of the sub-queries cannot be answered using set A, the algorithm proceeds to the second stage.
- Stage 2. This stage uses the result of the first stage: all sub-queries that can be answered using the attributes of set A, form the first element of the plan. Thus, these sub-queries will be executed in parallel. A join of their results is performed at the mediator level. The attributes returned after the execution of these sub-queries are added to set A. In the running example, only the sub-query SQ1 can be executed. It is the first sub-query in the chain. The attributes returned by SQ1, which are ISBN and Publisher are added to set A. A becomes = {Subject, Author, Publisher, Price, ISBN}.

- Stage 3. In this stage, we seek among the remaining sub-queries, a sub-query that can be executed using set A. If this sub-query exists, the set A is enriched with the attributes returned after its execution. In the example, SQ2 is selected and A becomes A = {Subject, Author, Publisher, Price, ISBN}. The same process is repeated until no more sub-queries must be executed. If at a given step, no sub-query can be executed using the attributes of set A, then there is no plan to execute the target query. We give a formal description of the algorithm.

```
Input: Set of sub-queries SQ={SQ1, SQ2,.., SQn}
       Set A
Output: Plan (if exists)
Begin
   // Stage 1
   Plan ← Ø, B ← Ø
   For each (SQi )i=1 to n
       if SQi can be answered using A
             B ← SQi
       if (B==SQ)
             Plan ← {SQ1, SQ2,.., SQn}
       Else
             Plan ← Ø
   // Stage 2
     If Plan == Ø
        Plan ← Plan. [B]// B contains sub-queries that will be joined
        A ← A U {attributes(B)}
        SQ ← SQ - {B}
   // Stage 3
     While SQ ? Ø
        For each SQi
             if SQi can be answered using A
                      N←SQi
                      Break
             Else
                      Return (Ø)//The plan does not exist
        Plan ← Plan. [N]
```

```
        SQ ← SQ - {N}
        A ← A U {attributes(N)}
Return (Plan)
END
```

PERFORMANCE EVALUATION

In this section, we analyse the performances of our framework WASSIT, when integrating DLs, through simulation. The performance index that we evaluate is the response time.

Performance Parameters

We study the influence of the key parameters on the response time, which is defined as the time elapsed between submitting a query to WASSIT and getting a response. In mediation systems, response time may be important. This is due to communication cost, source query processing costs and mediator processing cost. Furthermore, additional processing time is introduced by our *Optimisation* module. But this is still tolerable Since, we give to the user the guaranty to get a response in a finite time. Without our *Optimisation* module, the mediator may not answer some queries because of the limited query capabilities of the underlying DLs. Response time depends also on the bandwidth of the communication network, between mediator and data sources. The system load, which lies principally on queries frequency and size of sources' responses, has also an impact on the response time. We summarise these parameters in table.

Table. 8.4.The Key Parameters for Studying the System Performances.

Parameter	Meaning
N	Number of integrated sources
R_Size	Response size (Bytes)
F = 1/T	Queries frequency: number of queries addressed to WASSIT per time unit. T is the period of query arriving (seconds)
BW	Network Bandwidth table. The key parameters for studying the system performances

Bibliography

Aikens: *Theory and Practice of Online Learning*, New York: F.S. Crofts & Company, 2004.

Anderson, T.: *International Review of Research in Open and Distance Learning*, London: Waverly Book Company, 2003.

Anderson R.: *Handbook of Library Cataloguing*, New York: Lawrence Erlbaum, 2002.

Archer, W.: *Journal of the Asynchronous Learning Network*, USA: American school of Chicago, 2001.

Arbaugh, J.: *Multimedia Libraries: An Introduction*, Chicago: American Hotel Register Company, 2004.

Augustine: *Developing Multi-media Libraries*, Boston: William J. Nagel Company, 2001.

Berners-Lee, T.: *Developing Libraries Cataloguing*, San Francisco: Harper Bowling Green State University, 2000.

Burge, E.: *Managing Multimedia Libraries*, London: Methuen Publication, 2000.

Collins, A.: *Managing library Cataloguing*, Chicago: The Hotel Monthly Press, 2006.

Dalsgaard, C.: *The Multimedia Library: Materials Selection and Use*, London: Macmillan Publication, 2004.

Daniel, J.: *Video Collections and Multimedia in ARL Libraries*, London: Cambridge University, 2000.

Davie, L.: *Cataloguing Guide for Multimedia Libraries*, New York: Oxford: Pergamon Press, 2003.

Dixon, J.: *Multimedia Information Resources,* Chicago: The Hotel Monthly Press, 2005.

Dron, J.: *Multimedia Information Collection in Digital Libraries,* New York: The Ronald Press Company, 2000.

Eastin, M.: *Information Access Through Search Engines and Digital Libraries,* Boston: William J. Nagel Company, 2001.

Garrison, D.: *Libraries and Learning Resource,* Chicago: Hotel Monthly Press, 2001.

Holmberg, B.: *Theory and Practice of Library Science,* London: William J. Nagel Company, 2001.

Koper, R.: *Design and Usability of Digital Libraries,* Netherlands: Open University of the Netherlands, 2003.

Mason, R.: *Essential Cataloguing,* New York: Simon & Schuster Macmillan Press, 2002.

Palloff, R.: *Building Learning Communities in Cyberspace,* San Francisco: Jossey-Bass Publication, 2000.

Prensky, M.: *Digital Game-Based Learning,* New York: McGraw Hill Press, 2005.

Rogoff, B.: *Standard Cataloging for School and Public Libraries,* New York: Oxford University Press, 2006.

Salmon, G.: *Introduction to Cataloging and Classification,* London: Harvard University Press, 2005.

Vygotsky, L.: *Cataloging and Classification: An Introduction,* Cambridge: Harvard University Press, 2001.

Index